THE GLORY
OF HEAVEN

THE
GLORY
OF
HEAVEN

The Truth About Heaven,
Angels and Eternal Life

JOHN F. MACARTHUR

CROSSWAY BOOKS • WHEATON, ILLINOIS
A DIVISION OF GOOD NEWS PUBLISHERS

The Glory of Heaven

Published by Crossway Books
        a division of Good News Publishers
        1300 Crescent Street
        Wheaton, Illinois 60187

Edited by Leonard G. Goss

Cover design: Cindy Kiple

First printing, 1996

Printed in the United States of America

All Scripture quotations in this book, except those noted otherwise, are from the *King James Version* of the Bible.

References marked NASB are from *The New American Standard Bible*, copyright © 1960, 1962, 1963, 1968, 1971, 1972, 1973, 1975, and 1977 by The Lockman Foundation and are used by permission.

References marked NIV are from *The Holy Bible: New International Version*, copyright © 1973, 1978, 1984 by the International Bible Society. All rights reserved. Used by permission of Zondervan Publishing House. The "NIV" and "New International Version" trademarks are registered in the United States Patent and Trademark Office by International Bible Society. Use of either trademark requires the permission of International Bible Society.

Library of Congress Cataloging-in-Publication Data

MacArthur, John 1939-
   The glory of heaven : the truth about heaven, angels, and eternal
life / John F. MacArthur.
     p.   cm.
   ISBN 0-89107-849-5
   1. Heaven—Christianity. 2. Heaven—Biblical teaching.
3. Angels—Biblical teaching.   I. Title.
BT846.2.M32   1996
236'.24—dc20   96-20385

04	03	02	01	00	99	98	97	96
15	14	13	12	11	10	9	8	7	6	5	4	3	2	1

ACKNOWLEDGMENTS

My thanks to Phil Johnson, who has labored to meet editorial deadlines for me for the past fifteen years. But this book is dedicated to Phil's precious wife, Darlene, and their sons, Jeremiah, Jedidiah, and Jonathan, who have faithfully endured Phil's long days, late hours, and short attention span whenever those deadlines approach.

CONTENTS

INTRODUCTION

Heaven! The very word is synonymous with beauty, comfort, peace, satisfaction, and contentment. The adjectival form is often used to describe something wonderful, as in "This roast is heavenly," or "The scenery is heavenly in New Zealand." There's even a flavor of ice cream called "Heavenly Hash."

But heaven is far more than an adjective or an attitude. It is a *place*, a real place, where people of God go after they die. It is God's home, and the Bible gives us amazing insight into its splendrous glory.

In fact, the Bible is full of details about heaven. It is as if God has unwrapped some of the mystery about heaven and opened it so that we can see and desire.

However, because human nature is so tainted by the effects of sin, people left to their own instincts will inevitably corrupt *every* spiritual truth. Subjects like heaven, angels, and eternal life are certainly no exception to this rule. People lacking a biblical perspective always think wrongly about heavenly things. Either they ignore the spiritual realm altogether, choosing instead to live for this temporal world—or they become so absorbed in fantasies about the spirit world that they forfeit the truth.

This is evident everywhere you look. For example, visit any secular bookstore and you'll see shelves filled with books that reflect the materialistic bent—worldly "success" manuals, where *success* is inevitably defined in temporal terms only. Heaven is utterly irrelevant to this way of thinking.

But look around and you'll find other shelves lined with books that reflect an unhealthy, occultish obsession with heaven, angels, and the spiritual realm. Such books have risen sharply in popularity because of the influence of the New Age movement. Most of them are mystical, extrabiblical, sometimes even demonic.

Frankly, both perspectives are extremely harmful spiritually. Either approach will draw people far away from the truth, away from Scripture, and into spiritual bondage. Whether it is the materialistic or the occult variety, it is bondage just the same. And it causes multitudes to miss the true heaven and perish in hell.

As Christians we're supposed to oppose such trends, "destroying speculations and every lofty thing raised up against the knowledge of God, and . . . taking every thought captive to the obedience of Christ" (2 Cor. 10:5, NASB). We ought to confront every corruption of truth with biblical wisdom. After all, only the Bible provides reliable insight into heaven and the spirit world (1 Cor. 2:9-10). Too often, however, the church merely follows the world's fads.

You can see this by visiting the typical Christian bookstore. You'll find row after row of pragmatic "success manuals" that simply restate the secular books' advice, but using Christian terminology—reducing Jesus to the World's Greatest Salesman and similar nonsense, or arguing that the way to obtain church growth is to follow secular methods of marketing. On the other hand, you'll also find a number of books that recount people's mystical encounters with angels and spirit beings, near-death experiences, visions of "heaven," and other similar mystical phenomena.

Camouflaging temporal values with Christian terminology does not make them any less worldly. And painting one's mystical experiences with Christian imagery makes them no less occultic. "Evangelical" materialism and "evangelical" spiritualism are just as deadly as the secular varieties—perhaps even more so, because they wear the disguise of biblical terms.

Those concerns are not the only things that motivate me to write a book on heaven, however. I've been concerned for some time about a declining interest in heaven among Christians. Frankly, most North American Christians have things so good right here in this world that they don't really know what it is to long for heaven. God has blessed us with an abundance of earthly comforts—more than any prior generation in history. There is a danger that we become so comfortable in this life that we forget we are but strangers and pilgrims in this world. Like Abraham, we're supposed to think of ourselves as vagabonds here on earth, looking for a city with eternal foundations, whose builder and maker is God (Heb. 11:10).

Christians in less affluent and less comfortable cultures than ours tend to think more about heaven, because it promises things so different from what they have known in this world.

On a recent trip to an isolated city south of Siberia and on the back side of Tibet, I met with fifteen hundred impoverished Christians who had suffered greatly under Russian oppression for three quarters of a century. They were children of exiles, economically deprived, working hard daily just to find food. They wanted me to teach them from the Bible, and the subject they most desired to study was their future in the glory of heaven. I had the privilage of doing that over several hours, and many wept with joy.

How different is our response, coming from a more comfortable culture! I often meet Christians who live as if heaven would be an unwelcome intrusion into their busy schedule—an interruption of career goals or holiday plans.

Ever notice how the songs about heaven are mostly spirituals and other oldies? "This World Is Not My Home"; "Until that Day"; "Heaven Is a Wonderful Place." Almost no one writes songs about heaven these days. Most of us simply don't long for it like our ancestors did. We would rather be here.

But we dare not think of heaven as old-fashioned. Nothing is *less* old-fashioned. If you are a Christian, heaven *is* your future home for all of eternity. It is where all things are made new. The expression "old-fashioned" could hardly be less appropriate.

We need to have a better understanding of the glory of heaven. We must learn to set our affections on heavenly things, as we are commanded in Scripture. We need to see that as Christians even now, what God is doing in our lives is designed to fit us for heaven—not merely acclimate us to life here on earth. We need to realize, like Abraham, that "here have we no continuing city, but we seek one to come" (Heb. 13:14). "Our citizenship is in heaven" (Phil. 3:20, NASB). Our hearts should be there as well.

Jesus taught us to "lay up for [ourselves] treasures in heaven, where neither moth nor rust doth corrupt, and where thieves do not break through nor steal" (Matt. 6:20). Why? Because "where your treasure is, there will your heart be also" (v. 21). Clearly, His point is not that He wants our *treasures,* but that He wants our *hearts*. He was teaching us to fix our hearts on heaven, to long for the glory of heaven, and above all, to "seek those things which are above, where Christ sitteth on the right hand of God" (Col. 3:1).

Heaven is *His* realm. He has gone there to prepare a place for us to live with Him forever. That truth is what makes heaven so precious for the Christian. Our eternity there will be an eternity in the presence of Christ, sharing rich fellowship with Him personally, and living endlessly in the light of His countenance. That is heaven's chief appeal for the Christian whose priorities are straight. Christ Himself *is* the glory of heaven:

> The city had no need of the sun, neither of the moon, to shine in it: for the glory of God did lighten it, and the Lamb is the light thereof.
>
> —*Rev. 21:23*

THE MODERN ROMANCE WITH HEAVEN

THE RESURGENCE OF BELIEF
IN THE AFTERLIFE

More people are now talking about heaven, angelic beings, and life after death than any time in my memory. Several books on heaven and angels have had lengthy reigns at the top of all the bestseller lists. Heavenly interest abounds. I recently received a catalogue from a mail-order business that offers only "angelic" gifts. They specialize in stationery, jewelry, ceramics, and other gifts that feature images of angels. All kinds of media, from tabloid television to Hollywood movies to popular songs are being used to exploit the angels-and-the-afterlife craze.

Over a hundred books dealing with angels are currently in print as I write this. NBC recently aired a wildly popular special telecast, *Angels: The Mysterious Messengers*, then followed with *Angels II: Beyond the Light*. The original special was made into a book, joining a trend that has prompted some secular booksellers to devote entire sections of their bookstores to the angel craze. People traveling the "Information Superhighway" are also likely to encounter angels along the way. A search of the World Wide Web revealed dozens of sites dedicated to angels, many recounting dramatic personal testimonies about supposed angelic visitations.

At the same time an unprecedented fascination with the afterlife has arisen. People have been talking about near-death experiences since Dr. Elisabeth Kubler-Ross's 1970 book, *On Death and Dying*, rose to the top of the charts. Kubler-Ross recounted tales from several people who, it seemed, had literally been brought back from the dead—mostly resuscitated by surgeons in operating rooms or by paramedics at accident scenes. Many had fascinating tales to tell about what they supposedly had seen and experienced on the Other Side. Kubler-Ross said her research into this phenomenon altered her own views of the afterlife. She began her research holding to a skeptical rationalism, believing that only oblivion followed death. But studying people's near-death experiences made her a believer in the supernatural, she said.[1]

Another leading authority on near-death experiences for the past two decades has been Raymond A. Moody. His 1975 book, *Life After Life* was a runaway best-seller. He followed it with a sequel, *Reflections on Life After Life* two years later; *The Light Beyond* was published in 1989, *Coming Back* in 1990; and his latest is *Reunions: Visionary Encounters with Departed Loved Ones* (1993).[2]

DRAWN TO THE DARK SIDE

One might be tempted to think these are positive trends in the wake of so much rationalistic unbelief. But, sadly, such is not entirely the case. Accepting the reality of supernatural things is not the same as believing the truth about them. And when an unbelieving mind embraces the reality of the supernatural realm, the result can often be catastrophic. Both Elisabeth Kubler-Ross and Raymond Moody are living proof of this principle. Both began their research on near-death experiences as purely rationalistic scientists, convinced that there must be some perfectly reasonable natural explanation for the strange sensations reported by dying people. Both abandoned their skepticism for something potentially worse.

Kubler-Ross and Moody have veered off into the world of the occult. After her study of others' near-death experiences, Kubler-Ross reported that she had had a rather remarkable out-of-the-body experience of her own where she traveled the speed of light. She began experimenting with seances to contact the dead. She finally joined a bizarre religious cult led by Jay Barham, a man who claimed to be able to make spirits materialize in order to have sex with the living.[3] Now Kubler-Ross is a leading guru in the New Age movement.

Raymond Moody's forays into supernaturalism have also taken a sinister turn. His recent books smack of classic occult necromancy. He advocates crystal-ball gazing, "scrying," as it is known. He instructs people how to build "apparition chambers," special rooms with mirrors, in which he says it is possible to commune with the ghosts of one's departed loved ones. He has such a room in his own house and claims to have conversed there with his own dead grandmother.[4]

Obviously, evangelical Christians who accept the Bible as the Word of God must view this current fascination with the realm beyond death as something of a mixed blessing. As encouraged as we may be by evidence that an unbelieving rationalism has not utterly conquered faith, we must be deeply disturbed by any trend that seems to draw people into occultism, New Age philosophies, and superstition. And those are undeniably the roads traveled by most people caught up in the current angels-and-the afterlife fad. Because of their mounting popularity, we must look thoughtfully at them as we begin to seek the truth about heaven.

SEDUCED BY THE LIGHT

By far the most popular single account of one person's near-death experience is Betty J. Eadie's remarkable book, *Embraced by the Light.*

As of this writing the book is more than three years old and still rides atop the best-seller lists.

Mrs. Eadie recounts how she "died" in her hospital room while recovering after a hysterectomy in 1973. Her memories of what happened are extraordinarily vivid:

> My spirit was suddenly drawn out through my chest and pulled upward, as if by a giant magnet. My first impression was that I was free. There was nothing unnatural about the experience. I was above the bed, hovering near the ceiling. My sense of freedom was limitless and it seemed as if I had done this forever. I turned and saw a body lying on the bed. I was curious about who it was, and immediately I began descending toward it. Having worked as an LPN, I knew well the appearance of a dead body, and as I got closer to the face I knew at once that it was lifeless. And then I recognized that it was my own. That was *my* body on the bed. I wasn't taken aback, and I wasn't frightened; I simply felt a kind of sympathy for it. It appeared younger and prettier than I remembered, and now it was dead.[5]

Eadie goes on to describe how three robed men suddenly appeared by her side, telling her they had been with her for "eternities." She began to remember "an existence before [her] life on earth" and her relationship with these men "before."[6] She writes, "The fact of a pre-earth life crystallized in my mind, and I saw that death was actually a 'rebirth' into a greater life of understanding and knowledge that stretched backward and forward through time."[7]

At this point Eadie's near-death experience seems to have all the classic New Age overtones of reincarnation, out-of-body experiences, telepathy, and so on. She describes a ghostly visit to her own home, where she watched her children and was even able to look into their futures.

But then her story takes this extraordinary turn:

I saw a pinpoint of light in the distance. The black mass around me began to take on more of the shape of a tunnel, and I felt myself traveling through it at an even greater speed, rushing toward the light. I was instinctively attracted to it, although again, I felt that others might not be. As I approached, I noticed the figure of a man standing in it, with the light radiating all around him. As I got closer the light became brilliant—brilliant beyond any description, far more brilliant than the sun—and I knew that no earthly eyes in their natural state could look upon this light without being destroyed.[8]

Eadie describes a dazzling, golden "radiance" that surrounded this being. She says he reached out to her with pure, unconditional love. "There was no questioning who he was," she writes. "I knew that he was my Savior, and friend, and God. He was Jesus Christ."[9]

From this point on, Eadie's heavenly exploits center on this Jesus figure and what she says he taught her. She claims her mind assumed a supernatural ability to know and understand things—almost as if she were "remembering" what she had always known:

I understood, or rather, I *remembered,* his role as creator of the earth. His mission was to come into the world to teach love. This knowledge was more like remembering. Things were coming back to me from long before my life on earth, things that had been purposely blocked from me by a "veil" of for-getfulness at my birth.[10]

If it sounds like Eadie is claiming virtual omniscience for herself, that is precisely what she means to convey. She writes: "The word 'omniscient' had never been more meaningful to me. Knowledge permeated me. In a sense it *became* me, and I was amazed at my ability to comprehend the mysteries of the universe simply by reflecting on them."[11]

Eadie obviously believes she retained this understanding of "the mysteries of the universe" even after her return from heaven, and her book is filled with glib answers to questions she says had always perplexed her before her heavenly sojourn. For example, she writes,

> I wanted to know why there were so many churches in the world. Why didn't God give us only one church, one pure religion? The answer came to me with the purest of understanding. Each of us, I was told, is at a different level of spiritual development and understanding. Each person is therefore prepared for a different level of spiritual knowledge. All religions upon the earth are necessary because there are people who need what they teach. People in one religion may not have a complete understanding of the Lord's gospel and never will have while in that religion. But that religion is used as a stepping stone to further knowledge. Each church fulfills spiritual needs that perhaps others cannot fill. No one church can fulfill everybody's needs at every level. As an individual raises his level of understanding about God and his own eternal progress, he might feel discontented with the teachings of his present church and seek a different philosophy or religion to fill that void. When this occurs he has reached another level of understanding and will long for further truth and knowledge, and for another opportunity to grow.[12]

"Having received this knowledge," she concludes, "I knew that we have no right to criticize any church or religion in any way."[13]

Nevertheless, Eadie also emphasizes that there is a certain uniqueness about Christ: "Of all knowledge, however, there is none more essential than knowing Jesus Christ. I was told that he is the door through which we will *all* return. He is the only door through which we can return."[14]

Because she uses that kind of familiar Christian terminology and other biblical allusions in relating her account, many Christians have wrongly assumed that Betty Eadie herself is a true Christian. Rapt audiences across the nation have listened as she has retold her story, and many who call themselves Christians say they are convinced her experience should not be written off. I've heard from a surprising number of evangelical Christians who wonder if it is possible that Eadie's account of heaven and the afterlife might be a reliable and true account of what Christians can expect after death.

The answer is no. Many of Eadie's claims contradict Scripture, as we shall shortly see. Also, Eadie doesn't disclose it in her book, but she is a Mormon. Some of the truths she said she learned in heaven bear an uncanny resemblance to Mormon doctrines. In fact, despite her long discourse about the value of all religions, what Eadie does not say in her book—but apparently told a Utah reporter—is that during her visit to heaven she learned that the Church of Jesus Christ of Latter-Day Saints (the Mormon Church) is "the truest Church on the earth."[15] In a promotional package targeting Utah readers, Eadie's original publisher (a spin-off from a Mormon publishing house) inserted special promotional flyers into the first edition of the book. Titled, "Of Special Interest to Members of the Church of Latter-Day Saints," the flyers touted Eadie as a recent convert to Mormonism.[16]

In the wake of growing book sales, however, Eadie and her publisher have downplayed her church affiliation—almost to the point of seeming to want to obscure the fact that she is a Mormon. In an interview with *The Christian Research Journal*, she repeatedly refused to admit that she is a Mormon.[17]

Eadie's doctrine is not straight-up Mormonism, however. It is a curious mixture of Mormonism and New Age philosophy. There have been ripples of controversy about her teachings within the Mormon church itself, and church leaders, while pleased with the public-relations bonanza Eadie's book has been, have stopped short of treating her as an actual prophet.

In any case, Eadie's claims as a whole are plainly contrary to what Scripture teaches about heaven and the afterlife.

ON GUARD AGAINST
ANGELS OF DECEPTION

Scripture plainly warns us to be on guard against emissaries of Satan who appear to be angels of light (2 Cor. 11:13-15). The most influential false doctrines that have ever threatened the church have always been those that masquerade as orthodox, employing the familiar language of Scripture, but skewing the truth. In other words, using the *language* of biblical Christianity is not the same as being biblical.

So the fact that Betty Eadie is a pleasant woman who says she has had encounters with angels is certainly no guarantee that she is not deceived, or a deceiver, or both. In fact, the nature of her case gives us all the more warrant to examine her teachings with the most careful kind of scrutiny. Eadie is claiming to have received a comprehensive revelation of divine truth directly from the Lord Himself. Her description of her experience is more spectacular and far more detailed than the accounts of the Transfiguration in Matthew, Mark, and Luke. Her portrait of heaven goes miles beyond the apostle Paul's own meager account of his being caught up into the third heaven. If true, Eadie's story supersedes every recorded revelation of heaven found in Scripture. Moreover, if Betty Eadie is right, Christian theology needs to be completely revamped. According to her system, no one else has had it right in two thousand years of Christianity.

Obviously, it is extremely important to examine Mrs. Eadie's claims with the utmost care—like the Bereans, who were praised by the historian Luke because they subjected even the apostle Paul's inspired and infallible message to the careful scrutiny of the Old Testament—to see "whether those things were so" (Acts 17:11).

And if Eadie's claims fail the test of authenticity, they must be firmly rejected and exposed for what they are. Genuine love demands that we do this, for the sake of those who might otherwise be led into deception and false doctrine.

EMBRACED BY DARKNESS

Precisely what does Betty Eadie claim was revealed to her in heaven? Some of what she recounts are echoes of her Mormonism; other ideas are drawn from New Age teaching; and some are simply other unbiblical inventions that find their way into Eadie's retelling of her tale.

The Mormon Doctrines

Mormon influences are clearly evident throughout Eadie's account of heaven. Among the chief Mormon doctrines that find their way into her book are these:

PREEXISTENCE OF HUMAN SPIRITS. Betty Eadie claims all of us had an existence in the pre-mortal world. This is a key doctrine of Mormonism, but it is nowhere taught in Scripture.

We noted above that Mrs. Eadie claimed she could remember having had a previous relationship with her robed "monk" guides for "eternities." Elsewhere she writes,

> I *remembered* the creation of the earth. I actually experienced it as if it were being reenacted before my eyes. This was important. Jesus wanted me to internalize this knowledge. He wanted me to know how it felt when the creation occurred. And the only way to do that was for me to view it again and *feel* what I had felt before.

All people as spirits in the pre-mortal world took part in the creation of the earth.[18]

What does Scripture say of this? First of all, the biblical account of creation very clearly has the first human soul being created after the rest of creation was complete. The Bible says, "The Lord God formed man of the dust of the ground, and breathed into his nostrils the breath of life; and man became a living soul" (Gen. 2:7). Not until God was finished with creation did Adam become a living soul. There is no room for any sort of preexistence in the biblical account.

In fact, one of the crucial arguments for divine sovereignty posed to Job by God Himself was that when the universe was created, Job was nowhere around: "Where wast thou when I laid the foundations of the earth?" (Job 38:4). Job could not boast of having been there. He wasn't. Scripture nowhere suggests that our human souls existed prior to our conception—in fact, all the biblical data argues otherwise (cf. Ps. 51:5). God *alone* created the universe (Gen. 1:1; Col. 1:17).

MULTIPLE GODS. Eadie's account eliminates the doctrine of the Trinity. She writes, "I was still laboring under the teachings and beliefs of my childhood."[19] What were those teachings and beliefs? "My Protestant upbringing had taught me that God the Father and Jesus Christ were one being."[20] But her heavenly experience convinced Betty Eadie differently: "I understood, to my surprise, that Jesus was *a separate being from God,* with His own divine purpose."[21] This is perfectly in accord with Mormon doctrine but plainly at odds with Scripture, which from cover to cover teaches the unity of the divine Godhead (Deut. 6:4; 1 Cor. 8:6; 1 Tim. 2:5; Jas. 2:19). Jesus Himself said, "I and my Father are one" (John 10:30). There is no possibility of differing purposes between the Father and the Son (John 4:34; 5:30; 8:29).

Granted, the Trinity is a difficult concept to explain or understand, but Scripture clearly affirms, and every major branch of Christianity has agreed for nearly two thousand years, that while God the Father and Jesus Christ are distinct Persons, they are *not* separate beings, or separate gods. This is the clear teaching of Scripture: "Hear, O Israel: The Lord our God is one Lord" (Deut. 6:4).

THE DEIFICATION OF THE HUMAN SOUL. We have already noted that Betty Eadie claimed she enjoyed omniscience in heaven. This is in harmony with the Mormon notion that all believers are progressing toward godhood. Elsewhere, she writes, "I understood with pure knowledge that God wants us to become as he is, and that he has invested us with god-like qualities."[22]

Scripture does teach that in heaven we will be like Christ in holiness, but not that we will share the incommunicable attributes of God, such as His omnipotence and omniscience. Even in the glory of heaven, we will remain God's creatures. We will not attain a divinity of our own, or even share His deity. "I am the Lord," He says. "That is my name: and my glory will I not give to another" (Isa. 42:8).

EVE'S ACT SEEN AS NOBLE. Eadie echoes the Mormon notion that Eve's eating of the forbidden fruit was a noble act. A common Mormon view is that Eve willfully partook of the fruit as a sort of selfless sacrifice, so that she would be able to bear children and thus progress toward the state of divinity. Thus her disobedience becomes a positive act. *The Book of Mormon* says, "Adam fell that men might be; and men are, that they might have joy."[23]

Recounting what she learned when she was supposedly permitted to watch a replay of creation, Eadie writes,

> I had seen then the differences between Adam and Eve. I was shown that Adam was more satisfied with his condition in the Garden and that Eve was more restless. I was shown that she wanted to become a mother desperately enough that she was willing to risk death to obtain it. Eve did not "fall" to tempta-

tion as much as she made a conscious decision to bring about conditions necessary for her progression, and her initiative was used to finally get Adam to partake the fruit, then, they brought mankind to mortality, which gave us conditions necessary for having children—but also to die.[24]

Scripture, however, teaches plainly that Eve was deceived by Satan and that the Fall was wholly an act of sin (1 Tim. 2:14; 2 Cor. 11:3).

THE POSSIBILITY OF SALVATION AFTER DEATH. Mormonism is well known for the practice of baptizing people for the dead. Mormons believe that people who die without having heard the Mormon gospel will have an opportunity to hear and believe even after they die. Since baptism is viewed as essential to their salvation, the dead are baptized "by proxy"—that is, living Mormons stand in for the souls of people whom they know have died without being baptized in the Mormon church.[25]

Betty Eadie's book reflects the Mormon belief that death does not settle forever the question of a soul's eternal destiny. Her guides in the afterlife told her

that it is important for us to acquire knowledge of the spirit while we are in the flesh. The more knowledge we acquire here, the further and faster we will progress there. Because of lack of knowledge or belief, some spirits are virtual prisoners on this earth. [This echoes Mormon doctrine as well.] Some who die as atheists, or those who have bonded to the world through greed, bodily appetites, or other earthly commitments find it difficult to move on, and they become earthbound. They often lack the faith and power to reach for, or in some cases even to recognize, the energy and light that pulls us toward God. These spirits stay on earth until they learn to accept the greater power around them and to let go of the world. When I was in the black mass before moving towards the light, I felt the presence of such lingering spirits. They reside there as long as they want to in its love and warmth, accepting its healing influence, but eventually they learn to move on to accept the greater warmth and security of God.[26]

But Scripture says, "It is appointed unto men once to die, but after this the judgment" (Heb. 9:27). Scripture repeatedly teaches that the judgment of the wicked is based on works they do while on earth (Rom. 2:5-6; 2 Cor. 11:15).

The New Age Beliefs

So there are definite overtones of Mormonism in Betty Eadie's revelation of "heaven." But she is no doctrinaire Mormon. There are also some ideas in her book that seem more in harmony with the mysticism of the New Age movement than with the beliefs of orthodox Latter-Day Saints.

The New Age movement is a loosely-related array of ideas and philosophies that have much in common with both Hinduism and ancient gnosticism. New Age religions are *pantheistic* (believing in the divinity of creation as well as the Creator), *mystical* (viewing truth as something one finds within oneself), and *syncretistic* (blending and merging religious ideas from any number of sources). There is also a large dose of occult superstition in most New Age thought.

Many New Age doctrines are naturally fairly compatible with Mormonism. (There are, for example, obvious elements of pantheism, mysticism, and syncretism in Mormon belief as well.) But Betty Eadie's account draws more freely from New Age thought than traditional Mormonism normally would. These are the elements of New Age thought evident in her book:

UNIVERSALISM. Into Betty Eadie's heaven, everyone will ultimately attain entrance. Oddly enough, she juxtaposes her strongest statement about the exclusivity of Christ with an unqualified universalism. We noted earlier her acknowledgment that Jesus is the only door to salvation. Yet she states that through that Door *"all"* will one day enter.[27] In her description of the afterlife she never makes any reference to hell. She quite clearly does not believe anyone will spend eternity there.

This universalism is no doubt closely related to Eadie's suggestion, cited earlier, that all religions are equally necessary. In her way of thinking, it matters not what religion a person embraces while on earth, because everyone will eventually be fully enlightened in the afterlife. Thus religious error and false doctrine are seen as things that pose no real long-term danger. This kind of thinking is characteristic of New Age philosophy. In effect, it erases any important distinction between truth and error and easily suits Satan's design that proliferates forms of false religion. This he has done because he wants to offer something attrative to every person. He doesn't care what false religion people accept, because he is not trying to establish a false system. He only wants to destroy the truth of Christianity. As long as people do not accept the gospel truth of Scripture, Satan doesn't care what anyone believes. So all his false religions work together against the truth. Occultism, Mormonism, New Age religion, Hinduism, and whatever else attacks biblical truth furthers the aims of Satan's kingdom.

POSITIVE AND NEGATIVE ENERGIES. Here's a sample that demonstrates how profoundly Betty Eadie has been influenced by New Age teachings:

> Within our universe are both positive and negative energies, and both types of energy are essential to creation and growth. These energies have intelligence—they do our will. They are our willing servants. God has absolute power over both energies. Positive energy is basically just what we would think it

is: light, goodness, kindness, love, patience, charity, hope, and so on. And negative energy is just what we would think it is: darkness, hatred, fear (Satan's greatest tool), unkindness, intolerance, selfishness, despair, discouragement, and so on.

Positive and negative energies work in opposition to each other. And when we internalize these energies, they become our servants. Positive attracts positive, and negative attracts negative. Light cleaves to light, and darkness loves darkness. . . . There is power in our thoughts. We create our own surroundings by the thoughts we think.[28]

Eadie continues like that for several pages, reciting a litany that could well stand as the basic credo of the New Age movement.

SPIRITUAL HEALING. New Age advocates speak frequently about the healing properties of the mind. And if, as Betty Eadie believes, "We create our own surroundings by the thoughts we think," it stands to reason that we can heal ourselves by thinking positive thoughts. That is precisely what Eadie claims:

Our thoughts have exceptional power to draw on the negative or positive energies around us. When they draw at length on the negative, the result can be a weakening of the body's defenses. This is especially true when our negative thoughts are centered on ourselves. I understood that we are in our *most* self-centered state when we are depressed. . . .

All healing takes place from within. Our spirits heal our body. A doctor's sure hands may perform surgery, and medicine may provide ideal circumstances for health, but it is the spirit that effects the healing. A body without a spirit cannot be healed; it cannot live for long.[29]

Eadie states that there is spiritual power within us to enable us actually to alter our bodies' cells for healing. In fact, focusing on one's infirmities is a wrong use of negative energy and can be counter-productive:

> I saw that I had often yielded to negative "self-talk," such as, "Oh, my aches and pains," "I'm not loved," "Look at my sufferings," "I can't endure this," and more. Suddenly I saw the *me, me, me* in each of these statements. I saw the extent of my self-centeredness. And I saw that not only did I claim these negativisms by calling them mine, but I opened the door and accepted them as mine. My body then lived a sort of self-fulfilling prophecy: "Woe is me," was translated in the body as "I am sick." I had never thought of this before, but now I saw how clearly I had been a part of the problem.[30]

Of course, many others *have* thought of this before, including Mary Baker Eddy and virtually all the metaphysical science-of-mind cults that flourished a century or so ago. Such groups were the forerunners of the modern New Age movement, which holds very similar doctrines about healing and the mind.

CREATING ONE'S OWN REALITY. Another corollary of Betty Eadie's assertion that "we create our own surroundings by the thoughts we think" is the idea that truth and reality are subjective, unique to every individual. All our "surroundings"—including metaphysical realities—are merely the product of our thoughts. "If we understood the power of our thoughts," Eadie writes, "we would guard them more closely. If we understood the awesome power of our words, we would prefer silence to almost anything negative. In our thoughts and words we create our own weaknesses and our own strengths."[31] In other words, our thoughts determine what "reality" is.

The moral effects of such relativism are abominable. This means, for example, that people afflicted with illnesses and disabilities are viewed as having brought these things upon themselves. Eadie writes, "To my surprise I saw that most of us had selected the illnesses we would suffer, and for some, the illness that would end our lives."[32] On a "20/20" interview with Hugh Downs, Eadie stated that the victims of the Nazi Holocaust had chosen their own fate before birth.[33] This has the effect of trivializing human suffering and absolving the Nazi butchers of their crimes. An evangelical expert on the New Age movement, Doug Groothuis, has written, "If the Holocaust victims were not really victims at all but willing participants, then the Nazis should not have been morally condemned; they were simply enacting the wishes of their subjects. Surely, this is morally absurd."[34]

PANTHEISM. Pantheism is the notion that God and the universe are one. Pantheism is often expressed as a belief in the divinity of the creature as well as the Creator. No doubt the best-known example of New Age pantheism is actress Shirley MacLaine's claim that she is God. Such a claim is actually quite common in the world of the New Age; most New Age philosophies include the notion that God is embodied in all creation. That is why the New Age movement has such an affinity with those who want to deify nature and worship "Mother Earth."

Betty Eadie believes we all are divine. In her New Age and Mormon belief system, human spirits are literally the offspring of God and therefore essentially divine. As we have seen, she claimed omniscience for herself. Elsewhere she specifically states that human nature is "divine,"[35] and that prior to birth all human spirits possess "divine knowledge"—an omniscience that enables them to know exactly what they will face here on earth.[36]

Eadie describes one event in her heavenly travels where she noticed a rose by a river. As she looked at the rose, she says, its presence surrounded her. "I experienced it as if I *were* the flower! . . . I felt God in the plant, in me, his love pouring into us. We are all one!"[37] That is sheer pantheism.

As she describes her first meeting with the Jesus figure in her

vision, Betty Eadie writes, "I felt his light blending into mine, literally, and I felt my light being drawn to his. It was as if there are
two lamps in a room, both shining, their light merging together. It's
hard to tell where one light ends and the other begins; they just
become one light . . . I felt his enormous spirit and knew that I had
always been part of him, that in reality I had never been away from
him."[38]

There is a sense, of course, in which Scripture teaches that
Christians are united with Christ. But not in a way that obscures the
Creator-creature distinction, and certainly not in a way that harks
back to some eternal relationship between the human and the divine.
Betty Eadie's theology is non-Christian pantheism.

DUALISM. An unbiblical dualism also pervades all New Age belief.
Dualism is the notion that everything is reducible to two
fundamental principles—yin and yang, good and evil, light and
darkness, or whatever. To the dualist, all reality is explainable in
terms of the struggle between these two fundamental principles—
rather like *Star Wars'* The Force and The Dark Side of the Force.
In New Age philosophy the fundamental principles can be
described in terms of spirit and matter, light and darkness,
ignorance and knowledge, mind and body, heaven and earth—or
similar dualisms.

New Age dualisms color Betty Eadie's heaven. The juxtaposi-
tion of good-evil, spirit-body, and heaven-earth dualities is a running motif throughout her book, giving it a distinctly New Age
vocabulary. Dualism lies behind her concept of positive and negative energy. Dualism is the ground for her views on how spirit and
body work together in the process of healing. Dualism also frames
her view of sin and evil.

Dualism is inherently incompatible with a biblical view of sin. If
the dualistic worldview is correct, two fundamentally opposite forces
have held one another in tension from eternity past. Evil becomes

just as necessary as good. And that is the nature of things in Betty Eadie's heaven. As we have seen, she believes the Fall of Adam and Eve was a necessary evil. Furthermore, in Eadie's dualistic system, sin itself is not really an offense against a holy God, but rather the result of too much negative energy. Anger, hatred, envy, bitterness, and a lack of forgiveness are not so much *sins* for which we need atonement, but rather negative influences we must learn to "let go of."[39]

Eadie speaks of sin only occasionally, and as Groothuis notes, when she uses the word at all, she usually puts it in quotation marks.[40] In a classic example of her dualism, Eadie asserts that "our spirit bodies are full of light, truth, and love, [but] they must battle constantly to overcome the flesh."[41] That battle has the effect of strengthening the good in us, she says, and the resulting growth process is what will eventually free us from the influence of evil. Thus "sin" is simply a necessary force to be regulated and mastered by the normal mechanisms of spiritual growth. It is not seen as an enemy that can be ultimately destroyed and vanquished—nor is there any need for expiation through Christ's substitutionary atonement.

In fact, far from acknowledging the need for atonement, Betty Eadie declares that "sin is not our true nature. Spiritually we are at varying degrees of light—which is knowledge—and because of our divine, spiritual nature we are filled with the desire to do good."[42] That flatly contradicts Scripture, which says we are *by nature* children of wrath (Eph. 2:3), enemies of God (Rom. 5:10), incapable of being subject to God's laws (Rom. 8:7). Scripture says there is no one who does good, not even one (Rom. 3:12).

But according to Betty Eadie, "In the spirit world they don't see sin as we do here. *All* experiences can be positive."[43]

All dualism inevitably has this tendency to obliterate the moral significance of evil. If evil is an eternal cosmic force, then it is something to be tolerated and understood and even used—not an enemy that can ever be destroyed. Perhaps this explains Betty Eadie's nonchalant approach to humanity's sin problem. For example, Eadie says that while in heaven, she underwent a review of her entire life, displayed before her "in the form of what we might consider extremely well-defined holograms."[44] As she watched the replay of her life, she began to feel ashamed:

> I saw the disappointment I had caused others, and I cringed as their feelings of disappointment filled me, compounded by my own guilt. I understood all the suffering I had caused, and I felt it. I began to tremble. I saw how much grief my bad temper had caused, and I suffered this grief. I saw my selfishness, and my heart cried for relief. How had I been so uncaring?[45]

Eadie describes what she saw as the "ripple effect" of her wrong deeds. When she had wronged people, they had in turn wronged others, and so on. As she began to understand the far-reaching effects of her wrongs, she says, her pain multiplied and became unbearable.

In the midst of this, Eadie claims, the Savior stepped forward and urged her not to feel so bad about herself. "You're being too hard on yourself," she claims Jesus told her. Then he showed her that her good deeds had an equal and opposite "ripple effect."[46] All the good deeds in effect undid the bad ones—dualism again. "My pain was replaced with joy," she writes.

It's easy to see how this kind of thinking obliterates the need for atonement. One can supposedly cancel out one's own sin simply by doing enough good to undo sin's effects. Christ's work on the cross becomes superfluous. This is not true Christianity. This thinking is the result of a pagan dualism.

At this point we need to acknowledge that some people might think of Christianity itself as dualistic. After all, don't Christians understand the conflict of the ages as a battle between good and evil, or God and Satan? Is this not a proper dualism?

No, it is not. Satan is neither eternal nor equal to God. He is a created being. There is no fundamental, eternal principle besides

God himself. Evil is not an abiding challenge to His goodness. It is a condition into which creation has fallen and from which creation will be redeemed. Evil is *not* an eternal force on a par with God Himself. God and Satan are not equal opposites. Nor are good and evil.

In other words, true Christianity is inherently monistic. Christians believe in one, and only one, eternal principle—God Himself. He alone is sovereign over Satan and evil. Or in other words, in orthodox Christian thought, at the beginning of all reality and all existence, there is only God. "He is before all things and by him all things consist" (Col. 1:17). Even the doctrine of the Trinity does not alter Christianity's basic monism. God is three Persons in *one* essential Being.

So the nature of Christian truth rules out dualism. And history reveals that all who have tried to mix dualism with Christianity have fallen into serious heresy. The long history of gnosticism provides ample proof of this.

GNOSTICISM. Betty Eadie's doctrine, like all New Age philosophy, is infected with gnosticism. Gnosticism is a name for the various teachings of several unorthodox sects that flourished in the early centuries of Christianity. Gnosticism was dualistic, mystical, and always heretical. Strains of gnosticism survive in the New Age movement. In fact, one could say that the New Age movement *is* a revival of gnosticism. Though gnostics often use Christian language and a biblical vocabulary, gnostic ideas are hostile to true Christianity. Therefore, genuine believers must be on guard against the influx of neo-gnosticism.

The key idea underlying all gnosticism—the one from which it takes its name—is the belief that some higher knowledge than that found in the revealed truth of Scripture is available to enlightened souls. Gnostics don't always agree on *what* the "secret" to enlightenment is; but they agree that it is kept secret from all but enlightened ones, found in some "key" to truth that lies, inevitably, beyond Scripture.

Gnosticism is therefore inherently mystical—teaching people to look within themselves for the secret knowledge. This knowledge can be acquired through dreams and visions, angelic messengers, direct communication from God into the mind, biofeedback, one's own emotions, an out-of-body experience—or as in Betty Eadie's case, a combination of all of these, combined with a journey of the soul to the realm beyond.

Eadie's entire claim rests on the assertion that she is now, by virtue of her supposedly post-mortem experience, privy to the secrets of the universe. She claims to hold knowledge that goes beyond what Scripture reveals about heaven. Therefore she sets herself up as a higher authority on heaven than Scripture itself. This is classic gnosticism.

Other Unbiblical Ideas

Betty Eadie's book is filled with other unbiblical ideas—some lesser, some greater in importance. Here are a few of them:

THE SOVEREIGNTY OF THE HUMAN WILL. Mrs. Eadie espouses a radical free-will doctrine that erases the biblical doctrine of divine sovereignty. She describes her thoughts as she looked in on her own children from the realm of the dead: "They were individual spirits, like myself, with a intelligence that was developed before their lives on earth. Each one had their own free will to live their lives as they chose. I knew that this free will should not be denied them."[47] She says she realized that her children were living their lives according to an agenda that they had chosen for themselves before their births. And, according to Betty Eadie, their free-will choices could not be denied them. "There was no need for sorrow or fear."[48]

She expands on these notions later in the book, writing,

> I saw that in the pre-mortal world we knew about and even chose our missions in life. . . . We were given agency to act for ourselves here. Our own actions determine the course of our lives, and we can alter or redirect our lives at any time. I understood that this was crucial; God made the promise that he wouldn't intervene in our lives *unless we asked him*. And then through his omniscient knowledge he would help us attain our righteous desires. We were grateful for this ability to express our free will and to exercise its power. This would allow each of us to obtain great joy or to choose that which would bring us sadness. The choice would be ours through our decisions.[49]

Scripture teaches no such thing. Far from exalting the freedom of the human will, Scripture describes us as hopelessly in bondage to sin and wrong desires. "The carnal mind is enmity against God: for it is not subject to the law of God, neither indeed can be" (Rom. 8:7). We are subject to sin's bondage all our lives (Heb. 2:15).

Scripture also uses the metaphor of death to describe the spiritual condition of the human heart. We are said to be "dead in trespasses and sins" (Eph. 2:1). We live our lives enslaved to wrong desires, "in the lusts of our flesh, fulfilling the desires of the flesh and of the mind; and [are] by nature the children of wrath" (v. 3). Far from promising not to intervene unless we ask him, God's sovereign intervention is necessary for our salvation (vv. 4-5). Ours would be a hopeless situation indeed if God agreed to permit us to choose our own way and promised "that he wouldn't intervene in our lives unless we asked him."

Scripture plainly teaches that God's will is sovereign, not the sinner's. "It is not of him that willeth, nor of him that runneth, but of God that showeth mercy" (Rom. 9:16). He saves sinners in spite of their love for sin and their hatred of His righteousness. A choice was indeed made before the foundation of the world, but it was

God, not us, who chose that we should be holy and blameless before Him (Eph. 1:4).

HUMAN SELF-SUFFICIENCY. In addition to making the sinner's will sovereign, Betty Eadie's theology insists that humans are in and of themselves sufficient to meet all their own spiritual needs.

This doctrine renders God virtually unnecessary. No wonder Mrs. Eadie claims God has promised to stay out of human affairs. She believes people are capable of helping themselves without divine intervention: "I saw that we *always* have the right attribute to help ourselves, though we may not have recognized it or learned how to use it. We need to look within. We need to trust our abilities; the right spiritual tool is always there for us."[50] This is a damning doctrine to proclaim to sinners who are utterly incapable of doing anything to save themselves. Jesus' message was exactly opposite: "Without me you can do nothing" (John 15:5).

SALVATION BY HUMAN WORKS. Nonetheless, the notion that sinners are both sovereign in the exercise of their will and spiritually self-sufficient naturally puts the burden of salvation on the sinner's own back and establishes a system of works. This is a common failing of all cults and false doctrines.

By Betty Eadie's way of thinking, our earthly lives are simply part of an eternal growth process. Our sins are nothing but tools for us to learn by.[51] Divine grace is an unwelcome intruder in such a system, because when God does anything *for* us, it is virtually a lost growth opportunity. (That's why she suggests God has promised not to intervene unless we ask Him.) And since all our human deficiencies are simply imperfections that can be outgrown, we must pursue the process on our own. "We are to create our own lives, to exercise our gifts and experience both failure and success. We are to use our free will to expand and magnify our lives."[52]

And love is supreme.[53] "Love is really the only thing that matters."[54] It's all "so simple. *If we're kind, we'll have joy.*"[55]

AN UNDUE EMPHASIS ON ANGELS. Although Betty Eadie claims God doesn't want to intervene in human affairs, angels evidently have no compunctions about doing so. Eadie claims angels orchestrate the workings of providence.[56] They answer people's prayers.[57] Guardian angels hover around us all the time and are available to us virtually on command.[58] She says angels frequently come to us from the realm beyond, to prompt us to be faithful to the commitments we made before our birth.[59] Scripture, of course, teaches none of this.

MISCELLANEOUS UNBIBLICAL CLAIMS. Betty Eadie's book is filled with many other teachings that find no support whatsoever in Scripture, such as her claim that infant souls "can choose to enter their mother's body at any stage of her pregnancy."[60] She also suggests that prayers on behalf of departed people can be helpful to them in the spirit world.[61] And she completely omits any reference to the role of the Holy Spirit, evidently not believing in His personality.

ENCHANTED WITH ERROR

If it seems I have belabored the errors in Betty Eadie's account of heaven, it is because these are very serious errors, yet it appears that millions have been influenced by them. People are inexplicably enchanted with tales from the afterlife. And while *Embraced by the Light* is the best-known and most popular such account so far, it will in all likelihood not be the last.

In fact, other similar tales are beginning to appear already—some with even more ominous doctrinal overtones than Betty Eadie's. One such example is a book titled *Saved by the Light,* by Dannion Brinkley, which has already made it to *The New York Times* bestseller list.

Brinkley's journey into the afterworld occurred after he was struck by lightning. There are many close similarities between his account and Eadie's, but one major difference is that Dannion Brinkley is overtly hostile to Christianity, and biblical Christianity in particular. He suggests that Christianity is responsible for making people think that they are "not capable of being what it is that we truly are."[62]

Brinkley believes he was sent back to convey a message to the world. The message is this: The way mankind will go is not carved in stone. We have an opportunity to change things. In Brinkley's words, a heavenly being told him

> that I was to come back—just in case people didn't change, since the world as we know it was going to change and pass away; that religion would crumble and institutions would crumble, and governments would collapse because of the lies—and that what I had to do was prepare a system that people could come to that didn't have dogma, didn't have religion attached to it, and that they could go through an eight-step program to really find a way to renew themselves and their spirit in a world that was no longer secure, a world that you could not trust.[63]

Dannion Brinkley has found that "system without dogma" in the New Age movement, and now he is an evangelist for it. Asked how to reconcile his experience with Betty Eadie's, he said,

> People relate a little differently because of the cultural heritage or the religious heritage. Like the being of light I saw, Betty Eadie saw Jesus. Some see Mohammed, some see Krishna. Everybody has a name for it. *Nonetheless, it is still the same experience.* I have found in talking to Raymond [Moody] and talking to people myself, the near death experience is so uniform, so specific, that no matter what the culture, it's there, it exists—regardless of whatever particular dogma is attached to

it. . . . When you reach that spiritual level of consciousness, you see whatever your life's course has taught you.[64]

That is a virtual admission, from one of the leading advocates of near-death experiences, that such experiences can teach us nothing objective about life after death. They are inevitably shaped and interpreted by the person's existing worldview. They are no more reliable than dream analysis for giving us any reliable understanding of the unseen world.

People who draw their opinions about life after death and other spiritual matters from the stories of such experiences are playing with fire—hellfire! That is Satan's goal for them.

THINGS NOT LAWFUL
TO BE UTTERED

I've read many accounts of people's near-death experiences and visions of heaven. What is most remarkable to me in virtually all of them—even the ones that supposedly reflect a "Christian" perspective—is that they are not the least bit like the descriptions of heavenly visions in Scripture.

The centerpiece of heaven's glory in Scripture is always God Himself (cf. Isa. 6:1-3). Yet in the retelling of near-death experiences, it is inevitably the human subject who takes center stage. It was this way with Betty Eadie, for example. Instead of falling on her face in holy fear as Ezekiel did when he glimpsed God (cf. Ezek. 1:28), Eadie describes how *she* spelled out the terms under which she would agree to return to earth—and, she says, "They agreed to *my* terms."[65] Instead of trembling at her own uncleanness in the presence God as Isaiah did (Isa. 6:5), Eadie claims she couldn't tell where her own light left off and Jesus' light began to shine.[66] Instead of seeing Jesus Christ as "Alpha and Omega, the beginning and the end, the first and the last," the way the apostle John saw

Him (Rev. 22:13), Betty Eadie says she remembered how she had personally been with Him as an observer at Creation.

Such a vision of "heaven" plainly has nothing to do with the heaven spoken of in Scripture. In fact, the modern visionaries make a stark contrast to people in Scripture who were given glimpses of heavenly glory. The apostle Paul, for example, relates his account only reluctantly, fourteen years after the fact, framing it as a third-person narrative:

> *I knew a man in Christ above fourteen years ago, (whether in the body, I cannot tell; or whether out of the body, I cannot tell: God knoweth;) such an one caught up to the third heaven. And I knew such a man, (whether in the body, or out of the body, I cannot tell: God knoweth;) how that he was caught up into paradise.*
> *—2 Cor. 12:2-4*

When it comes to relating specific details of what he saw in heaven, the apostle is simply not very talkative. He only says that he "heard unspeakable words, *which it is not lawful for a man to utter*" (v. 4, emphasis added).

Here we learn that the apostle Paul, who had been called to one of the most important apostolic roles in the early church, regarded the details of what he saw and heard in his heavenly vision as unlawful things to recount. How does that compare with people today who fill up whole books, reporting what they supposedly saw and heard on their trips to heaven?

Clearly, because Scripture is the Word of God, we must reject every anecdotal account that contradicts what Scripture teaches. Ultimately, we are forced to conclude that the Bible is our *only* reliable source of information about heaven. There's no point in probing and dissecting people's near-death experiences, as if they would give us some important truth about the afterlife that we are lacking from Scripture. What Scripture teaches us about heaven, angels, and the afterlife is sufficient and accurate. God has already given us all we need to know to equip us fully for every good work (2 Tim. 3:17). There's nothing an eyewitness testimony could reliably add.

Furthermore, those who demand to know more than Scripture tells us are sinning: "The secret things belong unto the Lord our God: but those things which are revealed belong unto us and to our children for ever" (Deut. 29:29). The limit of our curiosity is thus established by the boundary of biblical revelation.

As we get into our study of what Scripture teaches, you'll see that although there are many questions left unanswered, Scripture does in fact give us a remarkably full and clear picture of heaven and the spiritual realm.

It is the inerrant biblical truth about heaven that should grip our hearts and minds—not a lot of fantastic and delusional ideas from someone's near-death experience.

When Scripture commands us to fix our hearts on heavenly things, it is teaching us that our focus should be on Christ, and on the true heavenly glory—not that we should immerse ourselves in fantasies about the heavenly life. Colossians 3:2—"Set your affection on things above, not on things on the earth"—is simply another way of phrasing the first and great commandment: "Thou shalt love the Lord thy God with all thy heart, and with all thy soul, and with all thy mind, and with all thy strength" (Mark 12:30).

NO EARTHLY IDEA ABOUT HEAVEN

Journeys to heaven and back are not the exclusive domain of cults and the New Age movement. Christian television is fairly crawling with people who recount fantastic stories of heavenly excursions they have made. For example, Richard Eby, who is a frequent guest on the worldwide Trinity Broadcasting Network (TBN) says he has visited *both* heaven and hell. Each time he tells his story, it seems, he embellishes it with more extrabiblical details.

Eby wrote a book about his heavenly experience titled *Caught Up into Paradise*.[1] He says he fell two stories off a balcony and landed on his head. He says he was taken to heaven, where he had a translucent body and the ability to float around at will. He has returned to TBN again and again to reveal more details about heaven.

Eby claims that during a TBN-sponsored tour of the Holy Land in 1977, he paid a visit to hell as well. While the tour group was seeing Lazarus's tomb in Bethany, Eby says, the lights suddenly went dark, and he realized Jesus was standing right next to him. He writes, "I heard the same wonderful Voice that had spoken to me from the cloud in my hospital room five years before: 'My son; I showed you heaven, now I show you hell. You must know about them both.'"[2]

Eby's tour of hell lasted only two minutes, but he says that was plenty long enough. According to him, hell is no pit of fire; it is cold and dank, "The kind [of cold] that sickens and chills every cell just enough to ache but not get numb. There was no way ever to get warm, not in that dank pit! And the smell! Horrid, nasty, stale, fetid, rotten, evil . . . mixed together and concentrated," Eby says. "Somehow I knew instantly that these were the odors of my Pit-mates. Stinking, crawling, demons seen mentally delighting in making me wretched."[3] And so Eby returned from Lazarus's tomb and from the realm of the dead with a story that is surely more fantastic than any Lazarus himself ever told about the afterlife! In recent years, Eby's vivid descriptions of hell have been recounted as frequently on TBN as his vision of heaven.

FOR HEAVEN'S SAKE—OR FOR EARTH'S?

A few years ago I wrote a book on the charismatic movement in which I examined the claims of several charismatic visionaries who claim to have seen heaven (or hell) firsthand and lived to tell the tale. One of these was Roberts Liardon, who says he made visits to heaven at least three times—all before he was even twelve years old. He is now a charismatic pastor in wide demand at conferences, where he recounts details of his multiple visits to heaven.

Liardon claims the most important detail he learned on his journey is that heaven contains warehouses full of body parts that are just there for people on earth to claim by faith. You need a new set of eyes? According to Roberts Liardon, if you had enough faith you could get some from the heavenly storehouses, which, incidentally, he says, are a mere "500 to 600 yards from the Throne Room of God." He claims Jesus personally showed him these warehouses. The scene he paints is surreal:

We walked into the first [warehouse]. As Jesus shut the front door behind us, I looked around the interior in shock!

On one side of the building were arms, fingers, and other exterior parts of the body. Legs hung from the wall, but the scene looked natural, not weird. On the other side of the building were shelves filled with neat little packages of eyes: green ones, brown ones, blue ones, etc.

This building contained all the parts of the human body that people on earth need, but they haven't realized these blessings are waiting for them in heaven. . . . And they're for saints and sinners alike.[4]

According to Liardon, Jesus told him, "These are the unclaimed blessings. This building should not be full. It should be emptied every single day. You should come in here with faith and get the needed parts for you and the people you'll come in contact with that day."[5]

Roberts Liardon's heaven *exists to serve earthly purposes.* Although Liardon's message is ostensibly about heaven, his focus is always, unwaveringly earthward. Liardon says there is a stadium in heaven where celestial inhabitants go to watch what is happening on earth. He says Jesus' whole purpose for taking him there in the first place was to commission him for an earthly ministry. Liardon's tour through heaven included such mundane pleasures as a playful splash-fight he claims he had with Jesus in the river of life.[6]

Liardon even says that one of his trips to heaven interrupted an episode of *Laverne & Shirley* he was watching. After the heavenly tour, he was returned to his living room. Then, Liardon says, Jesus "got up, walked back out through the door, the TV clicked back on, and I resumed watching *Laverne & Shirley.*"[7]

All this paints heaven in rather stark earth-tones. It implies that heaven is really subordinate to earth after all. Far from obeying the biblical command to set our affections on things above, this sort of teaching suggests that heaven itself is preoccupied with earthly realities, and that heaven's highest values are actually earthly goods.

Liardon's accounts of his heavenly visions therefore amount to anti-heaven absurdities. Such a fanciful perspective on heaven is every bit as worldly as the grossest kind of materialism.

EARTHBOUND AFFECTIONS

Despite the prevalence of heavenly visions like Betty Eadie's and Roberts Liardon's, however, surely *materialism* is by far the most widespread cause of wrong thinking about heaven these days. As damaging as these mystical visions of heaven may be to people who are duped by them, far more people are swept up in the worldliness and materialism of our generation and lose sight of heaven that way.

Let's be honest, too: materialism is not a problem for pagans only. A look at America's evangelical subculture reveals that materialism is alive and well among Bible-believing Christians. We now have modern megachurch complexes that include high-tech entertainment and special-effects facilities, health spas, fitness centers, bowling alleys, and even food courts. Dispensing material comforts to the flock has become more important for some churches than pursuing the prize of the heavenly calling. Little wonder if the people in the pews miss the point that materialism is sin.

We live in an era of immediate gratification. No generation prior to this has ever had access to so many means of fulfilling fleshly desires in a here-and-now fashion. For example, we have credit cards that allow us to own what we can't afford, go where we wouldn't be able to go, and do what would otherwise be impossible for us to do. Only later do we have to begin paying. The prevalence of uncontrolled credit-card debt is symptomatic of an attitude that says, "I want what I want *when* I want it!" The mindset of our age is against postponed pleasures of any kind. We prefer instant gratification, and we all too willingly sacrifice the future on the altar of the immediate.

Again, Christians are not exempt from this tendency. Rather than setting their affections on things above, many tend to become attached to the things of this earth. It's all too easy to become absorbed in temporal things and neglect what is eternal. Many spend their energy consuming and accumulating things that may promise gratification for now. But ultimately these things—along with any pleasure they bring—will perish. That's why we're commanded to accumulate our treasures in heaven, where they can never be destroyed or pass away. But having lost sight of the "sweet by and by," too many Christians busy themselves with the harried here and now.

Worse, certain high-profile media ministries, preaching a prosperity gospel, give multitudes the disastrous impression that this is what Christianity is all about. They promise people that Jesus wants them healthy, wealthy, and successful. Such teaching is extremely popular because it caters to the spirit of the age—and the desire to have everything in this life, right now. Roberts Liardon is part of this movement, and this very health-wealth-and-prosperity mentality is what has molded his warped view of "heaven."

Because the church doesn't *really* have heaven on its mind, it tends to be self-indulgent, self-centered, weak, and materialistic. Our present comforts consume too much of our thoughts, and if we're not careful, we inevitably end up inventing wrong fantasies about heaven—or thinking very little of heaven at all.

The main part of this book will be in-depth study of the *biblical* description of heaven, angels, and the afterlife. It is my hope and prayer that as we examine carefully what Scripture teaches about the spiritual realm, both you and I will be motivated to "seek those things which are above, where Christ sitteth on the right hand of God" (Col. 3:1).

THE PRECIOUSNESS OF HEAVEN

In reality, everything that is truly precious to us as Christians is in heaven.

The Father is there, and that's why Jesus taught us to pray, "Our

Father which art in heaven, Hallowed be thy name" (Matt. 6:9). *Jesus* Himself is at the Father's right hand. Hebrews 9:24 says, "Christ is not entered into the holy places made with hands, which are the figures of the true; but into heaven itself, now to appear in the presence of God for us." So our Savior is also in heaven, where He intercedes on our behalf (Heb. 7:25).

Many *brothers and sisters in Christ* are there, too. Hebrews 12:23 says that in turning to God we have come "to the general assembly and church of the firstborn, which are written in heaven, and to God the Judge of all, and to the spirits of just men made perfect." Our departed loved ones in the faith are there. Every Old and New Testament believer who has died is now in heaven.

Our names are recorded there. In Luke 10:20 Christ tells His disciples, who were casting out demons, "Rejoice not, that the spirits are subject unto you; but rather rejoice, because your names are written in heaven." And by saying that our names are written in heaven, Christ assures us that we have a title deed to property there. This is *our inheritance.* First Peter 1:4 says we are begotten in Christ "to an inheritance incorruptible, and undefiled, and that fadeth not away, reserved in heaven for you."

"*Our citizenship* is in heaven," according to Philippians 3:20 (NASB). In other words, heaven is where we belong. We're just "strangers and exiles on the earth" (Heb. 11:13). Our goals therefore should not include the accumulation of possessions here. Our real wealth—*our eternal reward*—is in heaven (Matt. 5:12). In Matthew 6:19-21 Jesus says that the only treasure we will possess throughout eternity is there.

In other words, everything we *should* love everlastingly, everything we rightly value, everything of any eternal worth is in heaven.

So self-indulgence and materialism in the church has a particularly destructive spiritual bent. It undermines everything the church should stand for. It tears Christians away from their heavenly moorings. And it makes them worldly.

The term *worldliness* almost sounds outdated, doesn't it? Many people think it sounds petty, legalistic, and unnecessarily old-fashioned. Our grandparents heard sermons against "the sin of worldliness." We think *we're* too sophisticated to concern ourselves with such trivia. But the real problem is that we are not sufficiently concerned with heavenly values, so we don't appreciate how wickedly sinful it is to hold on to earthly ones.

And that is the essence of worldliness: it involves love for earthly things, esteem for earthly values, and preoccupation with earthly cares. Scripture plainly labels it sin—and sin of the worst stripe. It is a spiritual form of adultery that sets one against God Himself: "Ye adulterers and adulteresses, know ye not that the friendship of the world is enmity with God? whosoever therefore will be a friend of the world is the enemy of God" (James 4:4).

I have actually heard Christians say they don't want to go to heaven until they've enjoyed all that the world can deliver. When all earthly pursuits are exhausted, or when age and sickness hamper their enjoyment, then they believe they'll be ready for heaven. "Please God, don't take me to heaven yet," they pray. "I haven't even been to Hawaii!"

But if you live your life without cultivating a love for heavenly things, you will never be fit for heaven. First John 2 says, "Love not the world, neither the things that are in the world. If any man love the world, the love of the Father is not in him. . . . The world passeth away, and the lust thereof: but he that doeth the will of God abideth for ever" (vv. 15, 17).

Some people who claim to know Christ actually love the world so much that frankly there may be good reason to wonder if they can possibly be citizens of heaven. As one of the old spirituals says, "Everybody talkin' 'bout heaven ain't goin' there."

Sadly, though, it is also true that everyone going to heaven isn't talking about it. "My brethren, these things ought not so to be"

(James 3:10). The hope of heaven should fill us with a joy of anticipation that loosens our hearts from this transitory world.

THIS WORLD IS NOT MY HOME

It may sound paradoxical to say this, but heaven should be at the
center of the Christian worldview. The term *worldview* has gained
great popularity over the past hundred years or so. It describes a
moral, philosophical, and spiritual framework through which we
interpret the world and everything around us. Everyone *has* a
worldview (whether consciously or not).

A proper Christian worldview is uniquely focused heavenward.
Though some would deride this as "escapism," it is, after all, the very
thing Scripture commands: "Set your affection on things above, not
on things on the earth" (Col. 3:2). The apostle Paul penned that
command, and his approach to life was anything but escapist.

In fact, Paul is a wonderful example of the proper biblical perspective between heaven and earth. He faced overwhelming persecution on earth and never lost sight of heaven. In 2 Corinthians
4:8-10 he says, "We are troubled on every side, yet not distressed;
we are perplexed, but not in despair; persecuted, but not forsaken;
cast down, but not destroyed; always bearing about in the body the
dying of the Lord Jesus, that the life also of Jesus might be made
manifest in our body." Then in verses 16-17 he adds, "We faint not;
but though our outward man perish, yet the inward man is
renewed day by day. For our light affliction, which is but for a
moment, worketh for us a far more exceeding and eternal weight
of glory." Elsewhere he told the church at Rome, "I reckon that the
sufferings of this present time are not worthy to be compared with
the glory which shall be revealed in us" (Rom. 8:18).

Paul was saying exactly what Peter told the scattered and persecuted believers he wrote to: we endure the sufferings of this
world for the sake of the glory of heaven (1 Peter 1:3-7). Whatever

we suffer in this life cannot be compared with the glory of the life to come.

In other words, we don't seek to *escape* this life by dreaming of heaven. But we do find we can *endure* this life because of the certainty of heaven. Heaven is eternal. Earth is temporal. Those who fix all their affections on the fleeting things of this world are the real escapists, because they are vainly attempting to avoid facing eternity—by hiding in the fleeting shadows of things that are only transient.

The irony is that all the things we can see and touch in this world are less substantive and less permanent than the eternal things of heaven—which we can grasp only by faith. The apostle Paul wrote, "We look not at the things which are seen, but at the things which are not seen: for the things which are seen are temporal; but the things which are not seen are eternal. For we know that if our earthly house of this tabernacle were dissolved, we have a building of God, an house not made with hands, eternal in the heavens" (2 Cor. 4:18—5:1).

It always amazes me when I encounter someone living as if this life is an unending reality. Nothing is more obvious than the transitory nature of human life. The fact that this earthly tabernacle—the human body—is "dissolving" becomes obvious at an all-too-early age. This tent is being torn down. "Indeed in this house we groan" (2 Cor. 5:2, NASB). Moreover, "the whole creation groaneth and travaileth in pain together until now" (Rom. 8:22). Nothing in this world is permanent. And that should be obvious to anyone who contemplates the nature of things.

There are many who mistakenly conclude that the brevity of life is a good justification for unbridled hedonism. After all, if there's nothing to life but what we can see and experience in the here and now, why not make the most of personal pleasure? A famous brewery used to advertise its beer by emphasizing the brevity of life: "You only go around once, so grab for all the gusto you can." In a similar vein, a shoe company now advertises, "Life is short. Play hard." How different that is from Jesus' advice to use this earthly life as an opportunity to lay up treasure in heaven!

But if this earthly life were the sum total of human existence, then our existence would be a tragic affair indeed. Remember the Peggy Lee song that was popular in the 1960s, "Is That All There Is?"

> *Is that all there is?*
> *Is that all there is?*
> *If that's all there is my friend,*
> *Then let's keep dancing.*
> *Let's break out the booze*
> *And have a ball,*
> *If that's all there is.*

As Christians we naturally lament the sense of futility and despair expressed in that song. But let's also acknowledge that the worldview the song expresses is the only logical alternative to Christianity. If our existence is the product of nothing and will lead to nothing, then all of life itself is really nothing. Or (as one skeptic expressed it), we are just protoplasm waiting to become manure. If that is the case, then there's really no good reason we should not simply eat, drink, and be merry while we wait to die.

But Scripture tells us that is the worldview of a fool (Luke 12:19-20). How much better to have the eternal perspective! I read somewhere an account of John Quincy Adams, who when asked late in life how he was doing replied, "John Quincy Adams is well, sir, very well. The house in which he has been living is dilapidated and old, and he has received word from its maker that he must vacate soon. But John Quincy Adams is well, sir, very well."

Paul says that when the earthly tabernacle of our body is gone, we will receive a new building from God, eternal in the heavens. To complete 2 Corinthians 5:2, which I quoted in part above, "in this house we groan, *longing to be clothed with our dwelling from heaven*"

(NASB, emphasis added). Romans 8:23 says that in heaven even our failing bodies will be redeemed. Our groaning will be ended when we are finally clothed with a heavenly body.

That alone would be good reason to fix all our hopes and affections on heaven, wouldn't it? My dear friend Joni Eareckson Tada knows this as well as anyone. Her earthly body was paralyzed from the shoulders down when she dived into shallow water as a teenager. As long as I've known her, she has had her heart set on heaven. It shows in her conversation, her songs, her radio messages, and her artwork. Often it seems as if talking with her draws one to the very edge of heaven where we can see in. Joni explains this in her recent book on the subject:

> I still can hardly believe it. I, with shriveled, bent fingers, atrophied muscles, gnarled knees, and no feeling from the shoulders down, will one day have a new body, light, bright, and clothed in righteousness—powerful and dazzling. . . .
>
> It's easy for me to "be joyful in hope," as it says in Romans 12:12, and that's exactly what I've been doing for the past twenty-odd years. My assurance of heaven is so alive that I've been making dates with friends to do all sorts of fun things once we get our new bodies. . . . I don't take these appointments lightly. I'm convinced these things will really happen.[8]

Whether or not the apostle Paul made appointments with people as he looked ahead to heaven, Scripture does not say. But clearly he had that very same kind of vivid expectation as he waited for heaven. Look again at these first few verses of 2 Corinthians 5:

> *We know that if our earthly house of this tabernacle were dissolved, we have a building of God, an house not made with hands, eternal in the heavens. For in this we groan, earnestly desiring to be clothed upon with our house which is from heaven: if so be that being clothed we shall not be found naked. For we that are in this tabernacle do*

groan, being burdened: not for that we would be unclothed, but clothed upon, that mortality might be swallowed up of life.

—vv. 1-4

In this body we groan because we are burdened by sin, sickness, sorrow, and death. Yet we don't want to be unclothed. In other words, we have no ambition to become disembodied spirits. *That's* not what we're yearning for. We want both our spirits and our bodies to enter the presence of God. And that is God's plan, too.

Some people have the notion that heaven is wholly ethereal, spiritual, and unreal. They envision it as a wispy existence in a dreamlike spiritual dimension. That is not the biblical conception of heaven. In heaven we will have real bodies—changed, glorified, made like Christ's resurrection body (Phil. 3:21)—*real,* eternal bodies, just as His was real (cf. John 20:27). And when I get my glorified knees I already have an appointment to go jogging with Joni Tada.

Paul says, "He who prepared us for this very purpose is God, who gave to us the Spirit as a pledge" (2 Cor. 5:5, NASB). The Greek word translated "pledge" is *arrabon*, the same word Paul used in Ephesians 1:14, also referring to the Holy Spirit. In modern Greek a form of *arrabon* refers to an engagement ring. In New Testament times it referred to a down payment or first install-ment—earnest money. So, the Holy Spirit is a token of God's pledge to us that even our bodies will be made new and imperish-able in the glory of heaven.

Paul goes on to apply this truth in very practical terms: "Therefore we are always confident, knowing that, whilst we are at home in the body, we are absent from the Lord: (For we walk by faith, not by sight:) We are confident, I say, and willing rather to be absent from the body, and to be present with the Lord" (vv. 6-8). This world held no fascination for Paul. He longed for the world to come.

Do you find it difficult to say honestly that those verses express the deepest desires of your heart? There is a tendency for most of us to hold tightly to this world because it is all that we know. It is familiar to us. All our dearest relationships are built here. We too easily think of it as home. So we become captive to this life. But when Paul says he is willing to be "present" with the Lord, he employs the Greek word *endemeō*, which literally means "to be at home." We are most truly "at home" only when we are finally with the Lord. Paul understood this. And the knowledge that he belonged in heaven was the very thing that helped him endure the struggles of this life.

We too should long to be clothed with our heavenly form. We should look forward to being absent from the body and present with the Lord. We should become more preoccupied with the glories of eternity than we are with the afflictions of today.

WHAT IS HEAVEN?

The *King James Version* of the Bible employs the word *heaven* 582 times in 550 different verses. The Hebrew word usually translated "heaven," *shamayim,* is a plural noun form that literally means "the heights." The Greek word translated "heaven" is *ouranos* (the same word that inspired the name of the planet Uranus). It refers to that which is raised up or lofty. Both *shamayim* and *ouranos* are used variously in Scripture to refer to three different places. (This explains why in 2 Corinthians 12:2 Paul refers to being caught up into "the *third* heaven.")

There is, first of all, *the atmospheric heaven*. This is the sky, or the troposphere—the region of breathable atmosphere that blankets the earth. For example, Genesis 7:11-12 says, "The windows of heaven were opened. And the rain was upon the earth forty days and forty nights." There the word "heaven" refers to the blanket of atmosphere around the world, which is where the hydrological cycle occurs. Psalm 147:8 says that God "covereth the heaven with clouds." That is the first heaven.

The planetary heaven, the second "heaven," is where the stars, the moon, and the planets are. Scripture uses the very same word for heaven to describe this region. For example, Genesis 1 says,

> *And God said, Let there be lights in the firmament of the heaven to divide the day from the night; and let them be for signs, and for seasons, and for days, and years: and let them be for lights in the firmament of the heaven to give light upon the earth: and it was so. And God made two great lights; the greater light to rule the day, and the lesser light to rule the night: he made the stars also. And God set them in the firmament of the heaven to give light upon the earth.*
>
> —*vv. 14-17*

The third heaven, the one Paul speaks of in 2 Corinthians 12, is *the heaven where God dwells* with His holy angels and those saints who have died. The other two heavens will pass away (2 Peter 3:10); this heaven is eternal.

Someone inevitably asks, If God is omnipresent, how can Scripture say heaven is His habitation? After all, how can an omnipresent Being be said to dwell *anywhere*? Solomon, when dedicating the Temple in Jerusalem, prayed, "Behold, the heaven and heaven of heavens cannot contain thee; how much less this house that I have builded?" (1 Kings 8:27).

It is certainly true that "the heaven and heaven of heavens" cannot contain God. He is omnipresent. There is no realm to which His presence does not reach. The psalmist, exalting God's omnipresence, said, "If I make my bed in hell, behold, thou art there" (Ps. 139:8).

So to say that God dwells in heaven is not to say that He is contained there. But it is uniquely His home, His center of operations, His command post. It is the place where His throne resides. And it is where the most perfect worship of Him occurs. It is in that sense that we say heaven is His dwelling-place.

This concept of heaven as the dwelling-place of God runs throughout Scripture. In the Old Testament, for example, Isaiah 57:15 says, "Thus saith the high and lofty One that inhabiteth eternity, whose name is Holy; I dwell in the high and holy place." So God specifically declares that He has a real dwelling-place. Isaiah 63:15 identifies that place: "Look down from heaven, and behold from the habitation of thy holiness and of thy glory." Psalm 33:13-14 says, "The Lord looketh from heaven; he beholdeth all the sons of men. From the place of his habitation he looketh upon all the inhabitants of the earth."

The same idea of heaven as God's dwelling-place is stressed throughout the New Testament. In fact, it is a running theme in Jesus' Sermon on the Mount. Our Lord said, "Let your light so shine before men, that they may see your good works, and glorify *your Father which is in heaven*" (Matt. 5:16). He cautioned those who were prone to make oaths that they should not swear by heaven, "for it is God's throne" (v. 34). And He instructs His hearers to love their enemies, "[so] that ye may be the children of *your Father which is in heaven*" (v. 45). Matthew 6:1 says, "Take heed that ye do not your alms before men, to be seen of them: otherwise ye have no reward of *your Father which is in heaven.*" He instructs His disciples to pray this way: "Our Father which art in heaven . . ." (v. 9). Nearing the end of the Sermon, He says, "If ye then, being evil, know how to give good gifts unto your children, how much more shall *your Father which is in heaven* give good things to them that ask him?" (7:11). And, "Not every one that saith unto me, Lord, Lord, shall enter into the kingdom of heaven; but he that doeth the will of *my Father which is in heaven*" (v. 21).

This same phrase echoes again and again in both the preaching and the private ministry of Jesus. Matthew 10:32-33 says, "Whosoever therefore shall confess me before men, him will I confess also before *my Father which is in heaven.* But whosoever shall deny me before men, him will I also deny before *my Father which is in heaven."* Matthew 12:50 says, "Whosoever shall do the will of *my Father which is in heaven,* the same is my brother, and sister, and mother." Jesus said to Peter, "Blessed art thou, Simon Barjona: for flesh and blood hath not revealed it unto thee, but *my Father which is in heaven"* (Matt. 16:17). He compared believers to little children and warned people against causing offense to them: "Take heed that ye despise not one of these little ones; for I say unto you, That in heaven their angels do always behold the face of *my Father which is in heaven"* (Matt. 18:10). He added, "It is not the will of *your Father which is in heaven,* that one of these little ones should perish" (v. 14). And, "if two of you shall agree on earth as touching any thing that they shall ask, it shall be done for them of *my Father which is in heaven"* (v. 19). He constantly referred to God as "my *heavenly* Father" (emphasis added throughout).

The concept of heaven as God's dwelling-place is also implicit in the New Testament teaching about the deity of Christ. He is described as "the bread of God . . . which cometh down from heaven" (John 6:33). Christ's own claim of deity is implicit in this statement: "I came down from heaven, not to do mine own will, but the will of him that sent me." He says of Himself, "I am the bread which came down from heaven" (v. 41). Numerous times in John 6 alone he makes this same claim (cf. vv. 50-51, 58). These claims were correctly understood by Jesus' hearers as straightforward assertions that He is God.

In fact, heaven is so closely identified with God in the Jewish conception that it actually became a euphemism for God Himself. *Heaven* was substituted for the name of God by people fearful of taking the Lord's name in vain. Particularly during the Intertestamental Period (the 400 years between the events of the Old Testament and those of the New), the Jewish people developed an almost superstitious fear of using God's name. They believed the covenant name of God (Yahweh or Jehovah) was too holy to pass through human lips. So they began substituting other terms in place of God's name, and "heaven" became a common substitute. By New Testament times that practice was so ingrained that the Jewish people understood most references to heaven as references to God Himself.

Instead of swearing by God's name, for example, they would swear by heaven. And since "heaven" was merely a substitute reference to God Himself, Jesus pointed out that swearing by heaven was a *de facto* violation of the commandment not to take His name in vain. Thus in Matthew 23:22 He says, "He that shall swear by heaven, sweareth by the throne of God, and by him that sitteth thereon." The word *heaven* stood for God Himself.

Such usage is common in the New Testament. Luke refers to "the Kingdom of God." But Matthew, writing to a predominantly Jewish readership, calls it "the kingdom of heaven" (cf. Luke 8:10; Matt. 13:11). We see another example of the use of heaven as a euphemism for God in Luke 15:18, for example, where the prodigal son, rehearsing what he would say to his father, says, "I will arise and go to my father, and will say unto him, Father, I have sinned against heaven, and before thee." He meant, of course, that he had sinned *against God*.

Although heaven is often used this way in place of God's name, we must not conclude that Scripture intends to equate heaven with God Himself. The terms are *not* synonyms. God transcends heaven. Heaven, in the end, is a *place*—the place where God dwells, the place where the elect will dwell with Him for all eternity, the heaven of heavens, the third heaven.

THE REALM OF GOD'S KINGDOM

This is not to suggest that heaven is limited by the normal boundaries of time and space. We have seen that Scripture teaches clearly that heaven is a real place that can be seen and touched and inhabited by beings with material bodies. We affirm that truth unequivocally.

But Scripture also reveals heaven as a realm not confined to an area delimited by height, width, and breadth. Heaven seems to span all those dimensions—and more. In Christ's message to the Philadelphian church, for example, He speaks of the eternal realm as "new Jerusalem, which cometh down out of heaven from my God" (Rev. 3:12). In the closing chapters of Scripture, the apostle John speaks of "that great city, the holy Jerusalem, descending out of heaven from God" (Rev. 21:10). The New Heaven and New Earth are seen blending together in a great kingdom that incorporates both realms. The paradise of eternity is thus revealed as a magnificent kingdom where both heaven and earth unite in a glory that surpasses the limits of the human imagination and the boundaries of earthly dimensions.

So heaven is not confined to one locality marked off by boundaries that can been seen or measured. It transcends the confines of time-space dimensions. Perhaps that is part of what Scripture means when it states that God inhabits eternity (Isa. 57:15). His dwelling-place—heaven—is not subject to the normal limitations of finite dimensions. We don't need to speculate about *how* this can be; it is sufficient to note that this is how Scripture describes heaven. It is a real place where people with physical bodies will dwell in God's presence for all eternity; and it is also a realm that surpasses our finite concept of what a "place" is.

There's another important sense in which heaven transcends normal time-space dimensions. According to Scripture, a mystery form of the kingdom of God—incorporating all the elements of heaven itself—is the spiritual sphere in which all true Christians live even now. The kingdom of heaven invades and begins to govern the life of every believer in Christ. Spiritually, the Christian becomes a part of heaven with full rights of citizenship here and now in this life.

That's exactly what Paul was saying when he wrote, "our citizenship is in heaven" (Phil. 3:20, NASB). There's a positional sense in which we who believe are already living in the kingdom of God.

In Ephesians 1:3 the apostle Paul says that God "hath blessed us with all spiritual blessings *in heavenly places* in Christ" (emphasis added). Ephesians 2:5-6 likewise says, "Even when we were dead in sins, [God] hath quickened us together with Christ . . . and hath raised us up together, and made us sit together *in heavenly places* in Christ Jesus." Note that in both passages, the verbs are past tense. Paul is speaking of an already-accomplished reality. We aren't yet in heaven bodily. But positionally we are seated with Christ in the heavenlies. Because of our spiritual union with Him, we have already entered into the heavenly realm. We already possess eternal life, and the spiritual riches of heaven are ours in Jesus Christ.

Christ Himself preached that the kingdom of heaven is at hand (Matt. 4:17). Yet He said to those who demanded to know when the visible kingdom would come, "The kingdom of God cometh not with observation: Neither shall they say, Lo here! or, lo there! for, behold, the kingdom of God is within you" (Luke 17:20-21).

Think about this: Heaven is where holiness, fellowship with God, joy, peace, love, and all other virtues are realized in utter perfection. But we experience all those things—at least partially—even now. The Holy Spirit is producing in us the fruit of "love, joy, peace, patience, kindness, goodness, faithfulness, gentleness, self-control" (Gal. 5:22-23, NASB). Again, those are the same traits that characterize heaven. Moreover, we have the life of God in us and the rule of God over us. We know joy, peace, love, goodness, and blessing. We have become part of a new family, a new kind of community. We have left the kingdom of darkness for the kingdom of light. We are no longer under the dominion of Satan but the dominion of God in Christ. Second Corinthians 5:17 says, "If any man is in Christ, he is a new creature; the old things passed away; behold, new things have come." We are new creations. *That's* what Jesus meant when He said, "The kingdom of God is within you."

Christ was not denying the reality of a literal, visible, earthly kingdom. Too many prophecies in both the Old and New

Testaments affirm that such a kingdom will one day exist. Nor was He suggesting that heaven is not a real *place*. He was simply teaching that heaven transcends all time-space limitations. He was focusing the Pharisees' attention on the important aspects of the heavenly kingdom that are available right here and now. Immediate entrance to the kingdom of heaven is the very thing the gospel message offers. That's why it is so often called "the gospel of the kingdom" (cf. Matt. 24:14).

When Jesus preached, He called people to enter the Kingdom (Luke 13:24). Sometimes He urged people to be saved (John 5:34). And other times He spoke of inheriting eternal life (Mark 10:30). All three expressions come together in the account of the rich young ruler. He asked Jesus, "What shall I do to *inherit eternal life?*" (Luke 18:18). When the young man turned away without believing, Jesus said, "With what difficulty shall they that have riches *enter into the kingdom of God!*" (v. 24). And the disciples, shocked at what transpired, asked, "Who then can *be saved?*" (v. 26). All three expressions point to the reality that occurs at conversion. When a person trusts Christ, that person is saved, inherits eternal life, and enters into the kingdom of God. Believers come under God's rule, not physically in heaven, but positionally in the heavenlies.

So while we do not yet live physically in heaven, we do have our spiritual citizenship in the heavenly realm. Therefore we should be preoccupied with heavenly things.

HEARTS IN HEAVEN

That is the whole point of this book. If my purpose were merely to dispel earthly myths about heaven, I could fill an entire book with biblical rebuttals of visions like Betty Eadie's and Richard Eby's and Roberts Liardon's—and a host of other similar claims. It is certainly crucial that we recognize the dangers of the gnostic approach to heaven and turn away from it.

But we dare not stop there. We must also seek to understand the *biblical* concept of heaven. We are commanded to contemplate heaven, to pursue it the way Abraham sought the city of God, to fix our affections there.

This means earnestly purging worldliness from our hearts. It means learning to wean ourselves from the preoccupations of this life. It means looking ahead to eternity and living in the expectation of a sure and certain hope. It means looking away from the mundane and temporal, and fixing our eyes steadfastly on Him who is the glory of heaven.

Those who live with this heavenly perspective discover abundant life as God intended it here on earth. Ironically, those who pursue earthly comforts are really the most *un*comfortable people on earth. As Puritan Richard Baxter wrote,

> A heavenly mind is a joyful mind; this is the nearest and truest way to live a life of comfort, and without this you must needs be uncomfortable. Can a man be at a fire and not be warm; or in the sunshine and not have light? Can your heart be in heaven, and not have comfort? [On the other hand,] what could make such frozen, uncomfortable Christians but living so far as they do from heaven? . . . O Christian get above. Believe it, that region is warmer than this below.[9]

Baxter went on to write,

> There is no man so highly honoureth God, as he who hath his conversation in heaven; and without this we deeply dishonour him. Is it not a disgrace to the father, when the children do feed on husks, and are clothed in rags, and accompany with none but beggars? Is it not so to our Father, when we who call ourselves his children, shall feed on earth, and the garb of our souls be but like that of the naked world, and when our hearts shall make this clay and dust their more familiar and frequent company, who should always stand in our Father's presence,

and be taken up in his own attendance? Sure, it beseems not the spouse of Christ to live among his scullions and slaves, when they may have daily admittance into his presence-chamber; he holds forth the sceptre, if they will but enter.[10]

Unfamiliarity with heaven makes a dull and worldly Christian. God has graciously bid us sample the delights of the world to come, and it is only a rebellious and perverse mindset that keeps us mired in the mundane and worldly. God has given us a down-payment on heaven. He has transferred our citizenship there. We "are no more strangers and foreigners, but fellowcitizens with the saints, and of the household of God" (Eph. 2:19). We therefore *cannot* ignore heaven's glory as if it had no significance. In Baxter's words, "There is nothing else that is worth setting our hearts on."[11]

I know few truths in Scripture that are more liberating to the soul than this: "our citizenship is in heaven" (Phil. 3:20, NASB). That is where our hearts should be. The cares of this world are nothing but a snare and a deadly pit. Jesus characterized "the cares of this world, and the deceitfulness of riches, and the lusts of other things" as that which "choke[s] the word, [so] it becometh unfruitful" (Mark 4:19). Similarly, the apostle John writes, "all that is in the world, the lust of the flesh, and the lust of the eyes, and the pride of life, is not of the Father, but is of the world" (1 John 2:16).

"But we have the mind of Christ" (1 Cor. 2:16). We can fix our hearts on the eternal glory of heaven, not on the things of this world, which inevitably come to nought anyway (1 John 2:17). We are members of a new family, having become the children of God (John 1:12). Galatians 4:26 says that the "Jerusalem which is above" is our mother. We have a new citizenship (Phil. 3:20), new affections (Col. 3:1), and a new storehouse where we are to deposit our treasures (Matt. 6:19-20).

And best of all, we can live in the glow of heaven's glory here and now, with our hearts already in heaven. This is to say that the

Christian life is meant to be like heaven on earth. Believers regularly taste the sweetness of the same heaven to which someday we will go to dwell forever. Praising and loving God with all your being, adoring and obeying Christ, pursuing holiness, cherishing fellowship with other saints—those are the elements of heavenly life we can begin to taste in this world. Those same pursuits and privileges will occupy us forever, but we can begin to practice them even now.

WHAT HEAVEN
WILL BE LIKE

G ustav Mahler's Fourth Symphony is based on a poem that describes heaven from a child's point of view. The music certainly *sounds* heavenly. The symphony's fourth movement features a soprano singing the German words to the poem *"Das himmlische Leben"*—"The Heavenly Life." English listeners might simply be moved by the serene beauty of the music. But the German words paint a peculiar picture of heaven.

In the first place, the inhabitants of this heaven are voracious carnivores. The poem speaks of Herod as a butcher who kills unsuspecting little lambs so that the inhabitants of heaven can eat all they like. And the oxen are so plentiful that the apostle Luke slaughters them "without giving it a thought."

The lyrics also have the inhabitants of heaven jumping and skipping and singing—but mostly gorging themselves on an endless supply of food. Peter catches fish, and Martha cooks them. So this child's vision of heaven turns out to be another "fools' paradise" where earthly appetites are indulged.

I'm intrigued by the way the unbelieving world portrays heaven. At one end of the spectrum is this view that heaven exists to gratify earthly lusts. At the other is a cynical suspicion that heaven will be unbearably monotonous. The classic caricature pictures heaven's inhabitants sitting on clouds and playing harps. I don't know if anyone really imagines heaven will be like that, but I have no doubt that many people think of heaven as a bland, boring place with nothing enjoyable to do. Some golfers think the game may lose its charm in heaven when everyone makes only holes in one.

A skeptic once told me, "I'd rather be in hell with my friends than in heaven with all the church people." Such a flippant attitude betrays a tragic lack of regard for the horrors of hell. It also grossly underestimates the blessedness of heaven.

This deep-seated suspicion that heaven may be an eternal bore reflects the sinful thinking of man. As sinners we are naturally prone to think a little sin is surely more enjoyable than perfect righteousness. It is hard for us to imagine a realm wholly devoid of sin and yet filled with endless pleasures.

But that is exactly how heaven will be. We will bask in the glory of God, realizing at last our chief end—to glorify God and to *enjoy* Him forever. The psalmist wrote, "In thy presence is fulness of joy; at thy right hand there are pleasures for evermore" (Ps. 16:11).

Such a thought is unfathomable to our finite minds. But Scripture repeatedly makes clear that heaven is a realm of unsurpassed joy, unfading glory, undiminished bliss, unlimited delights, and unending pleasures. Nothing about it can possibly be boring or humdrum. It will be a perfect existence. We will have unbroken fellowship with all heaven's inhabitants. Life there will be devoid of any sorrows, cares, tears, fears, or pain: "And God shall wipe away all tears from their eyes; and there shall be no more death, neither sorrow, nor crying, neither shall there be any more pain: for the former things are passed away. And he that sat upon the throne said, Behold, I make all things new" (Rev. 21:4-5). Murphy's law will finally be nullified. In heaven, whatever might go wrong can't.

The best of our spiritual experiences here are only small samples of heaven. Our highest spiritual heights, the profoundest of all our joys, and the greatest of our spiritual blessings will be normal in heaven. As we live now in the heavenlies, we are merely tasting the glories of the life to come. When we consider that Christ prayed for all who know Him to spend eternity with Him in unbroken fellowship (John 17:24), our hearts should overflow with gratitude and expectation.

The preacher of Ecclesiastes said, "The day of one's death is better than the day of one's birth" (7:1, NASB). He was merely being cynical about the meaninglessness and futility of this earthly life, but there is a valid sense for the Christian in which it is true that our death ushers us into an infinitely greater glory than our birth ever did. The confidence that heaven awaits us should fill us with a glorious hope. Paul said, "For to me to live is Christ, and to die is gain" (Phil. 1:21). The prospect of heaven made him joyful even in the face of death.

ABSENT FROM THE BODY, PRESENT WITH THE LORD

Paul also said he was "willing rather to be absent from the body, and to be present with the Lord" (2 Cor. 5:8). This was not a morbid death-wish on Paul's part. He was not saying he was fed up with living and eager to die. Rather, he was expressing his confidence that earthly existence is not the end of life at all for the Christian. Death immediately ushers the believer into a fuller, higher realm of more abundant life—in the very presence of the Lord.

If you are a Christian, trusting Christ *alone* for your salvation, Scripture promises that the moment you leave this life you go to heaven. To be absent from the body is to be present with the Lord. To depart this life is to be "with Christ" (Phil. 1:23). "To live is Christ, and to die is gain" (v. 21).

We need to have a heart like Paul's—yearning to be clothed with our heavenly form and to exchange this transient world for eternal joy. He wrote, "This corruptible must put on incorruption, and this mortal must put on immortality" (1 Cor. 15:53). Our mortality will be swallowed up by a more abundant life (2 Cor. 5:4).

Someone inevitably asks about the state of believers who die between now and the final consummation of all things. Are there compartments within heaven? Where did Old Testament believers go when they died? Do believers who die receive temporary bodies between now and the resurrection? What is the intermediate state like? And what about purgatory?

Some Wrong Views

A number of speculative views have been proposed to attempt to answer those questions. With regard to the state of Old Testament believers, for example, some teach that in the Old Testament, hades (the realm of the dead) was divided into two sections—one for the wicked and one for the righteous. They suggest that Old Testament saints who died went to the realm called "Abraham's bosom" (cf. Luke 16:22-23)—a sort of holding tank for the righteous. According to this theory, these believers were not brought into heaven until Christ conquered death in His resurrection.

Most of that is sheer conjecture with little, if any, real biblical support. Wilbur Smith writes, "However abundant the Scriptural data might be regarding the resurrection of believers and their life in heaven, the state of the soul between death and resurrection is rarely referred to in the Bible."[1] Scripture simply does not give much information about the intermediate state. But what we do know from Scripture is enough to debunk wrong theories.

SOUL SLEEP. One view held by many is that the soul of a believer who dies remains unconscious until the resurrection. This view is found in some of the non-canonical writings of the early church. Its best-known advocates today are the Seventh-Day Adventists.

They point out that the word "sleep" is often used in Scripture as a synonym for death. For example, Jesus told the disciples, "Our friend Lazarus sleepeth; but I go, that I may awake him out of sleep" (John 11:11). And Paul described the dead in Christ as "them also which sleep in Jesus" (1 Thess. 4:14).

But the "sleep" referred to in such imagery has to do with the body, not the soul. In his account of the crucifixion, Matthew wrote of a great earthquake: "And the graves were opened; and many bodies of the saints which slept arose" (Matt. 27:52). It is the *body,* not the soul, that "sleeps" in death. The body lies in rest utterly devoid of any sensation or awareness, awaiting reconstitution and resurrection in eternal perfection to join the soul already in heaven, since death. But the soul enters the very presence of the Lord. This was affirmed again and again by the apostle Paul in the verses I cited above, as he described his desire to be absent from the body, so that he could be "present with the Lord" (2 Cor. 5:8; Phil. 1:23).

The souls of the departed enter into their rest. But it is a rest from labor and strife, not a rest of unconsciousness. The apostle John was told to write, "Blessed are the dead which die in the Lord from henceforth: Yea, saith the Spirit, that they may rest from their labours" (Rev. 14:13). Yet he is clearly not describing a "rest" of unconscious sleep; in the scene John witnessed in heaven, the souls of the redeemed were there, actively singing and praising God (vv. 1-4).

Everything Scripture says about the death of believers indicates that they are immediately ushered consciously into the Lord's presence. In the words of the Westminster Confession of Faith, "The bodies of men after death return to dust, and see corruption; but their souls, (which neither die nor sleep,) having an immortal subsistence, immediately return to God who gave them. The souls of the righteous, being then made perfect in holiness, are received into the highest heavens, where they behold the face of God in light and glory, waiting for the full redemption of their bodies" (32.1).

PURGATORY. The Roman Catholic doctrine of purgatory is nowhere taught in Scripture. It was devised to accommodate Catholicism's denial of justification by faith alone. Here's why:

Scripture very clearly teaches that an absolutely *perfect* righteousness is necessary for entry into heaven. Jesus said, "I say unto you, that except your righteousness shall exceed the righteousness of the scribes and Pharisees, ye shall in no case enter into the kingdom of heaven" (Matt. 5:20). He then added, "Be ye therefore perfect, even as your Father which is in heaven is perfect" (v. 48)—thus setting the standard as high as it can possibly be set.

Later in His ministry, when the rich young ruler approached Jesus asking how he might enter heaven, Jesus upheld this same standard of absolute perfection. He began by declaring that "there is none good but one, that is, God" (Matt. 19:17)—not disclaiming sinless perfection for Himself, but plainly pointing out that such perfection is impossible for sinful humanity. Then, however, Jesus told the young man that in order to obtain eternal life, he must have a track record of perfect obedience to the law (vv. 17-21). Again and again, He made the required standard of righteousness impossibly high for all who would seek to earn God's favor on their own.

The young ruler clearly did not understand or acknowledge his own sinfulness. He assured Jesus that he had indeed kept the law from his youth up (v. 20).

Jesus subtly pointed out the young man's covetousness, which was a violation of the Tenth Commandment. From the outset of His conversation with the young man, the Lord was prodding him to confess that no one but God Himself is truly *good*. But the rich young ruler was unwilling to face his own sin, and so he finally went away without salvation.

The disciples marveled at this. The young man was evidently—from the human perspective—one of the most righteous individuals they knew. Notice that no one disputed his claim that he had obeyed the law. There must have been no overt sins in his life that anyone could point to. He was the best of men. So the disciples were floored when he walked away with no assurance of eternal life from Jesus. In fact, Jesus told them, "Verily I say unto you, That a rich man shall hardly enter into the kingdom of heaven" (v. 23).

Again, He was setting the standard at an impossible height. He was saying that the most fastidious legal observance is not enough. The most flawless external righteousness is not enough. All the worldly advantages of wealth are of no help. Only *absolute perfection* is acceptable to God. Our Lord kept underscoring these things because he wanted people to see the utter futility of seeking to earn righteousness by any system of works.

The disciples got the message. They asked, "Who then can be saved?" (v. 25).

And Jesus replied, "With men this is impossible; but with God all things are possible" (v. 26).

We know from Paul's treatise on justification in Romans 4 that God saves believers *by imputing to them the merit of Christ's perfect righteousness*—not in any sense because of their own righteousness. God accepts believers *in Christ*. He clothes them with the perfect righteousness of Christ. He declares them perfectly righteous because of Christ. Their sins have been imputed to Christ, who has paid the full penalty. His righteousness is now imputed to them, and they receive the full merit for it. That is what justification by faith means.

In other words, God does not first make us perfect, then accept us on that basis. He *first* justifies us by imputing to us an alien righteousness, *then* perfects us by conforming us to the image of Christ. He justifies the ungodly (Rom. 4:5).

Paul wrote, "Therefore being justified by faith, we have peace with God through our Lord Jesus Christ" (Rom. 5:1). And, "There is therefore now no condemnation to them which are in Christ Jesus" (Rom. 8:1). Those verses describe our justification as something already accomplished. They speak of it in the past tense. Jesus Himself described justification as an immediate event when He told how the repentant publican was saved after begging God for mercy: "This man went down to his house justified" (Luke 18:14). Justification is thus a completed fact for the believer; it is not an ongoing process. We stand before God fully acceptable to Him because of Christ's righteousness—not our own.

Roman Catholic doctrine denies all that. Catholicism teaches that justification is an ongoing process that depends on the degree of real, personal righteousness we achieve. According to official Catholic teaching, Christ's merit imputed to us is not enough to save; we must earn merit of our own through the sacraments and other good works we do. Righteousness is infused into us, then perfected by our own efforts. According to Catholic teaching, this real, personal righteousness that resides in us is the necessary ground on which God accepts us. And our justification is not complete until we are perfect. This reverses the order, suggesting that we must *first* be perfected, and only *then* is our justification complete.

The Catholic view of justification poses an obvious dilemma. We know too well that even the best Christians fall far short of perfection. No one (Catholic teaching actually says *almost* no one) achieves absolute perfection in this life. And if our own perfection is a prerequisite to heaven, it would seem no one could enter heaven immediately upon death. Any remaining imperfections would need to be worked out first.

The doctrine of purgatory is, therefore, necessary to solve this dilemma. Deny that we are justified by faith alone, and you must devise an explanation of how we can make the transition from our imperfect state in this life to the perfect state of heaven. Purgatory is where Roman Catholics believe most people go after death to be finally purged of their sins and gain whatever merit they may be lacking to enter heaven. Catholicism teaches that this will involve intense pain and suffering.

Oddly enough, although Catholic doctrine denies that the imputed righteousness of Christ is sufficient to save sinners in this life, it does allow the imputation of righteousness from earthly sinners to those in purgatory. Candles are lit, prayers are prayed, and Masses are said for the dead. Supposedly the righteousness earned via the sacrament is imputed to the person in purgatory, and that shortens his or her stay there.

The Biblical Response

As I have said, none of this is taught in Scripture. The sufferings of Christ were fully sufficient to atone for our sins. Our own sufferings can add nothing to the merit of Christ. As the writer of Hebrews says, there is no efficacious sacrifice for sin other than what Christ has provided; if Christ's sacrifice is not sufficient, or if we willfully turn away from it, "There remaineth no more sacrifice for sins, but a certain fearful looking for of judgment and fiery indignation, which shall devour the adversaries" (Heb. 10:26-27).

For all believers, because we are fully justified, there can be no condemnation. No post-mortem suffering is necessary to atone for remaining sin; *all* our sins are covered by the blood of Christ. No merit is lacking that must be made up. Every believer will be able to say with the prophet Isaiah, "I will greatly rejoice in the Lord, my soul shall be joyful in my God; for he hath clothed me with the garments of salvation, he hath covered me with the robe of righteousness, as a bridegroom decketh himself with ornaments, and as a bride adorneth herself with her jewels" (Isa. 61:10).

Some claim that the material in 1 Corinthians 3 describes purgatory, where the believer is put through a fiery judgment to purge out the dross of sin. But read that passage again. It describes the judgment of the believer's works, to see if they are "wood, hay, stubble," or "gold, silver, precious stones" (v. 12). At issue is whether our works endure or are burned up. And it is the works, not the saints themselves, that are tested in the purging fire. This is the judgment that will take place in the eschatalogical future, not an ongoing state of purgatory that believers pass through on their way to heaven:

> *Every man's work shall be made manifest: for the day shall declare it, because it shall be revealed by fire; and the fire shall try every man's work of what sort it is. If any man's work abide which he hath built thereupon, he shall receive a reward. If any man's work shall be burned, he shall suffer loss:* but he himself shall be saved; yet so as by fire.
>
> —*vv. 13-15, emphasis added*

Notice again that only the works, not the believers themselves, must go through the fire. Also note that rewards are what is at issue—not entrance to heaven.

Everything in Scripture indicates that the believer's entrance to heaven occurs immediately upon death. Let's examine a few key passages:

PSALM 16. Here we find the psalmist hopeful even as he faced death: "For thou wilt not leave my soul in hell [Heb., *sheol*, the realm of the dead]; neither wilt thou suffer thine Holy One to see corruption. Thou wilt shew me the path of life: in thy presence is fulness of joy; at thy right hand there are pleasures for evermore" (vv. 10-11). The psalmist anticipated that when he left this world, he would enter the presence of God, finding pleasure and fullness of joy. He had no fear of purgatorial sufferings. And he left no place for the notion of soul sleep.

PSALM 23. The final verse of this familiar psalm says, "Surely goodness and mercy shall follow me all the days of my life: and I will dwell in the house of the Lord for ever." David was certain that once his life was over, he would dwell in the house of the Lord forever (which can refer only to heaven). Notice that he goes immediately from "all the days of my life" to "dwell[ing] in the house of the Lord." The hope he expresses here is exactly the same as Paul's: "to be absent from the body and to be at home with the Lord" (2 Cor. 5:8, NASB).

LUKE 16. When the beggar Lazarus died, Jesus says he "was carried by the angels into Abraham's bosom" (v. 22). As we noted earlier, some think this expression "Abraham's bosom" describes a sort of holding tank where Old Testament saints went while awaiting heaven. I believe both Abraham and Lazarus were in the presence of God. In any case, this account rules out both soul sleep and purgatory.

To shed light on the expression "Abraham's bosom," we turn to a parallel expression that occurs in John 13. This is part of the apostle John's description of that final Passover celebration in the Upper Room. He writes, "Now there was leaning on Jesus' bosom one of his disciples, whom Jesus loved" (v. 23). The scene is a low table, where guests had to recline. This disciple (who was John himself—John 21:20, 24) was in a position so that his head was near Jesus' chest. They positioned themselves that way so they could converse while they ate with a free hand.

So when Jesus says Lazarus was carried to "Abraham's bosom" He indicates that the former beggar was reclining at a banquet table in a celebration of joy, next to Abraham, the father of the faithful. In other words, Lazarus was in the position of a guest of honor. Imagine the dismay of the Pharisees when Jesus portrayed an ordinary beggar reclining at the table next to the greatest of the Jewish Fathers!

Again, I believe this is heaven, not some intermediate state. Scripture never suggests Old Testament believers went to a special compartment where they had to wait for Christ to carry them into glory. In fact, the evidence points to a different conclusion.

MATTHEW 17. For example, when Christ was transfigured, Moses and Elijah appeared with Him (v. 3). Although Christ's death and resurrection hadn't yet occurred, Moses and Elijah were summoned from the realm of departed saints to the Mount of Transfiguration, where they conversed with Jesus about "His departure which He was about to accomplish at Jerusalem" (Luke 9:31, NASB). It seems obvious that they had not been shut away for ages in some intermediate compartment of hades, but were intimately familiar with Christ, partakers of His glory, and knowledgeable enough about His earthly work to discuss the details of what He was about to do. This is an amazing passage, a clear window into the kind of close fellowship we will share with Christ in eternity.

LUKE 23. This familiar passage describes that touching moment during the crucifixion when one of the thieves next to Jesus repented. "He said unto Jesus, Lord, remember me when thou comest into thy kingdom. And Jesus said unto him, Verily I say unto thee, To day shalt thou be with me in paradise" (vv. 42-43).

"Paradise" is the same word the apostle Paul used to describe being caught up into the "third heaven" in 2 Corinthians 12:4. Paradise is a synonym for heaven. It cannot be a reference to purgatory. And the promise of paradise *today* rules out not only purgatory, but soul sleep as well.

If anyone were a candidate for purgatory, this thief would be. Moments before, he had taunted Christ along with the unrepentant thief (Mark 15:32). His repentance was a last-minute change—while he was literally in his death throes. Yet Jesus promised to see him that very day in paradise.

Scripture contains many descriptions of heaven. Some of them are cast in apocalyptic or prophetic language filled with symbolism and mystery. Apocalyptic symbolism in Scripture always means that something of great consequence is under discussion. Don't make the error of thinking symbolic language means the thing described is unreal. As we have already established, the Bible asserts that heaven is a real place. And the descriptions of heaven, even the most apocalyptic ones, describe a real place.

Ezekiel's Wheel

One of the most dramatic descriptions of heaven in all Scripture comes from the prophet Ezekiel. Ezekiel was wonderfully transported to the very heart of heaven in a vision, and he describes in vivid detail what heaven and the throne room of God are like.

Ezekiel 1:4-28 (NASB) says this:

> And as I looked, behold, a storm wind was coming from the north, a great cloud with fire flashing forth continually and a bright light around it, and in its midst something like glowing metal in the midst of the fire. And within it there were figures resembling four living beings. And this was their appearance: they had human form. Each of them had four faces and four wings. And their legs were straight and their feet were like a calf's hoof, and they gleamed like burnished bronze. Under their wings on their four sides were human hands. As for the faces and wings of the four of them, their wings touched one another; their faces did not turn when they moved, each went straight forward. As for the form of their faces, each had the face of a man, all four had the face of a lion on the right and the face of a bull on the left, and all four had the face of an eagle. Such were their faces. Their wings were spread out above; each had two touching another being, and two covering their bodies. And each went straight forward; wherever the spirit was about to go, they

would go, without turning as they went. In the midst of the living beings there was something that looked like burning coals of fire, like torches darting back and forth among the living beings. The fire was bright, and lightning was flashing from the fire. And the living beings ran to and fro like bolts of lightning.

Now as I looked at the living beings, behold, there was one wheel on the earth beside the living beings, for each of the four of them. The appearance of the wheels and their workmanship was like sparkling beryl, and all four of them had the same form, their appearance and workmanship being as if one wheel were within another. Whenever they moved, they moved in any of their four directions, without turning as they moved. As for their rims they were lofty and awesome, and the rims of all four of them were full of eyes round about. And whenever the living beings moved, the wheels moved with them. And whenever the living beings rose from the earth, the wheels rose also. Wherever the spirit was about to go, they would go in that direction. And the wheels rose close beside them; for the spirit of the living beings was in the wheels. Whenever those went, these went; and whenever those stood still, these stood still. And whenever those rose from the earth, the wheels rose close beside them; for the spirit of the living beings was in the wheels.

Now over the heads of the living beings there was something like an expanse, like the awesome gleam of crystal, extended over their heads. And under the expanse their wings were stretched out straight, one toward the other; each one also had two wings covering their bodies on the one side and on the other. I also heard the sound of their wings like the sound of abundant waters as they went, like the voice of the Almighty, a sound of tumult like the sound of an army camp; whenever they stood still, they dropped their wings. And there came a voice from above the expanse that was over their heads; whenever they stood still, they dropped their wings.

Now above the expanse that was over their heads there was something resembling a throne, like lapis lazuli in appearance; and on that which resembled a throne, high up, was a figure with the appearance of a man. Then I noticed from the appearance of His loins and upward something like glowing metal that looked like fire all around within it, and from the appearance of His loins and downward I saw something like fire; and there was a radiance around Him. As the appearance of the rainbow in the clouds on a rainy day, so was the appearance of the surrounding radiance. Such was the appearance of the likeness of the glory of the Lord. And when I saw it, I fell on my face.

That is Ezekiel's description of God's throne in heaven. We can't fully understand all he described, and neither did he. But under the inspiration of the Holy Spirit he attempted within the limitations of human language and intelligence to describe what he saw: blazing light reflected off polished jewels and colored wheels of light mingled with angelic beings (the "living beings"). Around the throne of the eternal, glorious God, he saw a flashing, sparkling, spinning rainbow of brilliance.

How do we interpret such symbolism? Some strive to find meaning in every facet of Ezekiel's vision. (One source I consulted, for example, explains the faces of the angelic creatures like this: The lion refers to majesty and power, the man represents intelligence and will, the ox stands for patient service, and the eagle speaks of swift judgment.) But we must be cautious not to get carried away reading meaning into symbols that are not explained to us. This is not a secret message to be decoded; it is a large picture designed to display the sovereignty, majesty, and glory of God and the incredible beauty, symmetry, and perfection of His heaven. Although it's impossible to interpret the specifics definitively, we *can* understand that Ezekiel's aim was to put the glory of heaven on display. The wheels that moved in concert, the flashing lightning, the sparkling jewels, and the brilliant light—all picture God's glory.

So although Ezekiel's picture of heaven may be beyond our ability to fathom, we can certainly grasp the main idea: Heaven is a realm of inexpressible glory.

John's Apocalypse

John's extended vision of heaven is described throughout the book of Revelation. The Greek word translated "heaven" occurs more than fifty times in the book. Twice God is called "the God of heaven" (11:13; 16:11). The entire book is written from a heavenly perspective, though it deals largely with events that occur on earth.

There are many striking similarities between John's vision and Ezekiel's. John's is a fuller account, of course, but it blends beautifully with what Ezekiel described. In chapter 4, for example, John recounts being caught up into heaven: "After this I looked, and, behold, a door was opened in heaven: and the first voice which I heard was, as it were, of a trumpet talking with me; which said, Come up hither, and I will show thee things which must be hereafter. And immediately I was in the spirit; and, behold, a throne was set in heaven, and one sat on the throne" (vv. 1-2).

Notice that Ezekiel ended his vision of heaven with a description of God's throne and the inexplicable glory of heaven. John *begins* by describing that same throne. Repeatedly in this passage he mentions the throne, which is the center of heaven and the focal point of God's presence. From the throne of God emanates all the glory of heaven.

Verse 3 says, "He who was sitting was like a jasper stone." Jasper is an opaque, translucent crystalline quartz of differing colors, especially shades of green. (But the jasper of ancient times may actually have been a transparent stone.) Verse 3 adds that God was like "a sardius in appearance." Some suggest that the red sardius may speak of God as Redeemer, the One who provided a blood sacrifice—thus stressing the glory of God's redemptive character. Sardius and jasper were also the first and last of the twelve stones on the breastplate of the high priest (Ex. 28:17, 20).

It's impossible to ignore the fact that both Ezekiel and John are describing a scene of breathtaking glory and dazzling beauty—surpassing the limits of human language. John, like Ezekiel, is painting a big picture that portrays heaven as a realm of inexpressible glory. Again, let's not get so caught up in trying to read meaning into the symbols that we miss that rather obvious point.

Language fails when men try to describe divine glory, so John is using these comparisons to precious jewels to picture the breathtaking beauty of heavenly glory. The jewels he mentions were the most stunning, glorious images he could picture, so he resorts to them to make his point. Remember, though, that he is actually describing a glory that far exceeds that of any earthly jewel. If the scene is hard for you to visualize, that's fine. John is purposely painting a picture of glory that exceeds our ability to imagine.

Sounding much like Ezekiel, John continues, "There was a rainbow around the throne, like an emerald in appearance. . . . And from the throne proceed flashes of lightning and sounds and peals of thunder" (vv. 3-5, NASB). Again the imagery is designed to inspire awe and fear. It speaks of an immeasurable glory, power, and majesty.

The thunder and lightning are reminiscent of another scene in Scripture: Mount Sinai, where God came down to give the Law. The Israelites saw the divine glory in the form of thundering and lightning (Ex. 19:16). This language seeks to describe the indescribable. The sense it conveys is an awe that transcends any earthly awe.

John continues his description of the scene around the throne, giving another detail we ought to note carefully: "There were seven lamps of fire burning before the throne, which are the seven Spirits of God" (v. 5, NASB).

That verse confuses a lot of people. It does not suggest that there are seven Holy Spirits. The apostle Paul makes that clear in 1 Corinthians 12:4: "There are diversities of gifts, but the same Spirit" (cf. v. 11)—and in Ephesians 4:4: "There is one body, and *one* Spirit" (cf. Eph. 2:18, emphasis added). So this cannot be a reference to seven distinct Spirits of God. Obviously, that would violate what Scripture teaches elsewhere about the personality of the Holy Spirit.

The expression "seven spirits" is therefore to be understood as apocalyptic symbolism. John links it to seven lamps, which echo the lampstands of the churches in Revelation 2–3. And those in turn seem to have some relationship to the seven lamps in the original tabernacle (cf. Ex. 25:31-37). These were actually seven candles atop a *single* gold lampstand. The imagery the seven lamps conveys is therefore that of a seven-fold menorah. And the reference to "seven spirits" should be interpreted as a reference to the one, albeit "seven-fold," Spirit of God.

In what sense is the Spirit "seven-fold"? This could be a reference back to the Spirit's sovereignty over the seven churches in chapters 2–3. It could also be a reference to Isaiah 11:2, which describes "The spirit of [1] the Lord . . . the spirit of [2] wisdom and [3] understanding, the spirit of [4] counsel and [5] might, the spirit of [6] knowledge and of [7] the fear of the Lord." Whatever it means, it does not suggest that there is more than "one Spirit" by whom we are baptized into the Body of Christ (1 Cor. 12:13). That would run counter to the rest of Scripture (cf. also Eph. 2:18; John 14:16-17).

Look again at Revelation 4. Verse 6 says, "Before the throne there was, as it were, a sea of glass like crystal." Picture the beauty of that scene: a brilliant rainbow and the flashing colors of emerald, sardius, and jasper all splashing off a sea of crystal!

Again, all this color, light, and crystal reflect the splendor and majesty of the throne of God. This is familiar imagery in Scripture. In Exodus 24, we read: "Moses went up with Aaron, Nadab and Abihu, and seventy of the elders of Israel, and they saw the God of Israel; and under his feet there appeared to be a pavement of sapphire, as clear as the sky itself" (vv. 9-10, NASB). The flashing and sparkling light of God's glory is reflected by the crystal-clear, brilliant, sparkling sea of glass. Notice that the crystal sea is described as "pavement of sapphire" in Exodus 24—possibly because of the color reflecting off it. But both passages speak of its extraordinary "clearness." Ezekiel described it as "like the awesome gleam of crystal" (1:22, NASB). Again, it pictures heaven as a realm of unimaginable beauty, where every element of everything is designed as a backdrop to reflect the divine glory.

All this emphasis on brightness and clarity suggests that heaven is not a land of shadows and mists. In the biblical accounts, there is no hint of the long, dark tunnel that is ubiquitous in accounts like Betty Eadie's (see chapter 1). Instead, everything is described in terms of light and brilliance and clarity!

Even when John describes the other inhabitants of heaven, the focus remains on the glory of God. The seats of twenty-four "elders"—no doubt representing the whole body of the redeemed church—encircle the throne (Rev. 4:4). Verse 6 adds that four living creatures also encircled the throne—undoubtedly a reference to angelic creatures, perhaps the cherubim. So surrounding the throne are the angelic host and the church; occupying the throne is God Himself in all the glory of His majestic revelation.

It is significant that the book of Revelation alone mentions the throne of God at least thirty-nine times. All activity in heaven focuses in this direction, and all the furnishings of heaven reflect the glory that emanates from here.

IS THERE A TEMPLE
IN HEAVEN OR NOT?

In the ancient world, the two most important buildings of any national capitol were the palace and the temple. They represented civil and spiritual authority. In heaven the centrality of the throne of God emphasizes both His sovereignty and His worthiness to be worshiped. All heaven is His palace, and all heaven is His temple.

In Revelation 3:12 Christ says, "Him that overcometh [in Johannine writings this refers to every true believer, see pp. 98-99] will I make a pillar in the temple of my God, and he shall go no more out." In Revelation 7:15 one of the twenty-four elders, speaking of saints who have come out of the Great Tribulation, tells the apostle, "Therefore are they before the throne of God, and serve him day and night in his temple: and he that sitteth on the throne shall dwell among them."

Those verses teach that Christians will serve God forever in a heavenly temple. Other passages also speak of a temple in heaven. For example, Revelation 11:19 speaks of "The temple of God which is in heaven" and "the ark of His covenant . . . in His temple" (NASB). Later John describes "the temple of the tabernacle of the testimony in heaven" (15:5). Those passages make it clear that there is a temple in heaven.

In Revelation 21:22, however, describing New Jerusalem, John writes, "And I saw no temple therein: for the Lord God Almighty and the Lamb are the temple of it." Attempting to reconcile Revelation 21:22 with the rest of Revelation, some interpreters argue that presently there *is* a temple in heaven, but when God constructs the new heavens and earth, there *won't be*. That does not seem to capture the most obvious meaning of John's description. The temple in heaven is not a building; it is the Lord God Almighty Himself. Revelation 7:15 implies this when it says "He who sits on the throne shall spread his tabernacle over them." And Revelation 21:23, continuing the thought of *no temple*, adds, "The city had no need of the sun, neither of the moon, to shine in it: for the glory of God did lighten it, and the Lamb is the light thereof."

In other words, the glory of God both illuminates heaven and defines it as a temple. One might say all heaven is the temple, and the glory and presence of the Lord permeate it. Or, as John writes, "The Lord God Almighty and the Lamb *are* the temple of it" (v. 22).

A misunderstanding of such descriptions, unfortunately, has contributed to the notion that heaven is a dull, monotonous place. After all, who wants to be a pillar in a temple we can never leave (cf. Rev. 3:12)? But don't miss the import of what John is saying here. The point is not that we become immovable support posts in a building, but that we enter the limitless presence of the Lord in His own dimension and never again leave *Him*. Remember, *He* is the temple of which we are pillars. The imagery is tremendously rich, echoing Jesus' promise, "I will come again, and receive you unto myself; that where I am, there ye may be also" (John 14:3)—and the apostle Paul's great hope, "So shall we ever be with the Lord" (1 Thess. 4:17). Our place will forever be everywhere God dwells

Bear in mind that both Ezekiel and the apostle John are struggling to describe the indescribable. Even if God had revealed all the details about heaven, we wouldn't be able to comprehend them. It's unlike anything we know. But in Ephesians 2, Paul gives some insight into heaven from a slightly different perspective. Here Paul is describing our utter dependence on God for salvation, saying we were dead in our trespasses and sins (v. 1), by nature children of wrath (v. 3). Then he describes God's mercy and love toward us in saving us from our sins. The thought of God's grace reaching out to save us, when we deserved the opposite, ought to overwhelm us with gratitude and humility.

Now notice what Paul says in Ephesians 2:7: God saved us so "that in the ages to come he might show the exceeding riches of his grace in his kindness toward us through Christ Jesus." That verse won't satisfy people curious to understand what heaven *looks* like, but note the vivid description of what heaven will *be* like: it is a place where the riches of God's grace shine even more brightly than they do here on earth. That is what makes me long for heaven most. Heaven will be an eternity of God pouring out His kindness on His beloved children!

Stop and think of it. Every good thing we know here on earth is a product of God's grace (cf. James 1:17). And we who know Christ are going to heaven for this express purpose: so that God can showcase the infinite riches of His grace by showering His goodness on us endlessly. Does that not make your heart prefer the riches of heaven to the meager pleasures of earth?

NEW
JERUSALEM

Eternal heaven will be different from the heaven where God now dwells. As we noted in chapter 2, in the consummation of all things, God will renovate the heavens and the earth, merging His heaven with a new universe for a perfect dwelling-place that will be our home forever. In other words, heaven, the realm where God dwells, will expand to encompass the entire universe of creation, which will be fashioned into a perfect and glorious domain fit for the glory of heaven. The apostle Peter described this as the hope of every redeemed person: "We, according to his promise, look for new heavens and a new earth, wherein dwelleth righteousness" (2 Peter 3:13).

Even in the Old Testament this was what the righteous hoped for. We know that earthly Canaan was the Promised Land of the nation of Israel. But Hebrews 11 tells us that Abraham, to whom the promise was originally made, actually had his heart set on something more than a mere earthly land-promise. "By faith he sojourned in the land of promise, as in a strange country, dwelling in tabernacles. . . . For he looked for a city which hath foundations, whose builder and maker is God" (vv. 9-10). Abraham's vision was on the eternal, not the earthly. He made himself a nomad in this life, willing by faith to seek his only permanent dwelling in God's eternal city in the world to come.

The Old Testament prophesied a massive renovation of heaven and earth that would eventually make it the saints' eternal dwelling-place. Psalm 102:25-26 pictures the Lord changing our universe as if it were a worn-out garment: "Of old hast thou laid the foundation of the earth: and the heavens are the work of thy hands. They shall perish, but thou shalt endure: yea, all of them shall wax old like a garment; as a vesture shalt thou change them, and they shall be changed." (Interestingly, Hebrews 1:10-12 quotes this passage, attributing the words to God the Father, who is speaking to the Son. This is one of the notable proofs of Jesus' eternal deity.)

Clearly, a major cosmic remodeling has always been the plan of God. This was also God's gracious promise to His people through the Old Testament prophets. Speaking in Isaiah 65:17-19, God says,

> For, behold, I create new heavens and a new earth: and the former shall not be remembered, nor come into mind. But be ye glad and rejoice for ever in that which I create: for, behold, I create Jerusalem a rejoicing, and her people a joy. And I will rejoice in Jerusalem, and joy in my people: and the voice of weeping shall be no more heard in her, nor the voice of crying.

There God states that He will alter the present heaven and earth in a way that amounts to a whole new creation. Notice that in the new universe, New Jerusalem will be the focus of everything. The new heaven and new earth will be so glorious that it makes the first fade into insignificance ("The former shall not be remembered, nor come into mind"—v. 17). In the next and final chapter of Isaiah's prophecy, the Lord promises that this new heaven and new earth will remain forever, as will all the saints of God: "For as the new heavens and the new earth, which I will make, shall remain before me, saith the Lord, so shall your seed and your name remain" (66:22).

Revelation 21 gives what amounts to a full exposition of Isaiah's

promise. Here the apostle John describes his vision of the final consummation of all things. This chapter contains the Bible's most
exhaustive description of the new heaven and new earth—along
with His capital, the Holy City, New Jerusalem. What we see in
microcosm at the end of Isaiah is spelled out more fully at the end
of Revelation.

Here's the setting: The Battle of Armageddon has been fought
(Rev. 19), the earthly, millennial reign of Christ has come to an end
(20:7), and at the great white throne judgment God has sentenced
Satan and all the ungodly to eternal hell (20:11-15). Then the
whole universe will be dissolved ("the first heaven and the first
earth were passed away"—21:1). Everything we know will be made
perfect. Evil will be purged from the universe. Death and sin and
sadness and pain will be entirely done away with. The new heavens and new earth that take the place of the old will be the glorious
realm in which the people of God will dwell eternally.

THE OLD UNIVERSE DISSOLVES

Before we look closely at the description of heaven in Revelation
21, however, let's examine the process by which the current universe is destroyed and all things are made new. The apostle Peter
goes into detail on this, in a familiar passage that is well worth
examining.

Peter writes, "[Know] this first, that there shall come in the last
days scoffers, walking after their own lusts, and saying, Where is the
promise of his coming? for since the fathers fell asleep, all things
continue as they were from the beginning of the creation" (2 Peter
3:3-4). This predicts a time of apostasy and spiritual apathy when
unbelief and skepticism are prevalent. What Peter describes is a
common brand of mocking skepticism in our own time. You have
no doubt heard skeptics who claim that if Jesus hasn't returned after

two millennia, he's not going to return at all! (Which is something akin to thinking that because I haven't died yet I'm never going to.)

The skepticism Peter describes has special reference to cataclysmic judgment. These scoffers hold a belief similar to what geologists call *uniformitarianism*—the theory that all natural phenomena have operated uniformly since the origin of the earth. (Uniformitarianism undergirds the most popular evolutionary theories.) The scoffers' brand of uniformitarianism is metaphysical, however. They insinuate that God (if they acknowledge Him at all) has left the scene. "All we can observe are natural phenomena," they say. "The earth has continued to revolve, the rains have come and the sun has shone, and the water cycle has operated since the beginning of recorded history. There's no reason to think it can't go on evolving slowly forever, and certainly no reason to think a divine judge will intervene in any sort of destruction on a cosmic scale."

But theirs is an arrogant, false security. Peter continues: "This they willingly are ignorant of, that by the word of God the heavens were of old, and the earth standing out of the water and in the water: Whereby the world that then was, being overflowed with water, perished" (vv. 5-6). Those who say there has been no cataclysmic judgment on the earth forget (actually, they *willfully* reject) God's revelation about the great Flood, when God drowned the entire human race, sparing only Noah and his family, for which geological evidence also abounds.

Peter speaks of "the earth . . . formed out of water and by water" (v. 5, NASB). Many believe that prior to the Flood, a canopy of water or water vapor encircled the earth (cf. Gen. 1:7), protecting it from the sun's ultraviolet rays. Because of that protection, plant life flourished, and men and animals lived hundreds of years. (This would explain why, immediately after the Flood, the ages of people listed in the biblical genealogies began to decline sharply. Life expectancy was altered dramatically by the cataclysm.) Evidently the very canopy that was the earth's protection became the means of its judgment, as the breaking up of the canopy inundated the earth.

According to Scripture, the Flood was the only great catastrophe on the cosmic scale, right down to our own time. Things *have* pretty much continued as they have since the Flood, despite the fact that even Jesus said God's judgment was imminent in *His* day (cf. Matt. 3:2, 10-12).

Peter says no one should misinterpret God's delay as apathy, unfaithfulness, or slackness. In the first place, time is of no consequence to the Lord. A thousand years is no different from a single day. What Jesus said was imminent two thousand years ago is still imminent today.

But more important than that, the reason God delays His final judgment is because of His grace: "But, beloved, be not ignorant of this one thing, that one day is with the Lord as a thousand years, and a thousand years as one day. The Lord is not slack concerning his promise, as some men count slackness; but is longsuffering toward us, not willing that any should perish, but that all should come to repentance" (2 Peter 3:8-9).

God "is good to all: and his tender mercies are over all his works" (Ps. 145:9). Remember that in the aftermath of the Flood, God made a gracious promise never again to destroy the earth in such a way (Gen. 9:12-16)—and He confirmed His covenant with a rainbow. His grace, not His wrath, is currently on display.

However, we dare not presume that His grace rules out the day of His wrath. The wrath will come as well, when the Day of the Lord is unleashed. Peter reminds us, just as "the world that then was, being overflowed with water, perished," even so shall *this* world one day suffer cataclysmic destruction: "The heavens and the earth, which are now, by the same word are kept in store, reserved unto fire against the day of judgment and perdition of ungodly men" (2 Pet. 3:7).

So this time, instead of water, it will be fire—and fire unlike any known to humanity: "The day of the Lord will come as a thief in the night; in the which the heavens shall pass away with a great noise, and the elements shall melt with fervent heat, the earth also and the works that are therein shall be burned up" (v. 10). Atomic science has demonstrated to us that such destruction can occur. By splitting the atom, man unleashed the potential for unbelievable destruction—a chain reaction of atomic explosions could literally disintegrate this earth. Moreover, our earth has tremendous potential for fire. We live on the crust of a fireball; most of the earth's approximately eight thousand mile diameter is molten flame. The earth's core is a flaming, boiling, liquid lake of fire, which when it gets too close to the earth's crust, bursts through as a volcano.

But the fire Peter describes is no mere nuclear bomb. It is a meltdown of universal proportions. The heavens pass away with a great noise. The elements melt with fervent heat. Everything we know will be instantly burned up. This is the culmination of an eschatological period known as "the Day of the Lord," which is always associated in Scripture with the outpouring of divine wrath and judgment. The sudden, fiery demolition of the universe is the consummation of it all. This is uncreation! No effort on the part of most fanatical environmentalist will be able to preserve the planet. It is temporary, disposable, replaceable.

Peter's whole point has an intensely practical application: "Seeing then that all these things shall be dissolved, what manner of persons ought ye to be in all holy conversation and godliness, looking for and hasting unto the coming of the day of God, wherein the heavens being on fire shall be dissolved, and the elements shall melt with fervent heat?" (2 Peter 3:11-12). The answer is obvious: if everything in this life is perishable, we need to set our hearts on things that are imperishable. Like Abraham, the father of the faithful, we need to fix our hopes on a more permanent city—one whose architect and builder is God, and one that will never pass away. And so, Peter concludes, "We, according to his promise, look for new heavens and a new earth, wherein dwelleth righteousness" (v. 13).

But even this greatest of God's judgments ultimately has a gracious purpose, for only then will the universe stop groaning under the curse of sin (cf. Rom. 8:19-22).

A NEW HEAVEN AND A NEW EARTH

We return to Revelation 21 for a biblical description of the "new heaven and a new earth: for the first heaven and the first earth were passed away" (v. 1). The Greek word translated "new" (*kainos*) stresses that the earth God will create will not just be "new" as opposed to "old." It will also be *different*. Paul uses the same Greek word in 2 Corinthians 5:17: "If any man be in Christ, he is a new creature." It speaks of a change in quality. The new heavens and earth, like our newness in Christ, will be glorified, free from sin's curse, and eternal.

Scripture doesn't tell us what the new earth will look like, but we have reason to believe that it will in many respects be familiar. Jerusalem will be there—albeit an all-new Jerusalem. John's description concentrates on the Holy City, which has streets, and walls, and gates. John also mentions a high mountain, water, a stream, and trees. Best of all it is populated with the people of God—real people we will know and with whom we will share eternal fellowship.

All Things New

The new earth will also be utterly different, unfamiliar. John says, for example, "there will be no more sea" (Rev. 21:1). That's a significant difference immediately, because the current earth is covered mostly with water. Some Bible scholars think this stresses the erasure of all national boundaries. Others point out that the sea symbolized fear to the ancients, so they believe the absence of sea implies the absence of fear. Both may be true. In the new heaven and earth nothing will make us afraid, and nothing will separate us from other people. The only water described in heaven is "a pure river of water of life, clear as crystal, proceeding out of the throne of God and of the Lamb" (Rev. 22:1). This crystal-clear river flows right down heaven's main street (v. 2).

Revelation 21:3-7 outlines the most remarkable features of the New Heavens and New Earth:

> *And I heard a great voice out of heaven saying, Behold, the taber-nacle of God is with men, and he will dwell with them, and they shall be his people, and God himself shall be with them, and be their God. And God shall wipe away all tears from their eyes; and there shall be no more death, neither sorrow, nor crying, neither shall there be any more pain: for the former things are passed away. And he that sat upon the throne said, Behold, I make all things new. And he said unto me, Write: for these words are true and faithful. And he said unto me, It is done. I am Alpha and Omega, the beginning and the end. I will give unto him that is athirst of the fountain of the water of life freely. He that overcometh shall inherit all things; and I will be his God, and he shall be my son.*

Here Scripture promises that heaven will be a realm of perfect bliss. Tears, pain, sorrow, and crying will have no place whatsoever in the New Heaven and New Earth. It is a place where God's people will dwell together with Him eternally, utterly free from all the effects of sin and evil. God is pictured as personally wiping away the tears from the eyes of the redeemed.

Heaven is a realm where death is fully conquered (1 Cor. 15:26). There is no sickness there, no hunger, no trouble, and no tragedy. Just absolute joy and eternal blessings. It is frankly hard for our minds, which have never known anything but this sinful life and its calamities, to imagine.

How Can Heaven Be Perfect When There Is Such a Place as Hell?

Many people wonder how they can endure eternity knowing that some of their earthly loved ones will not be there. What about parents whose wayward son has departed from Christ and died in immorality and unbelief? How can heaven be perfect for them? What about someone whose earthly father died in sin, not knowing the Lord? How can that person endure the pain of eternal separation? What about the widow who comes to Christ after her beloved spouse has already died in a state of unbelief? How can heaven be pure bliss with no hope of reunion with these loved ones?

Scripture does not give a specific answer to that question. Some suggest that our memories of relationships on this earth will fade in the glory of heaven. And there is a hint in Scripture that this may be a factor: In the Isaiah 65 passage describing the New Heaven and New Earth, God says, "I create new heavens and a new earth: and *the former shall not be remembered, nor come into mind*" (v. 17, emphasis added). However, this cannot possibly mean we will forget everything about this earth and our life and relationships here. After all, we will continue many of those same relationships eternally. And we will spend eternity reciting the glory of how Christ has redeemed us. Since our redemption was accomplished by His work *on earth*, it is impossible that we will completely lose our memory of all earthly events and relationships.

But we will have a much clearer understanding of things from heaven's perspective. Now we see all things as in a cloudy mirror. Then we will know exactly as we are known (1 Cor. 13:12). All our earthly attachments will be overwhelmed by more satisfying relationships and more perfect affections. Just as God promises to be a father to the fatherless here on earth (Ps. 68:5), so He will personally fill the void left by any broken earthly relationships—and in an even more perfect way, because our feelings and our desires will be untainted by the effects of our sin. We will see and understand better the perfect justice of God, and we shall glorify Him for every detail of the outworking of His eternal plan—including His dealings with the wicked. The final verses of Isaiah's prophecy indicate that the destruction of the wicked will ultimately be something for which we will worship God (Isa. 66:22-24). The existence of hell will not dim the glory of heaven or taint its bliss in the least.

As for how this will operate in the minds of the redeemed, Scripture simply does not tell us. We're only promised that God Himself will dry our tears and give us supreme, undiminished joy and "pleasures for evermore" (Ps. 16:11). For now, it is enough to know that we can trust implicitly His infinite goodness, compassion, and mercy.

Furthermore, notice that when God says He will make all things new, He adds a message to the apostle John: "Write: for these words are true and faithful" (Rev. 21:5)—as if to add an exclamation mark to the reliability of these great promises. We who truly know the Lord know we can trust Him even with our unanswered questions. *All* His words are true and faithful, so when He says He is making all things new, it is a promise we can cling to, despite our inability to know precisely how all the difficulties will resolve. Heaven will be utterly perfect, no matter how impossible it may be for us to understand everything now.

One other thing is perfectly clear: God cannot be faulted for any lack of mercy or goodness, even though people perish eternally. He cannot be charged with any blame for their destruction. He freely offers the water of life to all who thirst (v. 6). People turn from God to sin willfully (cf. Rom. 1:18-23)

The Overcomers

The redeemed have a further promise. God says, "He that overcometh shall inherit all things; and I will be his God, and he shall be my son" (Rev. 21:7). God will elevate the redeemed to a position of unimaginable privilege—and bestow on them an inheritance beyond any earthly standard of measure.

"He that overcometh" includes *every* redeemed person. There is no partition in heaven between the "overcomers" and the "defeated Christians"—though some have attempted to teach this. One surprisingly popular view, for example, even goes so far as to claim that the "outer darkness" spoken of in Matthew 8:12 (where "there shall be weeping and gnashing of teeth") is a realm of heaven reserved for believers who do *not* overcome![1] Overcomers, in this view, are "a separate class of Christians who persevere."[2] Christians who are non-overcomers are banished to the outer regions of heaven, unable to share in its full blessedness. But that view is patently unbiblical.

According to Scripture there is no such thing as a true believer who does not persevere in the faith—because God Himself promises to keep us. We are "kept by the power of God through faith unto salvation" (1 Peter 1:5). And therefore all true Christians are ultimately "overcomers." Those who depart from the faith demonstrate that they were never really in Christ to begin with (1 John 2:19). This is the doctrine known as "perseverance of the saints."[3]

"He that overcometh," and parallel expressions, are common in John's writings. The apostle John quite plainly uses the concept of the "overcomer" as a synonym for the believer. By his definition, all Christians are ultimately "overcomers." He addresses both spiritual young men and spiritual fathers as those who have "have *overcome* the wicked one" (1 John 2:13-14, emphasis added). He warns all believers about the spirit of antichrist, then writes, "Ye are of God, little children, and *have overcome them:* because greater is he that is in you, than he that is in the world" (4:4, emphasis added). And to make it perfectly clear that he means *all* believers are overcomers, he writes, "Whatsoever is born of God overcometh the world: and this is the victory that overcometh the world, even our faith. Who is he that overcometh the world, but he that believeth that Jesus is the Son of God?" (5:4-5). There is therefore no such thing as a believer who is not an overcomer in this sense. This identificaton of believers as "overcomers" is also used in Christ's letters to the churches (cf. Rev. 2:7, 11, 17, 26; 3:5, 12, 21).

If Children, Then Heirs

When God says, "He that overcometh shall inherit all things," this is a promise to all believers. He will be our God; we shall be His children. Heaven will be our home, and we will dwell there not as mere guests, but with all the privileges of family members—children of the master of the house.

A study of the biblical passages related to our inheritance could be a book in itself. Scripture teaches that all who are believers are children of God (John 1:12)—"And if children, then heirs; heirs of God, and joint-heirs with Christ" (Rom. 8:17).

Perhaps not surprisingly, those who think heaven is divided between "overcomers" and mere run-of-the-mill Christians often suggest that only the "overcomers" share in the inheritance of the kingdom. Those left in "outer darkness" are disinherited, put outside the Father's house, cast out of the banquet hall, relegated to a secondary existence in the eternal realm—and not permitted in God's immediate presence.[4] This is a curious and wholly unbiblical idea of heaven! It makes the Christian's inheritance something to be merited by the believer's own works.[5] The notion that someone could get to heaven in that kind of spiritual limbo—devoid of any inheritance—is altogether foreign to everything Scripture has to say about heaven.

There are, of course, passages of Scripture that indicate there will be differing levels of honor in heaven. The parable in Luke 19:16-19, for example, portrays God as a nobleman who rewards two of his faithful servants by making them rulers over ten cities, and five cities, respectively. Also, Jesus speaks of the "least in the kingdom of heaven" (Matt. 11:11)—implying that there are varying degrees of standing in heaven. Our Lord taught repeatedly that believers will receive rewards for their faithfulness—and those rewards vary from person to person (Matt. 25:21-24).

How are these rewards determined? Our *works* will be tested for this very purpose. In that day when we stand before the judgment seat of Christ, the whole "edifice" of our earthly works will tested by the fire of God. Some impressive superstructures will be reduced to rubble, because they are built only for show—not out of lasting material. Like sets on a movie lot, these "buildings" may be magnificent and *appear* genuine even on close inspection, but the fire will test them for what they are made of, not for what they look like. All the wood, hay and stubble will be burned away. Scripture promises, "If any man's work abide which he hath built thereupon, *he shall receive a reward*" (1 Cor. 3:14, emphasis added). What about the person whose works are burned up? "He shall suffer loss: but he himself shall be saved; yet so as by fire" (v. 15). That evokes the notion of someone who is pulled from a burning building alive. He may be unharmed by the fire, but the smell of smoke is all over him—he has barely escaped destruction.

But don't be quick to relegate such a person to the confines of outer darkness, where there will be weeping and gnashing of teeth. Like the thief on the cross, like the workman hired at the last hour, that person will receive infinitely more than he or she has merited. Even those who barely escape the flames remain heirs of God and joint-heirs with Christ, sharing fully in the eternal blessing of heaven. The least in the kingdom of heaven is still greater than the greatest on earth (Matt. 11:11). In that realm the last are first and the first last—indicating that, as far as our *inheritance* is concerned, everyone finishes in a dead heat. And since whatever rewards we may earn will be cast before the throne of the Lamb (cf. Rev. 4:10), there cannot be a very pronounced hierarchy among the saved in the eternal state. Certainly there is no justification for teaching that some will be kept out of the heavenly banquets and consigned forever to the exterior realms of the kingdom.[6]

Our inheritance is something entirely different from our rewards. Our eternal inheritance is not merited by works, nor is it apportioned according to them. The apostle Paul ties our inheritance to our adoption as sons (Rom. 8:15-17). An *inheritance* by definition is not a reward for merit earned. It is a birthright.

Furthermore, there was a significant difference between Roman law and Jewish custom on the matter of a child's inheritance. By Jewish law, the eldest son always received a double portion of the inheritance. Under the Roman system, all children could receive equal shares. When Paul wrote, "if children, then . . . joint-heirs with Christ" (Rom. 8:17), he was addressing a Roman audience. The context indicates his emphasis was on the equality of God's children and the security of every Christian's inheritance.

Writing to the Galatians, Paul made a similar point: "And *if ye be Christ's,* then are ye Abraham's seed, and heirs according to the promise" (Gal. 3:29, emphasis added). He echoed the thought a chapter later: "And *because ye are sons,* God hath sent forth the Spirit of his Son into your hearts, crying, Abba, Father. Wherefore thou art no more a servant, but a son; and if a son, then an heir of God through Christ" (4:6-7, emphasis added). The inheritance is not a reward for a faithful servant (as were the rewards in most of Jesus' parables). It is a birthright for every child of the Father.

Plainly, Scripture is teaching that all Christians will receive a full share of the inheritance of heaven. *Every* believer will "inherit all things" (Rev. 21:7), so the inheritance isn't carved up and apportioned on the basis of worthiness. And when God says, "I will be his God, and he shall be my son"—He is saying that heaven will be not only our dwelling-place, but also our possession. We will be there not as boarders, but as full-fledged members of the family. What an inexpressible privilege that is!

THE HOLY CITY

Now look back at Revelation 21:2 for another important perspective on the heavenly realm. John writes, "I John saw the holy city, new Jerusalem, coming down from God out of heaven, prepared as a bride adorned for her husband."

Prepared as a Bride

As John watches, an entire city, magnificent in its glory, descends whole from heaven and becomes a part of the new earth. Heaven and earth are now one. The heavenly realm has moved its capital city intact to the new earth. Pay special attention to the key terms in this verse:

"Prepared" seems to imply that New Jerusalem had already been made ready before the creation of the new heavens and new earth. John does not say he saw the city being created. When he laid eyes on it, it was complete already. In other words, it was brought to the new earth from another place. Where is this other place?

"Coming down from God out of heaven" indicates that the city— already complete and thoroughly furnished—descended to the new earth from the heavenly realm, no doubt from the place Paul called "the third heaven." Again, this occurs immediately after the new heaven and earth are created. New Jerusalem, the capital city of the eternal realm, descends right before John's eyes, out of the very realm of God, where it has already been "prepared." Who "prepared" it? Evidently this incredible heavenly city is precisely what our Lord spoke of when He told His disciples that He was going away to "prepare a place" for them (John 14:3). Now at the unveiling of the new heavens and new earth, the city is finally prepared and ready.

"As a bride adorned for her husband." This speaks of the glory of this unimaginable city. Just think, when our Lord fashioned the mate-

rial universe at the beginning of time, He did it in seven days. He has been working on heaven for nearly two millennia. What a wonder it must be! The surpassing glory of this city is too rich to express in words.

You Have Come to Mount Zion

New Jerusalem is the very city Abraham was seeking, "whose architect and builder is God" (Heb. 11:10, NASB). The writer of Hebrews says to all the redeemed, "You have come to Mount Zion and to the city of the living God, the heavenly Jerusalem, and to myriads of angels, to the general assembly and church of the first-born who are enrolled in heaven, and to God, the Judge of all, and to the spirits of righteous men made perfect" (12:22-23, NASB).

That's a fascinating verse about heaven. Look at it for a moment. *Mount Zion* is adjacent to the temple mount in old Jerusalem. To dwell in Zion is to have one's residence right next to the Lord's own holy dwelling. This heavenly Zion will be the eternal home of all *"who are enrolled in heaven"*—all the redeemed of all ages. (Again this destroys the notion that some of the redeemed will be banished to a place outside the main core of heaven.) Here *"the spirits of righteous men"* (and women as well) will finally be *"made perfect."* We will be made fit to dwell amidst such unimaginable glory (1 John 3:2).

THE CROWN JEWEL OF HEAVEN

Revelation 21:10-27 describes in even more vivid detail John's vision of the holy city as it descended from heaven. An angel took John in his vision to a mountain on the new earth from which he could watch God's masterpiece, the capital city of the infinite heaven, descend from God, out of the third heaven, and become the crown jewel of the New Heaven and New Earth.

Notice that John describes the city as "having the glory of God" (v. 11). "Her light was like unto a stone most precious, even like a jasper stone, clear as crystal."

As we have already seen, this theme of light and glory is woven through everything Scripture has to say about the eternal realm. Heaven itself is an infinite, eternal expression of the divine glory. We might say that the essence of heaven is God's glory manifest in its midst. Isaiah 60:19 says, "The sun shall be no more thy light by day; neither for brightness shall the moon give light unto thee: but the Lord shall be unto thee an everlasting light, and thy God thy glory." Revelation 21:23 echoes an identical thought: "The city had no need of the sun, neither of the moon, to shine in it: for the glory of God did lighten it, and the Lamb is the light thereof." God Himself will light all of the infinite heaven—and particularly this sparkling celestial jewel called New Jerusalem.

When I was growing up, I used to go roller skating in Pasadena. Hanging in middle of the rink was a sphere covered with small, mirrored squares. When lights were aimed at it, the whole rink flashed and sparkled with light. In a mundane way that may picture what John is trying to communicate in this description of lights and jewels. He saw the eternal city coming down from heaven, and it resembled a sparkling, crystal, diamond-like stone blazing with the glory of God's very nature. And the splashing light of God's reflected glory literally covered the infinite new universe with breathtaking beauty.

Glorious Walls and Gates

Verse 12 says the city "had a wall great and high." Why would the heavenly city have a wall? Walls are for defense against one's enemies. But there will be no enemies in this realm; all the enemies of God will have already been cast into the lake of fire (Rev. 20:14-15). So this wall serves no *functional* purpose. Like everything else in heaven, it is a display of the glory of God. It also symbolizes the inviolable security of heaven.

Speaking of these same walls, Revelation 22:14-15 says, "Blessed are those who wash their robes, that they may have the right to the tree of life, and may enter by the gates into the city. Outside are the dogs and the sorcerers and the immoral persons and the murderers and the idolaters, and everyone who loves and practices lying" (NASB). That does not mean dogs and sorcerers and liars are camped just outside the gates of the city. Again, all who fit that description have already been banished to hell eternally (Rev. 20:15; 21:8).

John's description of the wall and its gates is interesting:

> *[The wall] had twelve gates, and at the gates twelve angels, and names written thereon, which are the names of the twelve tribes of the children of Israel: on the east three gates; on the north three gates; on the south three gates; and on the west three gates. And the wall of the city had twelve foundations, and in them the names of the twelve apostles of the Lamb.*
>
> *—21:12-14*

So the gates are named after the tribes of Israel and the foundations after the twelve apostles. This will be the dwelling-place of all the people of God for all time. Israel and the church are brought together in the eternal realm to form one people of God for all eternity.

The existence of gates implies that people are able to leave and enter the city. Don't think the city *contains* us. It will be our home, but we will not be confined there. We will have the infinite universe to travel, and when we do, we will go in and out through those gates.

Heavenly Measurements

In verses 15-16 John says, "The one who spoke with me had a gold measuring rod [probably about ten feet long] to measure the city, and its gates and its wall. And the city is laid out as a square, and its length is as great as the width; and he measured the city with the rod, fifteen hundred miles; its length and width and height are equal" (NASB). So the city is perfectly symmetrical, a massive cube, fifteen hundred miles square and fifteen hundred miles high. Some have suggested that this could actually describe a pyramid. While that is indeed a possible interpretation of these dimensions, it seems unlikely that Scripture would not say so if that's what it meant to convey. I take this as a description of a cube.

What is the significance of a cube-shaped city? Remember that in Solomon's Temple the Holy of Holies was a cube of twenty cubits (1 Kings 6:20). The New Jerusalem is the Holy of Holies for eternity. This *is* the very sanctuary of God Himself. It is His house, and our dwelling-place is part of the Father's own house (cf. Ps. 23:6; John 14:2). God has brought the very heart of the heavenly tabernacle—the Holy of Holies—to earth.

A height of fifteen hundred miles is frankly difficult to envision. On the current earth, something fifteen hundred miles high would extend well out of earth's atmosphere (which is only about a hundred miles deep). But remember that heaven and earth will then be merged, and atmosphere will have ceased to be an issue.

Are these great heights and distances merely symbolic? I'm inclined to think not. John describes the angel's measurement of the city wall: "He measured its wall, seventy-two yards, *according to human measurements, which are also angelic measurements*" (v. 17, NASB, emphasis added). The fact that such precise measurements are given seems to suggest that this describes a real place with real, earthly dimensions.

According to these measurements, the New Jerusalem covers a surface area of 2.25 million square miles. By comparison, all of greater London is 621 square miles. The actual City of London itself is an area of only one square mile, with a population of about 5,000. On that basis, the New Jerusalem would be able to house over a hundred billion people! And that does not even take into account the towering height of the city! Heaven will certainly be large enough for the "few" who find the narrow way (Matt. 7:13-14). And we'll discover in the glory of eternity that the "few" are really "a great multitude, which no man could number" (Rev. 7:9). Heaven will have plenty of room for all nonetheless.

How far is fifteen hundred miles? It is about the same as the distance from Maine to Florida. Imagine such an area squared off, then cubed, with multiple levels and millions of intersecting golden avenues. New Jerusalem is a place of immense size and unearthly majesty and beauty!

The Building Materials

Verse 18 tells us that the walls are made of jasper. That is a translucent, semi-opaque stone of varying colors. Some have suggested that in biblical times "jasper" was the name for a transparent, diamond-like semiprecious stone. In any case, the jasper stone allows the glory of God, radiating from the center of the city, to shine through. The city itself is "pure gold, like unto clear glass." Of course, the gold we're familiar with is not transparent. "Like unto clear glass" could refer to gold that is polished to a perfect sheen so that it reflects like a clear mirror. (Mirrors in ancient times were made of polished metal.). More likely it describes a variety of the precious metal so pure that it is translucent. Both Ezekiel and John describe much of heaven as being transparent like precious gems. The radiance of God's glory reflects the beauty of His presence through every diamond facet. That is what John saw. It must have sparkled with an unearthly brilliance and heavenly glow, but with a golden tone—so he recognized it as pure gold.

Verses 19-20 say, "The foundations of the wall of the city were garnished with all manner of precious stones. The first foundation was jasper; the second, sapphire; the third, a chalcedony; the fourth, an emerald; the fifth, sardonyx; the sixth, sardius; the seventh, chrysolyte; the eighth, beryl; the ninth, a topaz; the tenth, a chryso-prasus; the eleventh, a jacinth; the twelfth, an amethyst." Those are all colored jewels—various greens, sky blue, red, golden, violet, and other radiant hues. Along with the glasslike gold and translucent walls, this forms a picture of unbelievable and indescribable beauty. God has planted within us a love of beauty—and heaven's surpass-ing beauty will satisfy that love forever.

John adds, "And the twelve gates were twelve pearls: every sev-eral gate was of one pearl: and the street of the city was pure gold, as it were transparent glass" (v. 21). It is hard to imagine gates that big, each made of a single pearl. But that is what John describes. These won't be pearls from some giant variety of oysters, but per-fect pearls created by God's own hand.

WHAT HEAVEN LACKS

One is tempted to say nothing will be lacking in heaven, but hap-pily that is not the case. The apostle John lists a number of things utterly absent from heaven. You may be surprised by some of them.

No Temple

We already noted in chapter 3 that there is no temple in heaven. John writes, "I saw no temple in it, for the Lord God, the Almighty, and the Lamb, are its temple" (v. 22, NASB). So in one sense there is no temple in heaven. In another sense, however, God Himself *is* the temple.

In what sense is God the "temple" of heaven? A temple is where you go to worship. John is suggesting that in heaven when we worship, we will worship in the very presence of God. He is the place of worship. He spreads His tabernacle over all who are in heaven (Rev. 7:15, NASB). They serve Him day and night. The worship never stops.

Unfortunately, we tend to think of worship as starchy, formal, perhaps even a bit uncomfortable. Use the word *worship* to the typical Sunday-school boy, and he will think of something that makes him feel confined and somewhat awkward—a stuffy ceremony where he has to sit still and be quiet.

But that's far from the essence of worship. The biblical idea of worship incorporates all of life. That's why Paul could write to the Corinthians, "Whether therefore ye eat, or drink, or whatsoever ye do, do all to the glory of God" (1 Cor. 10:31). There's nothing *necessary* and *legitimate* in life that cannot be done to the glory of God. And since worship is simply glorifying God, this means there is nothing required of us that cannot be done as an act of worship. Therefore, if we were perfect beings, sinless in every regard, our lives would be non-stop worship.

That is exactly what heaven will be! In the familiar words of the first question from the Westminster Shorter Catechism, we will glorify God and enjoy Him forever. Far from being stuffy and uncomfortable, our worship in heaven will bring us sheer pleasure. It will be unhindered enjoyment of God, unadulterated by any taint of guilt or any fear of insecurity. None of our earthly pleasures can compare with the perfect delight we will derive from heavenly worship. All the joys we derive from earthly love, earthly beauty, and other earthly blessings are nothing in comparison to the pure bliss of heavenly worship before the very face of Him from whom all true blessings flow. Only those who know Him can even begin to appreciate the unadulterated pleasure this will be.

And the privilege of such perfect worship is part of the saints' inheritance. The psalmist wrote, "Whom have I in heaven but thee? and there is none upon earth that I desire beside thee. My flesh and my heart faileth: but God is the strength of my heart, and my portion for ever" (Ps. 73:25-26).

Isn't this the fulfillment of our very deepest desires? As the psalmist wrote, "One thing have I desired of the Lord, that will I seek after; that I may dwell in the house of the Lord all the days of my life, to behold the beauty of the Lord, and to inquire in his temple" (Ps. 27:4). In heaven that will be precisely our inheritance, and we will dwell forever in the house of the Lord (cf. Ps. 23:6)—a more glorious temple than we could ever imagine.

No Light Source

A temple building is not all that will be missing from heaven. As we noted earlier in this chapter, there will be no need of cosmic light sources. Revelation 21:23 says, "The city had no need of the sun, neither of the moon, to shine in it: for the glory of God did lighten it, and the Lamb is the light thereof."

The glory of heaven is a far more brilliant light than the light of the sun. In fact, Isaiah wrote, "Then the moon will be abashed and the sun ashamed, for the Lord of hosts will reign on Mount Zion and in Jerusalem, and His glory will be before His elders" (24:23, NASB). Next to the glory of God, the light of the sun and moon are paltry, flickering candles. Revelation 21:24 adds that "the nations shall walk by its light, and the kings of the earth shall bring their glory into it" (NASB). John is saying that even the kings of the earth will yield up their own glory in the face of the glory of heaven. All nations will walk in the light of God's presence, and all men, regardless of their position, will bow to His glory.

I once received a letter from an atheist who wanted to argue that if we take Scripture at face value, heaven will be hotter than hell. "Hell must be at or below the boiling temperature of brimstone (sulphur)—around 450 kelvins," he wrote. "And Isaiah 30:26 says that 'the light of the sun shall be sevenfold, as the light of seven days, in the day that the Lord bindeth up the breach of his people, and healeth the stroke of their wound.' Any competent physicist will tell you that a light source seven times the sun's brightness would cause the earth's surface to be well in excess of 450 kelvins. So if the Bible is true, heaven will be much hotter than hell."

But that argument does not really take Scripture at face value. In the first place, Isaiah 30:26 describes God's judgment on the earth, not the heavenly state. In the second place, the point of this passage in Revelation 21 is that there is no "light source" in heaven. The light there is not a radiant light, subject to Kelvin's scale. The only light is the glory of God. It permeates all heaven; it does not shine from any "source." It is a light unlike any light known on earth. It is the very light of Him who "is light, and in him is no darkness at all" (1 John 1:5). No reason exists to think of that light as emitting heat.

Again, this description pushes human language to the limit and aims to convey an idea that we cannot possibly imagine. But it is clear that the glory of heaven will be unimaginably brilliant.

Years ago, Lutheran scholar J.A. Seiss wrote these beautiful words about the light of heavenly Jerusalem:

> That shining is not from any material combustion,—not from any consumption of fuel that needs to be replaced as one supply burns out; for it is the uncreated light of Him who is light, dispensed by and through the Lamb as the everlasting lamp, to the home, and hearts, and understandings, of His glorified saints. When Paul and Silas lay wounded and bound in the inner dungeon of the prison of Philippi, they still had sacred light which enabled them to beguile the night-watches with happy songs. When Paul was on his way to Damascus, a light brighter than the sun at noon shone round about him, irradiating his whole being with new sights and understanding, and making his soul and body ever afterward light in the Lord. When Moses came down from the mount of his communion with God, his face was so luminous that his brethren could not

endure to look upon it. He was in such close fellowship with light that he became informed with light, and came to the camp as a very lamp of God, glowing with the glory of God.

On the Mount of Transfiguration, that same light streamed forth from all the body and raiment of the blessed Jesus. And with reference to the very time when this city comes into being and place, Isaiah says, "The moon shall be ashamed and the sun confounded,"—ashamed because of the out-beaming glory which then shall appear in the New Jerusalem, leaving no more need for them to shine in it, since the glory of God lights it, and the Lamb is the light thereof.[7]

No Security System

The apostle John further writes, "And the gates of it shall not be shut at all by day: for there shall be no night there" (Rev. 21:25). In an ancient city the gates were shut at night to protect the people from robbers, bandits, and invading armies. Gates that are always open speak of perfect security and protection. There will be absolutely no threat to the security of heaven, so there will be no need of closed gates.

Verse 26 repeats the thread of thought from verse 24—the idea of kings bringing their glory to the throne of God.: "They shall bring the glory and honor of the nations into it." In other words, there will be no rival to the glory or the authority of God. The cosmic conflict of the ages will be finally ended forever, and God and His people will dwell in utter security.

John says, "Nothing unclean and no one who practices abomination and lying, shall ever come into it, but only those whose names are written in the Lamb's book of life" (v. 27, NASB; cf. 22:15). Only the elect of God—those who have put their trust in Christ—will enter that great city. Satan and his wicked minions will already have been banished forever from the scene.

No Needs

In Revelation 22:1-2 the angel shows John "a pure river of water of life, clear as crystal, proceeding out of the throne of God and of the Lamb. In the midst of the street of it, and on either side of the river, was there the tree of life, which bare twelve manner of fruits, and yielded her fruit every month: and the leaves of the tree were for the healing of the nations." This crystal-clear, celestial river flows out of the throne and through the middle of the New Jerusalem. Imagine what a river meant to someone living in a barren place like Palestine. It was a welcome place of comfort and rest, refreshment and sustenance. A river meant cool water to a mouth parched by the desert heat. Cities were built next to rivers. And imagine the joy of someone who lived in the desert finding a tree with fruit! The New Jerusalem will be the epitome of everything precious—a city, a river, and trees.

Psalm 46:4-5 speaks of the same river: "There is a river, the streams whereof shall make glad the city of God, the holy place of the tabernacles of the most High. God is in the midst of her; she shall not be moved."

In Eden there was also a beautiful river that watered the garden (Gen. 2:10). Eden had "the tree of life also in the midst of the garden" (Gen. 2:9). So the scene in heaven seems to be the final perfection of everything Eden represented.

"The tree of life" might actually describe one, two, or three trees. The Greek expression lacks a definite article, so this could actually be translated, "In the middle of the street and on either side of the river was a tree of life"—signifying three trees, one in the street and two on either side of the river. Alternatively, "In the middle of the street" might describe the position of the river, as these verses are rendered in a modern translation: "He showed me a river of the water of life, clear as crystal, coming from the throne of God and of the Lamb, in the middle of its street. And on either side of the river was the tree of life" (22:1-2, NASB).

In any case, the fruit of the tree of life is indescribably wonderful. It bears twelve kinds of fruit, one for each month—like a "fruit-of-the-month" tree. The privilege of eating from this tree is granted to all overcomers (Rev. 2:7).

In heaven we will eat for enjoyment, not sustenance. Nevertheless, the tree has a wholesome, beneficial effect on those who partake. Even its leaves are "for the healing of the nations" (22:2). The Greek word translated "healing" is *therapeia*, from which we get the English word *therapeutic*. John is saying that the leaves of the tree of life somehow enrich the heavenly life—if only through the pure joy of eating. The water of life is also there for the sheer pleasure of drinking. No food will be *needed* in heaven, but incredible gourmet delights will nonetheless be enjoyed. Again this underscores the truth that God's design for us is that we may *enjoy* Him forever. Much of heaven is designed for sheer pleasure—both the pleasure of God and the pleasure of His people.

No Curse

If any aspect of heaven stirs my heart with eager anticipation, it is this:

> *And there shall be no more curse: but the throne of God and of the Lamb shall be in it; and his servants shall serve him: and they shall see his face; and his name shall be in their foreheads. And there shall be no night there; and they need no candle, neither light of the sun; for the Lord God giveth them light: and they shall reign for ever and ever."*
> *—Rev. 22:3-5*

The curse will be overturned and erased forever, with all its painful and detestable ramifications. Pain, the agony of toil, sweat, thorns, disease, sorrow, and sin will have no place whatsoever in heaven.

As the apostle Paul wrote, "Eye hath not seen, nor ear heard, neither have entered into the heart of man, the things which God hath prepared for them that love him" (1 Cor. 2:9). The delights of heaven are beyond the scope of our wildest imaginations. But for the believer, we can taste it even now: "God hath revealed them unto us by his Spirit" (v. 10). We have "tasted of the heavenly gift" (cf. Heb. 6:4). And having had a foretaste of heaven, we ought to have our hearts fixed firmly there.

Unfortunately, many Christians think that fellowship with God and enjoyment of heaven is impossible until we actually arrive there. But the real truth is that for Christians, eternal life is a present possession, not merely a future hope. We're supposed to live as if our hearts are in heaven already. We can commune and fellowship with God even now—not face to face, but through prayer and the study of His Word.

In heaven the difference will be that we will be "with him" on a face-to-face basis (1 Cor. 13:12). First Thessalonians 4:17 says that from the time we are caught away to be with the Lord, through all eternity, "so shall we ever be with the Lord." "He hath said, I will never leave thee, nor forsake thee" (Heb. 13:5).

So when the apostle John says in heaven we will see His face (Rev. 22:4), this implies the ultimate perfection of our intimacy, communion, and fellowship with the Lord. Having His name on our forehead speaks of both His ownership of us and our unflagging commitment to Him.

These, then, are the consummate blessings of the eternal state: We will be forever in the presence of the eternal, holy God. We will have intimate, unbroken fellowship with Christ. We will be joint-heirs with Christ. We will rule and reign with Christ. The full riches of heaven will be ours to possess and enjoy however we please.

All those statements would be blasphemous if God Himself had not promised these things to us.

WHAT WE WILL BE LIKE IN HEAVEN

Perfection.

Most of us understand the concept but have a hard time envisioning anything truly perfect. Everything in our earthly experience is flawed, imperfect.

And for those who know and love the Lord, the imperfections we are most deeply aware of often tend to be our own. I'm not speaking of the frailties of our bodies—though we feel those all too well. But the imperfections that trouble us most are not that superficial. The real problem is a sinfulness that comes straight from the heart (cf. Mark 7:21-23).

Of course, we have a tendency to be more tolerant of our *own* imperfections than we are of others'. We try to cover for ourselves, but in our hearts we really know that we are woefully and sinfully imperfect. What Christian cannot echo the sentiment Paul expresses in Romans 7:24: "O wretched man that I am! Who shall deliver me from the body of this death?"

We're not alone in this. The entire universe suffers the effects of human sin. Paul also writes, "We know that the whole creation groaneth and travaileth in pain together until now" (Rom. 8:22). That's why *all* we can know on earth is imperfection. All creation agonizes under the cruel effect of sin's curse, waiting for the consummation of all things, when the curse will be finally removed.

At that time, everything will be perfect. Pain, sorrow, and the groaning of creation will finally be no more. "The ransomed of the Lord shall return, and come to Zion with songs and everlasting joy upon their heads: *they shall obtain joy and gladness, and sorrow and sighing shall flee away*" (Isa. 35:10, emphasis added).

Not only that, but *we* shall be gloriously perfected. The whole person—body and soul—will be made completely new, flawless. As the apostle John wrote, "Beloved, now are we the sons of God, and it doth not yet appear what we shall be: but we know that, when he shall appear, we shall be like him; for we shall see him as he is" (1 John 3:2).

We can't envision it now—"it doth not yet appear"—but we will finally be wholly and completely Christlike. This is the very purpose for which God chose us in eternity past: "to be conformed to the image of his Son" (Rom. 8:29). "He hath chosen us in him before the foundation of the world, that we should be holy and without blame before him in love" (Eph. 1:4). He has already begun this good work in us, and He will faithfully "perform it until the day of Jesus Christ" (Phil. 1:6). And when we see Christ, we will instantly and summarily be made utterly perfect, for we shall see Him as He is.

Heaven is the perfect place for people made perfect. Perfection is the goal of God's sanctifying work in us. He's not merely making us better than we are; He is conforming us to the image of His Son. As much as glorified humanity can resemble incarnate, exalted deity, we will resemble our Lord. He is making us fit to dwell in His presence forever. The utter perfection of heaven is the consummation of our salvation. It is the purpose for which He chose us before the foundation of the world.

CHANGED FROM THE INSIDE OUT

God begins the process of perfecting us from the moment we are converted from unbelief to faith in Christ. The Holy Spirit regenerates us. He gives us a new heart with a new set of holy desires (Ezek. 36:26). He transforms our stubborn wills. He opens our hearts to embrace the truth rather than reject it. He enables us to believe rather than doubt. He gives us a hunger for righteousness and a desire for Him. And thus the new birth transforms the inner person. From that point on, everything that occurs in our lives—good or bad—God uses to move us toward being like Christ (Rom. 8:28-30).

In a positional sense, we are declared perfect immediately. We are clothed with a perfect righteousness (Isa. 61:10; Rom. 4:5), which instantly gives us a standing before God without any fear of condemnation (Rom. 5:1; 8:1). This is the great position of privilege Scripture refers to when it says God has "blessed us with all spiritual blessings in heavenly places in Christ" (Eph. 1:3). And when Paul writes that God has "raised us up together, and made us sit together in heavenly places in Christ Jesus" (Eph. 2:6), he is again speaking of this position of favor with God that we have been granted by grace alone. We are not literally, physically seated with Christ in the heavenlies, of course. But in the eternal court of God, that is the high legal standing we enjoy.

But God does not stop there. Having judicially declared us righteous (Scripture calls that *justification*) God never stops conforming us to the image of His Son (that is *sanctification*). Although our legal standing is already perfect, God is also making *us* perfect. Heaven is a place of perfect holiness, and we would not be fit to live there unless we too could be made holy. In a sense, then, the blessing of justification is God's guarantee that He will ultimately conform us to the image of His Son (that is *glorification*). "Whom he justified, them he also glorified" (Rom. 8:30).

The seeds of Christlikeness are planted at the moment of conversion. Colossians 2:10 says we are made "complete" in Christ. Peter adds that believers have been granted "all things that pertain unto life and godliness" (2 Peter 1:3). If you are a Christian, the life of God dwells in your soul, and with it all that you need for heaven. The principle of eternal life is already in you, meaning you *have* title to heaven as a present possession. You have already passed from death to life (John 5:24). You are a new person. Whereas you were once enslaved to sin, you have now become a slave of righteousness (Rom. 6:18). Instead of receiving the wages of sin, which is death, you have received God's gift of eternal life (Rom. 6:23). And eternal life means abundant life (John 10:10). It is like an artesian well of spiritual power within us, satisfying and enabling us to live the life we are called to (John 7:38). As Paul writes, "If any man be in Christ, he is a new creature: old things are passed away; behold, all things are become new" (2 Cor. 5:17).

Now let's be honest. Even for the most committed Christian, it doesn't always seem like "all things are become new." We don't always *feel* like a "new creature." Usually we are more keenly aware of the sin that flows from within us than we are of the rivers of living water Christ spoke of. Although we "have the firstfruits of the Spirit, even we ourselves groan within ourselves" (Rom. 8:23). And we groan this way all our lives. Remember that it was a mature apostle, not a fragile new Christian, who cried in Romans 7:24, "O wretched man that I am! Who shall deliver me from the body of this death?"

Here's the problem: Like Lazarus, we came forth from the grave still bound in graveclothes. We are incarcerated in human flesh. "Flesh" in the biblical sense refers not just to the physical body, but to the sinful thoughts and habits that remain with us until our bodies are finally glorified. When Paul speaks of "flesh" and "spirit," he is not contrasting the material and the immaterial the way gnosticism and New Age dualism do. He uses the word *flesh* to speak of a tendency to sin—a sin principle—that remains even in the redeemed person.

He clearly spells out the problem from his own experience in Romans 7. Here Paul writes:

> That which I do I allow not: for what I would, that do I not; but what I hate, that do I. If then I do that which I would not, I consent unto the law that it is good. Now then it is no more I that do it, but sin that dwelleth in me. For I know that in me (that is, in my flesh,) dwelleth no good thing: for to will is present with me; but how to perform that which is good I find not. For the good that I would I do not: but the evil which I would not, that I do. Now if I do that I would not, it is no more I that do it, but sin that dwelleth in me. I find then a law, that, when I would do good, evil is present with me.
>
> —vv. 15-21

If you are struggling to understand how the apostle Paul employs the term *flesh*, this last phrase can virtually be taken as his definition: *The flesh* is "the principle that evil is present in me, the one who wishes to do good" (v. 21, NASB). It includes all the sinful habits and thought patterns that we acquired in our lives before Christ. These fleshly influences have yet to be done away with, and we are severely troubled by them all our lives.

Therefore, although in the depths of our beings we are new creatures, vested with everything necessary for life and godliness, we cannot appreciate fully this newness because of the persisting presence of sin.

Like Paul, we "delight in the law of God after the inward man" (v. 22). Only the principle of eternal life in us can explain such a response of love for the law of God. But at the same time, the flesh constricts and fetters us, like tightly-bound graveclothes on someone just up out of the tomb. This flesh principle is at war against the principle of new life in Christ. Although we delight in the law of God, there is "another law" in us, "bringing [us] into captivity to the law of sin which is in [our] members" (v. 23).

How can this be? After all, Paul earlier wrote in this very epistle that our bondage to sin is broken. We are supposed to be "free from sin, and . . . servants to God" (6:22). How can he now portray us as being in "captivity to the law of sin"?

But being a slave is not quite the same thing as being a captive. As unredeemed sinners, we were willing bondservants of sin. As Christians who are not yet glorified, we are "captives," unwilling prisoners of an already-defeated enemy. Although sin can buffet and abuse us, it cannot destroy us. Sin's authority and dominion are broken. It is "present" in the believer's life (7:21), but our real allegiance is now to the principle of righteousness (v. 22). It is in this sense that "all things are become new" (2 Cor. 5:17)—even though it often seems we fall into old patterns of sinful thinking and behavior.

God is changing us from the inside out. He has planted the incorruptible seed of eternal life deep in the believer's soul. We have a new desire and a new power to please God. We have a new heart and a whole new love for God. And all those are factors that contribute to our ultimate growth in grace.

Paul makes a fascinating point about the inside-out transformation of believers. In 2 Corinthians 3, he contrasts the effects of our salvation with what happened to Moses when he encountered God's glory on Sinai. Paul reminds the Corinthians that when Moses came down from the mountain after the giving of the law, his face glowed. It glowed so brightly that he had to put a veil over his face so that people could look at him without hurting their eyes (Ex. 34:29-33). Yet that was a fading glory (2 Cor. 3:7), and it was a reflected glory.

In contrast, "the glory which shall be revealed in us" (Rom. 8:18) is an ever-growing glory that is not reflected, but comes straight from within. Paul writes, "We all, with unveiled face beholding as in a mirror the glory of the Lord, are being transformed into the same image from glory to glory, just as from the Lord, the Spirit" (2 Cor 3:18, NASB).

In other words, the Spirit of God conveys us from one level of glory to another. As we look in the "mirror," what we see is a reflection of "Christ in [us], the hope of glory" (Col. 1:27). And as we gaze on His glory, the glow of our Christlikeness grows brighter. One day we shall see Him not merely in a dim reflection; instead we shall stand bodily in His presence: "For now we see in a mirror dimly, but then face to face" (1 Cor. 13:12). And with one face-to-face glance at the person of Christ, we will be instantly transformed into His likeness. "We shall be like him; for we shall see him as he is" (1 John 3:2).

Although sin has crippled our souls and marred our spirits— though it has scarred our thoughts, wills, and emotions—we who know Christ have already had a taste of what redemption is like. And so we long for that day when we will be completely redeemed. We yearn to reach that place where the seed of perfection that has been planted within us will bloom into fullness and we will be completely redeemed, finally made perfect (Heb. 12:23). That is exactly what heaven is all about.

A REDEEMED SOUL

In heaven we will finally lose all traces of human fallenness. In fact, no one will ever enter heaven or dwell there who isn't absolutely perfect. This is often symbolized in Scripture by the imagery of white robes that are worn by the redeemed in heaven. Revelation 6:11 says this about the martyrs of the Apocalypse: "White robes were given unto every one of them; and it was said unto them, that they should rest yet for a little season, until their fellowservants also and their brethren, that should be killed as they were, should be fulfilled." The white robes symbolize holiness, purity, and absolute perfection. In Revelation 7:14 one of the elders says, "These are they which came out of great tribulation, and have washed their robes, and made them white in the blood of the Lamb." Repeatedly, the Bible emphasizes the perfection of those who enter heaven.

Scripture tells us that apart from holiness, "no man shall see the Lord" (Heb. 12:14). God doesn't merely justify us and clothe us with a positional righteousness, then leave us bound in the grave-clothes of the flesh. He lovingly, graciously conforms us—heart, soul, mind, and flesh—to a standard befitting the lofty position He has elevated us to.

But don't misunderstand. This is not to say our own personal holiness is the ground on which we are granted entrance into heaven or acceptance with God. If that were the case, none of us could ever gain enough merit to deserve heaven. We are graciously granted entry into heaven solely and exclusively because of Christ's perfect righteousness, which is imputed to us in our justification. The holiness gained in our sanctification is by no means meritorious.

Moreover, the holiness our sanctification produces could never be sufficient to fit us for heaven by itself. In heaven we will be *perfectly* Christlike. Sanctification is the earthly process of growth by which we press toward that goal; *glorification* is the instantaneous completion of it. God graciously and instantaneously glorifies us and admits us into His presence. As we noted in chapter 3, there is no waiting period, no soul sleep, and no purgatory.

Misunderstanding on this point runs deep. No less a Protestant thinker than C. S. Lewis wrote,

> Our souls *demand* Purgatory, don't they? Would it not break the heart if God said to us, "It is true, my son, that your breath smells and your rags drip with mud and slime, but we are charitable here and no one will upbraid you with these things, nor draw away from you. Enter into the joy"? Should we not reply, "With submission, sir, and if there is no objection, I'd *rather* be cleaned first." "It may hurt, you know."—"Even so, sir."[1]

But nothing in Scripture even hints at the notion of purgatory, and nothing indicates that our glorification will in any way be painful. On the contrary, as we have noted already, Scripture suggests that the moment a believer dies, his soul is instantly glorified and he enters God's presence. To depart this world is to be with Christ (Phil. 1:23). And upon seeing Christ, we become like Him. It is a graceful, peaceful, painless, instantaneous transition. Paul says, "To be absent from the body" is "to be at home with the Lord" (2 Cor. 5:8, NASB).

Notice that Paul indicates Christians in heaven at this moment are "absent from the body." The body goes to the grave; the soul is admitted immediately to heaven. Hebrews 12:23 also suggests that all the saints who have died and are now in heaven are there without their bodies; it describes heaven as the dwelling-place of "*the spirits* of righteous men made perfect" (NASB, emphasis added). But we do not remain mere spirits throughout eternity. Our glorified spirits will be united with glorified bodies at the final resurrection. (We'll return to that subject later in this chapter.)

What will the perfected soul be like? The most obvious truth is that it will finally be perfectly free from evil forever. We will never again have a selfish desire or utter useless words. We will never perform another unkind deed or think any sinful thought. We will be perfectly liberated from our captivity to sin, and finally able to do that which is absolutely righteous, holy, and perfect before God. Can you imagine yourself behaving in such an incredible way? I frankly have a hard time envisioning myself as utterly perfect. But there will be no imperfection in heaven!

Revelation 21:27 says, "Nothing unclean and no one who practices abomination and lying, shall ever come into it" (NASB). No one who has any stain of sin will ever enter the heavenly city; therefore sin will never again pose any threat whatsoever.

What about the stain of *our* past sins? Revelation 22:14-15 says, "Blessed are those who wash their robes, that they may have the right to the tree of life, and may enter by the gates into the city. Outside are the dogs and the sorcerers and the immoral persons and the murderers and the idolaters, and everyone who loves and practices lying" (NASB). Sin may define who we once were, but no longer. We are now new creatures in Christ, completely forgiven, thoroughly washed, and forever made perfect. As Paul wrote the Corinthians,

> *Know ye not that the unrighteous shall not inherit the kingdom of God? Be not deceived: neither fornicators, nor idolaters, nor adulterers, nor effeminate, nor abusers of themselves with mankind, nor thieves, nor covetous, nor drunkards, nor revilers, nor extortioners, shall inherit the kingdom of God.* And such were some of you: but ye are washed, *but ye are sanctified, but ye are justified in the name of the Lord Jesus, and by the Spirit of our God.*
> —1 Cor. 6:9-11, emphasis added

All believers can rest in this confidence: God has already justified us in order to free us from the guilt of sin. He is now sanctifying us in order to deliver us from the corruption of sin. And one day He will glorify us in order to liberate us from the very presence of sin—forever!

If you are not a Christian, you need to lay hold of this truth by faith: the sin that will keep you out of heaven has no cure but the blood of Christ. If you are weary of your sin and exhausted from the load of your guilt, He tenderly holds forth the offer of life and forgiveness and eternal rest to you: "Come unto me, all ye that labour and are heavy laden, and I will give you rest" (Matt. 11:28). No one will be turned away: "and him that cometh to me I will in no wise cast out" (John 6:37). All are invited: "The Spirit and the bride say, Come. And let him that heareth say, Come. And let him that is athirst come. And whosoever will, let him take the water of life freely" (Rev. 22:17).

In heaven there will be no sin, suffering, sorrow, or pain. We will never do anything to displease God. There will be no temptation because the world, the flesh, and the devil will all be conspicuously absent. There will be no persecution, division, disunity, or hate. In heaven there will be no quarrels or disagreements. There will be no disappointments. Prayer, fasting, repentance, and confession of sin will cease because the need for them will cease. There will be nothing to confess and nothing to pray for. There will be no weeping because there will be nothing to make us sad. With sin and its effects erased forever, it will be a life of unimaginable blessing!

We will then know *perfect pleasure*. Psalm 16:11 says, "In Thy presence is fullness of joy; at thy right hand there are pleasures forever." Everything that now makes us groan will finally be done away with, and we will find ourselves in the very presence of God, where the purest and truest kind of pleasure is possible. Whatever pleasures we have known here on earth while living under the curse of sin are trivial, paltry diversions compared to the pure delights of heaven. When our souls are made anew we will finally be able to glorify God perfectly, and enjoy Him forever, as He intended. Since nothing is better or greater than God, the pure enjoyment of Him must be the very essence of bliss.

In heaven we will also have *perfect knowledge*. Paul writes, "Then shall I know even as also I am known" (1 Cor. 13:12). Since we are known comprehensively, this must mean we will know comprehensively. This cannot speak of absolute omniscience, for omniscience is one of the incommunicable attributes of God. To embrace all knowledge, one would have to *be* God. But this does indicate that our knowledge will be as complete as we could ever desire. We will have no more unanswered questions, no confusion, no ignorance, and no more need to walk by faith rather than by sight.

We will live in *perfect comfort*. We will never experience one uncomfortable moment. In Jesus' account of the beggar Lazarus and the rich man, Abraham says to the rich man in hell, "Child, remember that during your life you received your good things, and likewise Lazarus bad things; but now he is being comforted here, and you are in agony" (Luke 16:25, NASB). Hell is agony; heaven is eternal comfort.

We will finally know *perfect love.* First Corinthians 13:13 says, "Now abideth faith, hope, charity, these three; but the greatest of these is charity." Why is love the greatest of these three virtues? Because it is the only one that is eternal. In heaven all our hopes will be realized. "Hope that is seen is not hope: for what a man seeth, why doth he yet hope for?" (Rom. 8:24). All that we have laid hold of by faith will be ours to enjoy forever. Faith will be swallowed up by sight. But we will love perfectly and will be loved perfectly for all eternity. John 13:1 says Christ loved His disciples *eis telos*—to the end; to utter perfection. That same love will engulf us forever. And we will finally be able to love perfectly in return.

We could summarize by saying that heaven is a place of *perfect joy.* Our joy in this life is always mixed with sorrow, discouragement, disappointment, or worry. Sin, grief, and sorrow inevitably dampen happiness. An honest look at life in this world produces more tears than real joy. Our lives here begin with the joy of new birth, but inevitably end in the sorrows of death and separation. But in heaven things will be different. Heaven is a place of undiluted joy. At the end of the parable of the talents in Matthew 25, our Lord tells the faithful steward, "Well done, good and faithful servant . . . enter thou into the joy of thy lord" (v. 23).

That Jesus chose this terminology indicates that one of the dominant characteristics of heaven is joy. Best of all, it's an unending and never-diminishing joy. It must be, because heavenly perfection is never altered.

A GLORIFIED BODY

But as we have already stressed, heaven is not merely a state of mind. It is a real place, where the redeemed will have real bodies, like the resurrection body of Jesus Christ.

The Necessity of Our Resurrection

God made man body and soul—we consist of an inner man and an outer man (Gen. 2:7). Therefore our ultimate perfection demands that both body and soul be renewed. Even the creation of a new heaven and earth demands that we have bodies—a real earth calls for its inhabitants to have real bodies. An honest approach to Scripture does not permit these realities to be spiritualized or allegorized away. Eternal life as a mere state of mind would defeat the whole point of many of the promises of Scripture.

Death results in separation of the body and the soul. Our bodies go to the grave, and our spirits go to the Lord. The separation continues until the resurrection: "The hour is coming, in the which all that are in the graves shall hear his voice, and shall come forth; they that have done good, unto the resurrection of life; and they that have done evil, unto the resurrection of damnation" (John 5:28-29). Right now the souls of believers who have died are in heaven. But someday their bodies will be resurrected and joined to their spirits, and they will enjoy the eternal perfection of body and soul.

Similarly, the bodies of unbelievers who have died are in the grave, and their souls are in hell. There will also be a day when the bodies of the ungodly will be raised from the graves and joined to their spirits. They will then stand, body and soul, before the judgment throne of God, and will then be cast bodily into the lake of fire (cf. Matt. 5:30).

Christians need not dread that judgment. There is no possibility of condemnation for those who are in Christ Jesus (Rom. 8:1). We *eagerly* await the redemption of our bodies (v. 23). "In this [body] we groan, earnestly desiring to be clothed upon with our house which is from heaven" (2 Cor. 5:2). Precisely what does this mean? Is it implying that we will receive all new bodies? Will they be anything like our current bodies? Will we look anything like what we do now?

First of all, note that our resurrection bodies *are* our earthly bodies, glorified. The bodies we receive in the resurrection will have the same qualities as the glorified resurrection body of Christ. For "we know that, when he shall appear, we shall be like him" (1 John 3:2).

Christ's resurrection body was the same body as before, not a whole new one. After He arose, the tomb was empty. The body itself was resurrected—the very same body, but in a glorified state. The wounds from His crucifixion were still visible (John 20:27). He could be touched and handled—He was not merely an apparition or a phantom (Luke 24:39). He looked human in every regard. He conversed a long time with the disciples on the road to Emmaus, and they never once questioned His humanity (Luke 24:13-18). He ate real, earthly food with His friends on another occasion (vv. 42-43). Yet His body also had other-worldly properties. He could pass through solid walls (John 20:19). He could appear in different forms so His identity was not immediately obvious (Mark 16:12). He could suddenly appear out of nowhere (Luke 24:36). And He could ascend directly into heaven in bodily form (Luke 24:51; Acts 1:9).

Our bodies will be like that. Paul writes that the Lord "shall change our vile body, that it may be fashioned like unto his glorious body" (Phil. 3:21). They will be real, physical, genuinely human bodies—the very same bodies we have dwelt with on this earth—yet wholly perfected and glorified. Second Corinthians 5:1 calls the resurrection body "a house not made with hands, eternal in the heavens."

First Thessalonians 4 describes the resurrection of believers who have died, and the simultaneous catching away to heaven of believers who are still alive:

I would not have you to be ignorant, brethren, concerning them which are asleep, that ye sorrow not, even as others which have no hope. For if we believe that Jesus died and rose again, even so them also which sleep in Jesus will God bring with him. For this we say unto you by the word of the Lord, that we which are alive and remain unto the coming of the Lord shall not prevent [precede] them which are asleep. For the Lord himself shall descend from heaven with a shout, with the voice of the archangel, and with the trump of God: and the dead in Christ shall rise first: Then we which are alive and remain shall be caught up together with them in the clouds, to meet the Lord in the air: and so shall we ever be with the Lord.

—vv. 13-17

Believers who are dead are first united with their perfected bodies, then those who are still alive will be caught up and instantly "changed"—glorified. So every Christian still living on the earth when Christ comes will be perfected. And, again, notice that both the living and the dead will have their old bodies made new and glorified.

This doctrine of bodily resurrection is absolutely essential to the Christian message. In 1 Corinthians 15 (the definitive chapter on the subject), Paul severely rebukes anyone who would doubt or question this reality: "But someone will say, 'How are the dead raised? And with what kind of body do they come?' You fool!" (vv. 35-36). That is one of the most caustic retorts in all the Pauline writings. But in Paul's estimation, this doctrine is fundamental. To deny it is to embrace something other than genuine Christianity: "For if the dead rise not, then is not Christ raised: And if Christ be not raised, your faith is vain; ye are yet in your sins" (vv. 16-17).

Resurrection Illustrated

Paul uses a series of illustrations to explain the resurrection of the body. The first is an illustration borrowed from Christ's own teaching. Jesus said, "Except a corn of wheat fall into the ground and die, it abideth alone: but if it die, it bringeth forth much fruit" (John 12:24).

The apostle applies the same imagery to the bodily resurrection: "That which thou sowest is not quickened, except it die: and that which thou sowest, thou sowest not that body that shall be, but bare grain, it may chance of wheat, or of some other grain" (1 Cor. 15:36-37). When you plant a seed, the first thing it does is die. The process of fermentation and decomposition is what triggers the new life. Similarly our bodies will die, be placed in a grave, and then be raised, just as a seed dies and produces a plant that is far more glorious than the seed.

Also, the seed contains the pattern for the plant that grows. All the genetic code for an entire oak tree is contained inside the kernel of the acorn. Likewise, our resurrection bodies will bear a resemblance to the body that is buried—but with a far greater glory. We will be ourselves, only perfect. And the decomposition of the earthly will only facilitate the remaking of a glorified resurrection body—with none of the flaws of the old, but with all that is necessary for a perfect existence in heaven.

That answers the question "How are the dead raised up?" (v. 35). Paul employs a second illustration to reply to the doubter's second challenge, "With what body do they come?" The scoffer's question suggests that it is absurd to think normal human flesh would be fit for life in heaven. Paul's reply points out that it is absurd to think of the resurrection body as "normal" human flesh. After all, even in our limited earthly knowledge, "All flesh is not the same flesh: but there is one kind of flesh of men, another flesh of beasts, another of fishes, and another of birds" (v. 39). The resurrected body will no doubt be a different variety of flesh than we know from earthly experience. It will be literal human flesh, but gloriously and perfectly so—as different from the earthly kind as human flesh is from that of birds.

Continuing in a similar mode of thought, Paul says, "There are also celestial bodies, and bodies terrestrial: but the glory of the celestial is one, and the glory of the terrestrial is another. There is one glory of the sun, and another glory of the moon, and another glory of the stars: for one star differeth from another star in glory" (vv. 40-41). Since God made everything from a tiny, crawling bug to a massive star system, He can make any kind of body He wants. God's creation is rich with infinite variety. Why question His ability to create any kind of resurrection body He wants?

Tying all these illustrations together, Paul concludes: "So also is the resurrection of the dead. It is sown in corruption; it is raised in incorruption: It is sown in dishonour; it is raised in glory: it is sown in weakness; it is raised in power: It is sown a natural body; it is raised a spiritual body. There is a natural body, and there is a spiritual body" (vv. 42-44).

Like a seed, the resurrection body is sown and is raised. The graveyards of men are the seed plots of resurrection. But the resurrection body is new, changed in virtually every way imaginable. It was sown in death and decay; it is raised to be *imperishable*. It is buried as a thing of defilement, ingloriously placed under the earth; but it is raised as something *glorious*. When entombed it is dead, utterly inanimate and impotent; but it is raised to be *powerful*. It is planted as a lifeless material thing; yet raised as something full of life and *spiritual*.

All this is to say that in heaven we will have real bodies that are permanently and eternally perfect. You will never look in a mirror and notice wrinkles or a receding hairline. You will never have a day of sickness. You won't be susceptible to injury, or disease, or allergies. There will be none of those things in heaven. There will only be absolute, imperishable perfection.

We will no doubt have unimaginable abilities in heaven. Remember that the heavenly city is fifteen hundred miles high. Don't think you'll be waiting for elevators to get you to the top.

You'll no doubt have the ability to fly—or if you desire, simply be transported there in an instant—in the same way that Christ's resurrection body could seemingly disappear and reappear in another place at will.

Above all, we will be *Christlike*. Paul writes,

> *And so it is written, The first man Adam was made a living soul; the last Adam was made a quickening spirit. Howbeit that was not first which is spiritual, but that which is natural; and afterward that which is spiritual. The first man is of the earth, earthy: the second man is the Lord from heaven. As is the earthy, such are they also that are earthy: and as is the heavenly, such are they also that are heavenly.*
>
> —*1 Cor. 15:45-48*

In that passage Paul contrasts the heads of two families. Adam is our father according to the flesh, meaning that he is the head of the human race. Christ is our spiritual head, and the first among the redeemed race. Just as our earthly bodies are descended from Adam's so that we resemble him, so in heaven we will be like Jesus Christ, who is incorruptible, eternal, glorified, powerful, and spiritual.

So the best picture of what we'll be like in heaven is the resurrection body of Jesus Christ. We will have a body fit for the full life of God to indwell and express itself forever. It can eat but won't need to. It will be a body that can move at will through space and matter. It will be ageless and not know pain, tears, sorrow, sickness, or death.

It will also be a body of brilliant splendor. Christ's glorified body is described as shining like the sun in its strength (Rev. 1:16). And in an Old Testament promise, Scripture compares our glorified bodies to the shining of the moon and stars: "They that be wise shall shine as the brightness of the firmament; and they that turn many to righteousness as the stars for ever and ever" (Dan. 12:3).

Do you see why it is irrational to seek our highest joy and comfort in this life? God's plan, to make us like Christ, is infinitely better. Why would we ever set our affections on the fleeting things of this earth? To have such a perspective is only to seek what will never satisfy. That kind of thinking only aggravates our misery.

PERFECT RELATIONSHIPS

So far we have barely touched on the question of relationships in heaven. Yet this is one of the major issues most Christians wonder about. Will we recognize our loved ones? Will we remember our earthly relationships? What kind of relationships will we have? Will we have family love and fellowship in heaven? Will our relationships in heaven be anything like they are here?

The question I'm most often asked about heaven is, *"Will I be married to the same spouse in heaven?"* Most are saying, "I don't want to lose my relationship with my wife; I can't imagine going to heaven and not being married to her." (Others, however, may be secretly hoping for a different answer. I'm not certain why so many ask this one!)

Scripture speaks specifically to many of these questions. On the issue of marriage and family, for example, Paul said,

> *This I say, brethren, the time has been shortened, so that from now on those who have wives should be as though they had none; and those who weep, as though they did not weep; those who rejoice, as though they did not rejoice; and those who buy, as though they did not possess; and those who use the world, as though they did not make full use of it; for the form [Gk., schema] of this world is passing away.*
>
> *—1 Cor. 7:29-31, NASB*

The apostle lists several of the things that are passing away: marriage, weeping, earthly rejoicing, and ownership. All the *schema* of the world is passing away. *Schema* refers to fashion, manner of life, and a way of doing things.

Paul was saying we should take what life brings, yet keep from being engulfed in it, because all those things are part of a *schema* that is temporary. Although the privileges of marriage are wonderful and its responsibilities enormous, don't allow your marriage to become an excuse for failure to serve God, to put treasure in heaven, or to set your affections on things above.

Paul is not questioning the legitimacy of earthly blessings such as marriage, normal human emotions, and earthly ownership. But he is saying that we must never allow our emotions and posses-sions to control us so that we become entangled by this passing world.

Marriage and other business of this life can sometimes intrude on more important matters of eternal concern. Paul writes, "He that is unmarried careth for the things that belong to the Lord, how he may please the Lord: but he that is married careth for the things that are of the world, how he may please his wife" (1 Cor. 7:32-33). So if you can remain single, do. Concentrate on the things of the Lord, because marriage is only a temporary provision.

If you're already married, however, this does not mean you may become indifferent to your marriage. Too much elsewhere in Scripture elevates the importance of marriage and commands hus-bands and wives to seek to honor God through the marriage rela-tionship. But this passage simply underscores the temporal nature of marriage. While married couples are heirs together of the grace of *this* life (cf. 1 Peter 3:7), the institution of marriage is passing away. There are higher eternal values.

Jesus Himself taught that marriage is an earthly union only. Matthew 22 records an incident when some Sadducees came to Him to try to trick Him with a puzzle. The Sadducees did not believe in the afterlife. They had a running dispute with the Pharisees about this very issue. The Pharisees taught that after the resurrection each person would have the same relationships he has here. They believed men would remain married to their earthly wives and retain their earthly families forever. The Sadducees wanted to get Jesus to take sides, so they tried to paint an absurd moral dilemma using the Pharisees' theology in the guise of asking Jesus a question.

They said, "Master, Moses said, If a man die, having no children, his brother shall marry his wife, and raise up seed unto his brother" (v. 24). (That was indeed a Mosaic principle taught in Deuteronomy 25—designed to protect a family's line of inheritance.) They presented a hypothetical scenario:

"Now there were with us seven brethren: and the first, when he had married a wife, deceased, and, having no issue, left his wife unto his brother: Likewise the second also, and the third, unto the seventh. And last of all the woman died also. Therefore in the resurrection whose wife shall she be of the seven? for they all had her."

—vv. 25-28

Jesus' reply was a sharp rebuke for their ignorance of the Scriptures: "Ye do err, not knowing the scriptures, nor the power of God. For in the resurrection they neither marry, nor are given in marriage, but are as the angels of God in heaven" (vv. 29-30).

In other words, angels don't procreate. Neither will we in heaven. All the reasons for marriage will be gone. Here on earth man needs a helper, woman needs a protector, and God has designed both to produce children. In heaven, man will no longer require a helper because he will be perfect. Woman will no longer need a protector because she will be perfect. And the population of heaven will be fixed. Thus marriage as an institution will be unnecessary.

Some believe Jesus' reply to the Sadducees means we will all be genderless creatures in heaven. But that is not a necessary conclusion from what Jesus actually said. Nor does Scripture elsewhere picture the redeemed in heaven as without gender. Certainly the resurrected body of Christ does not appear to have been turned into an androgynous figure. When Mary saw Him after the resurrection, she supposed that He was the gardener—a man's occupation —and spoke to Him as "Sir" (John 20:15). Others recognized Him for who He was. Our gender is part of who we are. Nothing in Scripture suggests that men will cease to be men or that women will cease to be women. But there will be no marrying or giving in marriage. Marriage as an institution will pass away.

But what are those of us who are happily married supposed to think of this? I love my wife. She's my best friend and my dearest companion in every area of life. If those are your thoughts about your spouse as well, don't despair! You will enjoy an eternal companionship in heaven that is more perfect than any earthly partnership. The difference is that you will have such a perfect relationship with every other person in heaven as well. If having such a deep relationship with your spouse here is so wonderful, imagine how glorious it will be to enjoy a perfect relationship with every human in the whole expanse of heaven—forever!

"Will we really know each other?" may be the second most frequently-heard question about heaven. And the answer is yes. We will forever be who we are now—only without any of our faults or infirmities. Everything in Scripture seems to confirm this.

For example, in the Old Testament, when a person died, the biblical writers said he was "gathered to his people" (cf. Gen. 25:8; 35:29; 49:29; Num. 20:24; Jud. 2:10). In 2 Samuel 12, when David's infant child died, David confidently said, "I shall go to him, but he shall not return to me" (v. 23). David evidently expected to see the child again—not just a nameless, faceless soul without an identity, but that very child.

The New Testament indicates even more clearly that our identities will remain unchanged. While sharing the Passover meal with

His disciples, Christ said, "Take this [cup], and divide it among yourselves: For I say unto you, I will not drink of the fruit of the vine, until the kingdom of God shall come" (Luke 22:17-18). Christ was promising that He and His disciples *would* drink the fruit of the vine together again—in heaven. Elsewhere Jesus makes a similar, but even more definite, promise: "Many shall come from the east and west, and shall sit down with Abraham, and Isaac, and Jacob, in the kingdom of heaven" (Matt. 8:11).

All the redeemed will maintain their identity forever, but in a perfected form. We will be able to have fellowship with Enoch, Noah, Abraham, Jacob, Samuel, Moses, Joshua, Esther, Elijah, Elisha, Isaiah, Daniel, Ezekiel, David, Peter, Barnabas, Paul, or any of the saints we choose.

Remember that Moses and Elijah appeared with Christ on the Mount of Transfiguration. Even though they died centuries before, they still maintained a clear identity (Matt. 17:3). Moreover, Peter, James, and John evidently recognized them (v. 4)—which implies that we will somehow be able to recognize people we've never even seen before. For that to be possible, we must all retain our individual identities, not turn into some sort of generic beings.

When the Sadducees tried to trap Jesus about the resurrection, He cited God's words to Moses in Exodus 3:6: "I am the God of thy father, the God of Abraham, the God of Isaac, and the God of Jacob." Then Jesus commented, "God is not the God of the dead, but of the living" (v. 32). His plain meaning was that Abraham, Isaac, and Jacob were still living, and that God continued to be their God. Moreover, Jesus' account of the rich man and Lazarus indicates that *both* men maintained their identities—though Lazarus was in heaven and the rich man in hell.

Another common question is this: *"Will I be reunited with my family and friends in heaven?"* Obviously, the answer to this question is implied by all that we have seen so far: yes. We will be reunited not only with our own families and loved ones, but with the people of God from all ages. In heaven we will all be one loving family. The immense size of the family will not matter in the infinite perfection of heaven. There will be ample opportunity for close relationships with everyone, and our eternity will be spent in just that kind of rich, unending fellowship.

Describing the Lord's appearing and the resurrection of the saints who have died, Paul writes, "We which are alive and remain shall be caught up *together with them* in the clouds, to meet the Lord in the air: and so shall we ever be *with the Lord*" (1 Thess. 4:17, emphasis added). Paul's purpose in writing was to comfort some of the Thessalonians who evidently thought their dying loved ones would miss the return of Christ. He says in verse 18, "Comfort one another with these words." The *comfort* comes from the prospect of reunion. Little comfort this would be if in the reunion we could not even recognize one another. But Paul's promise that we will all be "together" forever implies that we shall renew fellowship with all whom we have known.

Theologian A.A. Hodge wrote,

Heaven, as the eternal home of the divine Man and of all the redeemed members of the human race, must necessarily be thoroughly human in its structure, conditions, and activities. Its joys and its occupations must all be rational, moral, emotional, voluntary, and active. There must be the exercise of all faculties, the gratification of all tastes, the development of all talent capacities, the realization of all ideals. The reason, the intellectual curiosity, the imagination, the aesthetic instincts, the holy affections, the social affinities, the inexhaustible resources of strength and power native to the human soul, must all find in heaven exercise and satisfaction.[2]

If you're worried about feeling out of place in heaven, don't. Heaven will seem more like home than the dearest spot on earth to you. It is uniquely designed by a tender, loving Savior to be the place where we will live together for all eternity and enjoy Him forever—in the fullness of our glorified humanity.

Is it any wonder that the psalmist said, "Precious in the sight of the Lord is the death of his saints" (Ps. 116:15)?

UNBROKEN FELLOWSHIP WITH GOD

Without question, the most marvelous thing of all about heaven—heaven's supreme delight—will be unbroken fellowship with God Himself.

First John 1:3 defines our salvation in terms of fellowship with God: "Our fellowship is with the Father, and with his Son Jesus Christ." When we become believers, we enter into close spiritual fellowship with God. His life becomes ours. His will becomes our will, and His purpose our purpose. Even though sin hinders our walk with Christ on earth, the deepest part of our regenerated soul is united with the living God and in fellowship with the living Christ.

In other words, salvation brings us into communion with God. We can talk and commune with Him. We pray to Him as our dear Father—"Abba," in Paul's favorite terminology. We hear Him speak to us in His Word. He moves providentially in our lives to reveal Himself. We enjoy real spiritual communion with Him.

But that communion is nonetheless incomplete, shrouded from our plain view. As Paul writes "Now we see through a glass, darkly; but then face to face: now I know in part; but then shall I know even as also I am known" (1 Cor. 13:12). He's talking about our fellowship with God. In heaven it will be perfect, unhindered, unclouded by any sin or darkness.

This is one of the main things that was on Jesus' heart and mind as He prayed the night of His betrayal. John 17 records our Lord's high-priestly prayer. This is a prayer for the disciples—and also for every believer of all time. Jesus says so plainly (v. 20). Anticipating the completion of His work on earth, our Lord asks the Father to return Him to the glory He had before the world began. He prays, "Father, I will that they also, whom thou hast given me, be with me where I am; that they may behold my glory" (v. 24). He wants us to be *with Him*. But that's not all. Notice the kind of relationship He prays for among all believers: "That they all may be one; as thou, Father, art in me, and I in thee, *that they also may be one in us*" (v. 21, emphasis added). His design for us is perfect fellowship with Him—much like the unity that exists between Father and Son!

This is such an incredibly profound concept that there's no way our finite minds can begin to appreciate it. But it was obviously the foremost thought on Jesus' mind whenever He spoke of the promise of heaven to the disciples. Earlier that same night on the eve of His crucifixion, He told them, "Where I go, you cannot follow Me now; but you shall follow later" (John 13:36). Later, knowing the disciples were troubled at the thought of His leaving them, He expanded the same promise:

> "Let not your heart be troubled: ye believe in God, believe also in me. In my Father's house are many mansions: if it were not so, I would have told you. I go to prepare a place for you. And if I go and prepare a place for you, I will come again, and receive you unto myself; that where I am, there ye may be also."
>
> —John 14:1-3,
> emphasis added

Simply put, we're going to be with a Person as much as we are going to live in a place. The presence of Christ is what makes heaven heaven. "The Lamb is the light thereof" (Rev. 21:23). And perfect fellowship with God is the very essence of heaven.

Notice how crucial is the notion of fellowship in the Bible's final summary of heaven: "Behold, the tabernacle of God is with men, and he will dwell with them, and they shall be his people, and God himself shall be with them, and be their God" (Rev. 21:3). That verse emphasizes God's intimate presence "with men"—among humanity. The idea is that God Himself will pitch His tent among men and dwell among them. All believers will forever enjoy the pleasure of God's company.

This will not be in the same manner that God had His tabernacle among the Israelites in the wilderness. There, God's tent—the tabernacle—was in the middle of the camp, but it was such holy a place that strict rules governed when and how people could come and go into the tabernacle. No one was permitted into the Most Holy Place, where God Himself dwelt—except for the high priest, and that was only once a year. But Revelation 7:15 tells us that "He who sits on the throne shall spread His tabernacle over them" (NASB)—indicating that God actually brings us into His own dwelling.

Jesus told the disciples, "In My Father's house are many dwelling-places," then added, "I go to prepare a place for you" (John 14:2, NASB). He is personally preparing rooms in the Father's own house for each one of the elect! That promises us the most intimate fellowship imaginable with the living God.

In heaven we will actually see the Lord face to face. This is impossible in the earthly realm. After all, God said, "No man can see Me and live!" (Ex. 33:20, NASB). John 1:18 and 1 John 4:12 both say, "No man hath seen God at any time." First Timothy 6:16 declares that God "alone possesses immortality and dwells in unapproachable light; whom no man has seen or can see" (NASB). Indeed, God is "of purer eyes than to behold evil, and [cannot] look on iniquity" (Hab. 1:13). As long as we are tainted by sin, we cannot see God. The view of such perfect righteousness would destroy us.

God is therefore inaccessible to mortal man on a face-to-face basis. This is what made Christ's incarnation so wonderful:

although no man has ever seen God at any time, "the only begotten Son, which is in the bosom of the Father, he hath declared him" (John 1:18). Christ "tabernacled among us" (John 1:14)—"and we beheld his glory, the glory as of the only begotten of the Father." He came to our world to dwell among us, and He did it in order to redeem us and take us to heaven, where Father, Son, and Holy Spirit will dwell in our midst in perfect fellowship. What a breath-taking reality!

In heaven, since we will be free from sin, we will see God's glory unveiled in its fullness. That will be a more pleasing, spectacular sight than anything we have known or could ever imagine on earth. No mere earthly pleasure can even begin to measure up to the privilege and the ecstasy of an unhindered view of the divine glory.

Matthew 5:8 says, "Blessed are the pure in heart: for they shall see God." The Greek verb translated "see" (*horao*) is in a tense that denotes a future, continuous reality. In heaven we will continually be seeing God. Kings generally seclude themselves from direct contact with their people. It is a rare privilege to have an audience with a king. But believers in heaven will forever have perfect, unbroken fellowship with the King of Kings!

This has always been the deepest longing of the redeemed soul. The psalmist said, "As the hart panteth after the water brooks, so panteth my soul after thee, O God. My soul thirsteth for God, for the living God: when shall I come and appear before God?" (Ps. 42:1-2). And Philip, speaking for all the disciples, said to Christ, "Show us the Father, and it sufficeth us" (John 14:8).

Revelation 22:3-4 seals the promise: "The throne of God and of the Lamb shall be in it; and his servants shall serve him: *and they shall see his face*" (emphasis added).

David wrote, "As for me, I will behold thy face in righteousness: I shall be satisfied, when I awake, with thy likeness" (Ps. 17:15). What really satisfies you? New clothes? A new job? A promotion?

A new house or car? A great meal? A fun time? A vacation? Don't set your heart on such paltry earthly pleasures. The redeemed will be able to *see God*.

David knew every station in life, from that of a lowly shepherd to the honor of being a great warrior to the status of being king. He tasted every earthly pleasure. And he knew ultimate satisfaction would come only when he could see the face of God and be like Him in holiness.

As Christians, our highest satisfaction will come when we see our God and His Son, Jesus Christ, and when we stand before Them in perfect uprightness. Heaven will provide us with that privilege—an undiminished, unwearied sight of His infinite glory and beauty, bringing us infinite and eternal delight. We can begin to understand why Peter, after seeing only a faint glimpse of that glory, wanted to make a camp on the Mount of Transfiguration and stay there permanently! (Matt. 17:4).

In "My Savior First of All," eighteenth-century hymn writer Fanny Crosby wrote:

> *When my life work is ended, and I cross the swelling tide,*
>> *When the bright and glorious morning I shall see,*
> *I shall know my Redeemer when I reach the other side,*
>> *And His smile will be the first to welcome me. . . .*
>
> *Thru the gates of the city in a robe of spotless white,*
>> *He will lead me where no tears will ever fall;*
> *In the glad song of ages I shall mingle with delight*
>> *But I long to meet my Savior first of all.*

Those words have special significance—Fanny Crosby was blind. She knew the first person she would ever see would be Jesus Christ.

In a way, the same thing is true of us all. Our sight here on earth is virtually like blindness compared to the clearer vision we will have in heaven (1 Cor. 13:12). We ought to be eagerly looking for that day when our vision will be enlightened by the glory of His presence. I sincerely hope that's your deepest desire.

THE
HEAVENLY HOST

A discussion of heaven would not be complete without giving some attention to the angels.

As I mentioned at the outset of this book, angels are a very popular subject these days. "Angelmania" has swept popular culture and is the hottest New Age trend at the moment. Recently five of the top ten books on a list of religious best-sellers were books dealing with the subject of angels.

One book that has topped the charts for many months is a how-to guide instructing people on methods for contacting angels, communicating with them, and even receiving guidance from them.[1] One well-known secular publisher lists all these titles in its catalogue: *Angel Letters*, *Angel Power*, *An Angel to Watch Over Me*, *Angel's Bidding*, *Angels and Aliens*, *Angels Over Their Shoulders*, *The Angels Weep*, *The Angels Within Us*, *Angels: The Mysterious Messengers* and *Ask Your Angels*. And that's only in the listings under "A"!

Communicating with angels is serious business, according to books like these. According to the publisher's promotional material for the most popular of these books, "The authors show us how we can draw on the power of angels to reconnect with our lost

inner selves and to achieve our goals, whether they be better relationships, healing an illness, or recovery from addiction."
Supposedly this book will teach the reader "how to align with the
angelic energy field and learn to talk with your angels."

Here are some other verbatim quotations from various publishers' comments about their latest angelic books:

• Through the easy techniques presented in this book, you can
learn to access and attune to beings such as guardian angels, nature
spirits and elementals, spirit totems, archangels, gods and god-
desses—as well as family and friends after their physical death. Also
reveals which acupressure points stimulate your intuitive faculties,
how to protect yourself from lower-level discarnates, and how to
conquer fears of the unknown.

• Everyone has a Spirit Guide or guardian angel who assists
him in keeping on a chosen Karmic path. [This cassette tape] helps
you get in touch with yours.

• [You can learn to] contact your guardian angel and be recep-
tive to the angelic realm in your daily life. Learn how to attune to
the higher frequencies of Spirit, to be more aware of angels and
nature spirits, and to communicate with these loving beings in
order to develop a deeper appreciation of our own place in Creation.

• [This book] enables us to begin to open our hearts to these
joyful and comforting protectors, so we can raise our consciousness
to a new dimension.

• All the pieces in this unique collection stress the cooperation
between humans and angels in the creation of our inner life and
even of nature. The reader experiences a rich and variegated view
of these ancient, elusive spirits that have inspired us for so long.

• The authors teach you nine specific ways your personal angel
protects you, how to call out to your guardian angel, and how to get
your angel to answer your cry for help and assistance in matters big
and small. You'll also find out about the Angelic Hierarchy and
learn the actual language of the Angelic Kingdom!

• Shows us how to co-create with the angels and the
Kingdom of Heaven on Earth. Specific exercises and meditations

help you communicate with angels who are waiting to be invited into your life!

• Inspiration from the angels and Muses is always available. Along with writing and art exercises, the reader will explore the angelic realm through guided journeys, focusing on mandalas, knowing how to use the seasonal forces, learning how colors influence us and how the angels use color and light as their own language. Case histories of how many people became aware of their creative talents when they began playing with the angels are included.

• Offers a complete method for bringing the healing light of the soul, the Solar angel, and the angelic healers into the physical body. Taught in workshops for the past eight years, these easy-to-learn processes have helped thousands to heal and upgrade the cells in their body. The healing angels will work with whatever healing path or healing treatment you are now using. Includes a chart of healing questions, colors, and images for use with specific illnesses.

• By utilizing a combination of your birth sign and a specific colored candle, you can obtain the magic and wisdom you want in life by calling upon the angels. This book contains many spiritual secrets that will guide the reader to success and power.

Much of this, of course, is little more than occult divination, sorcery, and typical New Age-style mysticism. Everything we said about the dangers of mystical "visits to heaven" in chapter 1 applies equally to these attempts to consort with spirit beings.

Indeed, I have no doubt that some who claim to commune with angels really have been able to establish a link with angelic beings—though not in they way they seek. Scripture warns us plainly that Satan and his messengers often appear as angels of light (2 Cor. 11:13-15). In other words, demonic beings take advantage of the gullibility of people who are actively seeking to communicate with the spirit world. "Angelmania" turns out to be sheer occultism, with all its horrible effects. Many people have been drawn into serious demonic bondage by these practices, and Christians should be strongly warned against them.

Unfortunately, the evangelical response to Angelmania has been weak. Already there are "Christian" angel books, enthusiastically recounting "Real-Life Stories About Angels" and glowing tales of Christians who have conversed with angels. Typically, evangelicals are merely getting swept up in the world's fads. Unfortunately, this one poses some particularly serious hazards.

As 2 Corinthians 11:15 suggests, "it is no great thing" for a demon to disguise himself as a good angel. Furthermore, despite the prevalence of stirring tales about angelic interventions (angels who rescue missionaries from cannibals and similar tales), there is no way any of these stories can be verified—except for the biblical ones. That doesn't mean it *wasn't* an angel whose invisible hand mysteriously steadied you when you were about to take a tumble down the stairs. But it means you cannot possibly know for sure whether it was an angel or not. We *do* know for sure that it is God whose providence preserves us from various disasters. Whether in a given instance He employs angels as His instruments or not, *it is God who should be the focus of our praise and gratitude, not the angelic beings.*

Scripture does teach that angels minister to the saints (Heb. 1:14), and that *some* "have entertained angels without knowing it" (Heb. 13:2, NASB). And for that very reason we are instructed to show kindness and hospitality to strangers. But the language of Scripture indicates that these incidents are rare, and the key to understanding this verse is the phrase *without knowing it*. It is certainly possible, according to Scripture, that you might play host to an angel. But in all likelihood, if that occurs, it will occur without your knowing it. Nowhere does Scripture encourage us to have an angel-fetish, or to look for evidence of angels in everyday life.

The tales that fill today's angelic-encounter books are unverifiable stories—extraordinary displays of divine providence, perhaps, but not necessarily authentic accounts of angelic intervention. The whole fixation is of questionable value, and undoubtedly it is causing far more spiritual harm than good.

WHAT DOES SCRIPTURE SAY ABOUT ANGELS?

A recent issue of *Moody* featured an excellent cover article critiquing the angel craze. The article included a quotation from theology professor Ed Glasscock, who stated, "The Bible never really explains angels. It just makes casual references to their activities."[2] I agree. Gleaning our information solely from the biblical data, we come up with far more unanswered questions about angels than detailed knowledge. We know that angels minister to humans and even intervene from time to time in human affairs, but as to *how* this happens we know very little. And we are discouraged from looking into all spiritual matters beyond what is revealed for us in Scripture: "The secret things belong unto the Lord our God: but those things which are revealed belong unto us and to our children for ever" (Deut. 29:29).

Nevertheless, there is a considerable body of information in Scripture about these wonderful creatures, the angels. And since we will spend eternity with them in heaven, it is helpful to this study of heaven to learn all we can from Scripture about the angels and their role.

Scripture uses several expressions to describe the angels. They are called "the sons of the mighty" in Psalm 89:6; "sons of God" (Job 1:6; 2:1; 38:7); *elohim* (literally, "gods"—Ps. 8:5); "holy ones" (Ps. 89:5, NASB); "morning stars" (Job 38:7), "princes" (Dan. 10:13); and "principalities and powers" (Eph. 3:10).

Study the Bible and you will find angels in the third heaven, where God dwells. There they worship Him continuously. You'll find them in the second heaven, traversing the universe, serving

God in various ways. And you'll find them in the first heaven, even intervening from time to time in human affairs.

How Angels Were Created

Angels are created beings. They are not demigods. They do not have attributes of deity, such as omniscience or omnipresence. They did not exist in eternity past. They are creatures. Nehemiah 9:6 says, "Thou, even thou, art Lord alone; thou hast made heaven, the heaven of heavens, *with all their host,* the earth, and all things that are therein, the seas, and all that is therein, and thou preservest them all; and *the host of heaven worshippeth thee*" (emphasis added). That clearly indicates that God created the angels. It also suggests that angels—like all other intelligent creatures—were designed to render worship to God, not to receive worship themselves. In fact, in every case in Scripture, whenever angels are offered any form of worship, they always rebuke the worshiper and redirect all worship to God alone (cf. Rev. 19:10; 22:8-9).

Psalm 148 confirms that the angels are created beings who worship the Creator:

> *Praise ye him, all his angels: praise ye him, all his hosts. Praise ye him, sun and moon: praise him, all ye stars of light. Praise him, ye heavens of heavens, and ye waters that be above the heavens. Let them praise the name of the Lord:* for he commanded, and they were created.
>
> —*vv. 2-5, emphasis added*

Both Nehemiah 9:6 ("Thou, even thou, art Lord [Heb. *yhwh*] alone; thou hast made heaven . . . with all their host") and Psalm 148:5 ("the Lord *[yhwh].* . . commanded, and they were created") identify *Jehovah* as the One who created the angels. One of the strongest proofs of Jesus' deity is the biblical assertion that *He* is the One who created all things, including the angels. Colossians 1:16

says: "By him were all things created, that are in heaven, and that are in earth, visible and invisible, whether they be thrones, or dominions, or principalities, or powers: all things were created by him, and for him." Here Paul is explicitly defending Christ's deity against the teaching of some who said He was merely a created being. (To this day, the Jehovah's Witnesses sect teaches that Christ is an archangel—the highest of created beings.) Paul carefully refutes all such teaching, by declaring that Christ Himself is the One who created everything—*including* all angelic beings and everything else that exists. Therefore Christ *is* Jehovah incarnate. He cannot be a mere angel Himself.

Paul often refers to the angels as "principalities and powers" who dwell and rule in heavenly places (cf. Eph. 6:12). We're not told precisely what the hierarchy of heaven is, but evidently the angels are organized in a divinely-ordered chain of command. They are described throughout Scripture as a huge heavenly army. And as their Creator, Christ is set far above them in authority. He alone is at the Father's right hand, "far above all principality, and power, and might, and dominion, and every name that is named, not only in this world, but also in that which is to come" (Eph. 1:21). Again Scripture repeatedly makes this stark distinction between Christ, who is eternal (John 1:1), and the angels, who are merely created beings. Christ "is before all things, and by him all things consist" (Col. 1:17).

Moreover, the doctrine that angels are created beings is in perfect harmony with 1 Timothy 6:15-16, which states that Jesus Christ is "is the blessed and only Sovereign, the King of kings and Lord of lords; *who alone possesses immortality*" (NASB).

It appears that the angels were created early in the process of creation. Job 38 describes the laying of earth's foundation: " . . . when the morning stars sang together, and all the sons of God shouted for joy?" (v. 7). So the angels were there to witness the formation of our world. And since there is no procreation among angels (Matt. 22:30), they must have all been created at once—in a sweeping creative act. God instantly commanded, and untold numbers of creatures came into existence, each one independently unique. They do not reproduce, so there can never be any increase in the number. They do not die, so there's no decrease.

How many angels are there? Scripture doesn't give us a number. But at the birth of Christ there appeared "a multitude of heavenly host" (Luke 2:13). At His arrest Jesus said if He wanted to, He could simply pray to the Father and immediately call forth *twelve legions* of angels. That would be somewhere between 78,000 and 144,000 angels. Think of it: if Jesus needed 144,000 angels, they'd be there instantly. But there's no reason to think "twelve legions" exhausts the ranks of the angels. In fact, there is biblical evidence that the total number is much higher.

Scripture often describes the immense number of angels by comparing them to the stars. The angels and the stars are even spoken of in terms that are used interchangeably. "The host of heaven" sometimes speaks of the stars (cf. Deut. 17:3) and sometimes speaks of the angels (1 Kings 22:19). The angels are even called "the morning stars" in Job 38:7. No doubt the emphasis is on their glory and innumerable expanse. Scientists say there are multiplied billions of stars in the universe. Could there be such a large number of angels?

Yes. In Revelation 5:11, the apostle John writes, "And I beheld, and I heard the voice of many angels round about the throne and the beasts and the elders: and the number of them was ten thousand times ten thousand, and thousands of thousands." If we take the numbers literally, it figures to more than a billion. But this is probably an expression the apostle uses to convey the idea of a number so large that it cannot be counted.

That is precisely what Hebrews 12:22 indicates: "Ye are come unto Mount Zion, and unto the city of the living God, the heavenly Jerusalem, and to *an innumerable company of angels.*" Like the stars of heaven and the grains of sand on a beach, the number is simply too high to count meaningfully. No doubt God Himself knows the precise number. But it is a number so high we would not be able to comprehend the immensity of it.

When Angels Fell

Satan and the demons are fallen angels. All that is known about Satan's fall is conveyed to us rather subtly by Scripture. Satan seems to be the real target of a couple of messages addressed to earthly rulers. These rulers are themselves so evil that we may assume they were indwelt by Satan. Thus the messages addressed to the evil kings seem actually to be meant for Satan. For example, the words of Isaiah 14:12-15, though addressed to the king of Babylon, actually refer to Satan, addressing him as "Lucifer," (literally, "Star of the Morning"):

> *How art thou fallen from heaven, O Lucifer, son of the morning! how art thou cut down to the ground, which didst weaken the nations! For thou hast said in thine heart, I will ascend into heaven, I will exalt my throne above the stars of God: I will sit also upon the mount of the congregation, in the sides of the north: I will ascend above the heights of the clouds; I will be like the most High. Yet thou shalt be brought down to hell, to the sides of the pit.*

Evidently Satan aspired to usurp God's very throne, and as a result was cast out of heaven.

Ezekiel 28 includes a message to the king of Tyre that clearly goes beyond the king himself and applies to Satan, who must have indwelt him. We know this, because it alludes to his deception of Eve in the Garden:

> *Thus saith the Lord God; Thou sealest up the sum, full of wisdom, and perfect in beauty. Thou hast been in Eden the garden of God; every precious stone was thy covering, the sardius, topaz, and the diamond, the beryl, the onyx, and the jasper, the sapphire, the emerald,*

and the carbuncle, and gold: the workmanship of thy tabrets and of thy pipes was prepared in thee in the day that thou wast created. Thou art the anointed cherub that covereth; and I have set thee so: thou wast upon the holy mountain of God; thou hast walked up and down in the midst of the stones of fire. Thou wast perfect in thy ways from the day that thou wast created, till iniquity was found in thee. By the multitude of thy merchandise they have filled the midst of thee with violence, and thou hast sinned: therefore I will cast thee as pro-fane out of the mountain of God: and I will destroy thee, O cover-ing cherub, from the midst of the stones of fire.

—vv. 12-16

When Lucifer fell, he took a third of the angels with him (Rev. 12:3-4). These fallen angels are nothing but demonic beings, some of whom are still troubling the earth to this very day—and will continue to do so until they are destroyed by the hand of God's judgment (Rev. 20:10).

What Angels Are Like

Angels are persons. That is, they are beings with all the attributes of personality: intellect, feelings, and volition. They have personalities.

In the Ezekiel 28 passage that describes the fall of "the anointed cherub that covereth," God says to him: "Thou sealest up the sum, full of wisdom, and perfect in beauty" (v. 12). Evidently the archangel who fell and became Satan was the most intelligent of all God's creatures.

Angels are almost always portrayed in Scripture as highly intelligent beings. In Matthew 28:5, when the two Marys found Jesus' tomb empty on the morning of the resurrection, "The angel answered and said unto the women, Fear not ye: for *I know* that ye seek Jesus, which was crucified" (emphasis added). The angels communicate. They have conversations. They know things. They obviously are creatures of intellect.

Angels are not omniscient, however. First Peter 1:12 says the gospel contains truths that "the angels desire to look into." So there are some things they do not understand. Yet even their desire to know more proves that they are intelligent beings.

Angels also express emotion. Remember that they sang together at creation (Job 38:7). Luke 15:10 says "There is joy in the presence of the angels of God over one sinner that repenteth." I believe that verse speaks of *God's* joy over the salvation of His elect. But there is a sense in which that joy is also shared by angels. The parable Jesus tells in this context describes a woman who has lost a coin. She sweeps the house, takes a candle, and looks everywhere until she finds it. Then "she calleth her friends and her neighbours together, saying, Rejoice with me; for I have found the piece which I had lost" (v. 9). Then verse 10 says, "*Likewise*" there is joy over the salvation of a sinner. This clearly implies that God rejoices in the angels' presence so that they may share His joy! There is every reason to believe they are able to express themselves with emotions.

Meaningful worship is impossible apart from emotion I believe. Of course, sheer blind emotion does not equate to real worship, but "worship . . . in spirit and in truth"—the kind of worship God seeks (John 4:23)—is not possible apart from authentic feelings. The purest worship involves rejoicing in the truth (cf. 1 Cor. 13:6). And the fact that angels are often seen worshiping around the throne of God indicates that they do have emotions. Look at Isaiah's description of angelic worship around the throne of God:

> *I saw also the Lord sitting upon a throne, high and lifted up, and his train filled the temple. Above it stood the seraphims: each one had six wings; with twain he covered his face, and with twain he covered his feet, and with twain he did fly. And one cried unto another, and said, Holy, holy, holy, is the Lord of hosts: the whole earth is full of his glory.*
>
> *—Isa. 6:1-3*

Isaiah's description of these majestic creatures makes clear that they are not mere machines, or animals, but both highly intelligent and capable of the profoundest emotions associated with the highest kind of worship.

It is also evident that they have a will. Lucifer's sin was a willful pride. He said in his heart, "*I will* ascend into heaven, *I will* exalt my throne above the stars of God: *I will* sit also upon the mount of the congregation, in the sides of the north: *I will* ascend above the heights of the clouds; *I will* be like the most High" (Isa. 14:13-14, emphasis added).

God Himself appeals to the wills of the angels. Hebrews 1:6 records God the Father's command to the angels at the birth of His son: "And let all the angels of God worship him." Obedience to any command involves an act of the will.

Not only do angels have all the attributes of personality, but they are also lofty creatures, slightly higher in majesty and authority than humans. When Christ became a man, Scripture says He was made "a little lower than the angels" (Heb. 2:7). So angels occupy a higher state than we do—at least for the time being. Someday redeemed humanity will judge the angels—and this may imply that we will also rule over them in heaven. Paul wrote, "Know ye not that we shall judge angels? How much more things that pertain to this life?" (1 Cor. 6:3). Jesus promised the churches of Asia Minor, "To him that overcometh will I grant to sit with me in my throne, even as I also overcame, and am set down with my Father in his throne" (Rev. 3:21). Sharing the throne of Christ may imply that we will have rule over the angels. If so, this is a stunning concept.

WHAT DO ANGELS DO?

The life and the world of angels is as involved and as active and as complex as ours is. They dwell in another dimension, but our worlds intersect often, and at least some of their business is related to the affairs of this world. Hebrews 1:14 calls them "ministering spirits, sent forth to minister for them who shall be heirs of salvation."

Martin Luther believed that an angel is a spiritual creature without a body created by God for the service of Christendom and the church. Whether that is really the *main* function of angels or not, we simply are not told, but it certainly is *one* of their duties. (The fact that they are organized in a highly structured chain of command may suggest that angelic duties are varied according to rank.)

As ministering spirits who minister to the elect, angels are no doubt active in human affairs, though usually unseen. Undoubtedly they do many things on our behalf, but nowhere does Scripture encourage us to look further into how this occurs. We are never encouraged to try to discern the unseen work of angels in our lives. We're merely reminded to exhibit a Christlike hospitality, because we never know when or in what form an angel may be our guest. Colossians 2:18 warns believers not to become angel-worshipers, and not to develop our doctrine from visions.

Hebrews 1:14 specifically calls the angels "spirits," which implies that they do not have material bodies. Nonetheless, they may appear in visible form when God chooses to let them be manifest. And whenever Scripture describes any such angelic appearance, the angel always appears as a man. Masculine pronouns are invariably used to refer to them. For example, in Genesis 18–19, when angels came to visit Abraham and paid a visit to Sodom, they were fully human in appearance. They sat down with Abraham. They ate with him. They walked with him. They conversed in human language. Every detail of their visible form was in appearance human.

At other times angels appear as men, but with extraordinary, even supernatural, qualities. In Matthew 28:3, for example, the angel who appeared at Jesus' empty tomb was no normal-looking man: "His countenance was like lightning, and his raiment white as snow."

Biblical appearances of angels—unlike those of popular lore—often cause trauma and great fear. When an angel appeared to Mary, from the moment that he greeted her, "she was troubled at his saying, and cast in her mind what manner of salutation this should be" (Luke 1:29). When another angel appeared to the shepherds who attended His birth, "they were sore afraid" (Luke 2:9). When the Roman soldiers guarding Jesus' tomb spotted the angel there, "for fear of him [they] did shake, and became as dead men" (Matt. 28:4).

Whenever angels do appear to people in Scripture, it is in the role of a messenger. In fact, "messenger" is the primary meaning of the Greek word *angelos*. So the angels provide a sort of heavenly messenger service, and we get glimpses of this throughout Scripture. The angel who appeared to Mary at the Annunciation identified himself: "I am Gabriel, that stand in the presence of God; and am sent to speak unto thee" (Luke 1:19). On this particular occasion, perhaps because of the sacred importance of the message, the highest-ranking archangel from the very presence of God was sent to Mary to deliver the word.

Finally, as we have seen, angels are constantly ministering around the throne of God in worship. Worship is plainly one of their chief functions (cf. Isa. 6:3; Rev. 4:6-9; 5:9-12).

HOW WILL WE RELATE TO THE ANGELS IN HEAVEN?

Scripture indicates that in heaven we will join the angels in worshiping God around His throne. Revelation 4:4 describes the very first scene John witnessed in his vision of heaven: "Round about the throne were four and twenty seats: and upon the seats I saw four and twenty elders sitting, clothed in white raiment; and they had on their heads crowns of gold." Those elders represent the church. The fact that permanent seats are there for them indicates that the redeemed people of God will perpetually be worshiping there alongside the angels.

John goes on to describe the incredible creatures who worship nonstop around God's throne, and adds this in verse 8: "They rest not day and night, saying, Holy, holy, holy, Lord God Almighty, which was, and is, and is to come." Never tiring of their ministry, they offer the purest, most perfect worship around the clock, exactly as Isaiah described it in his vision (cf. Isa. 6:3).

> *And when those beasts give glory and honour and thanks to him that sat on the throne, who liveth for ever and ever, the four and twenty elders fall down before him that sat on the throne, and worship him that liveth for ever and ever, and cast their crowns before the throne, saying, Thou art worthy, O Lord, to receive glory and honour and power: for thou hast created all things, and for thy pleasure they are and were created.*
>
> *—Rev. 4:9-11*

Revelation 5:8-12 portrays a similar scene, with multiplied thousands of voices singing of the worthiness of God and the Lamb.

That is the song of heaven. I cannot wait to hear it. I cannot wait to sing it with a glorified voice, and be part of the great chorus of the redeemed, with the entire host of heaven joining in.

Instantly, when we hear that sound, all earth's troubles will recede into utter insignificance. All our labors will be over, all our tears will be dried, and there will be nothing left but the sheer bliss of heaven and our perfect enjoyment of God—forever.

A FINAL WORD TO THE READER

We have reached the end of our brief study of heaven and its inhabitants. Whatever sense of the glory of heaven I have been able to convey through mere words on a page is paltry indeed compared to what heaven's glory will be like when we see it in all its spectacular fullness. Nonetheless, I hope your heart is stirred, as my own is, by the matchless grace of a God who would manifest His goodness to unworthy creatures like you and me—people who have sinned against Him repeatedly—and bring us into His own dwelling-place forever. To think that He would permit us to share in the glory of heaven is a wonder too great for the human mind to fathom. Such grace and mercy are impossible for us even to begin to appreciate. Only in the eternity of heaven will we be able to verbalize adequately the worship and thanksgiving that is due Him for this. And even there, we will sing of it for all eternity—and never begin to exhaust the wonder and glory of it.

If this study has in any way aroused a desire within you to participate in the glory and blessedness of heaven, then my design for writing it has been met.

My prayer for you, dear reader, is that you will look beyond the fading realities of this world and see just a glimpse of the glory of heaven. And having caught that tiny ray of heaven's glory, may you be like the man who found a treasure in a field, and sold all his earthly possessions in order to buy it (Matt. 13:44). If you have never trusted Christ for salvation, may you flee to Him right now for forgiveness and cleansing, and receive the pure white robe of His righteousness.

All that is glorious, all that is noble, and all that is blessed awaits us in heaven. I hope you are headed there, and that your heart yearns for reunion with Christ.

And heaven may be closer than you think. As the apostle Paul wrote,

> *Knowing the time, that now it is high time to awake out of sleep: for now is our salvation nearer than when we believed. The night is far spent, the day is at hand: let us therefore cast off the works of dark-*

ness, and let us put on the armour of light. Let us walk honestly, as in the day; not in rioting and drunkenness, not in chambering and wantonness, not in strife and envying. But put ye on the Lord Jesus Christ, and make not provision for the flesh, to fulfil the lusts thereof.
—*Rom. 13:11-14*

APPENDICES

THE JEWELS IN OUR HEAVENLY CROWN

BY RICHARD BAXTER [1]

Let us draw near and see from the pure fountain of the Scriptures what excellencies the saints' everlasting rest affords. May the Lord hide us in the clefts of the rock, and cover us with the hands of indulgent grace, while we approach to take this view. And may we put off from our feet the shoes of irreverence and fleshly thoughts while we stand upon this holy ground.

These truths are like jewels in the Christian's heavenly crown:

HEAVEN IS PURCHASED FOR US WITH CHRIST'S OWN BLOOD

It is a most singular honor and ornament in the style of the saints' heavenly rest to be called *the purchased possession;* meaning it is the fruit of the blood of the Son of God. Yea, it is the chief fruit—the end and perfection of all the effects and efficacy of that blood.

Surely love is the most precious ingredient in the whole composition; and of all the flowers that grow in the garden of love, can there be brought one more sweet and beautiful to the garland than this blood? Greater love than this there is not—to lay down the life of the lover. And to have this our Redeemer ever before our eyes, and the liveliest sense and freshest remembrance of that dying, bleeding love upon our souls! Oh, how will it fill our souls with perpetual ravishments to think that we have passed through all, and here arrived safely at the breast of God! We shall behold, as it were, the wounds of love with eyes and hearts of love forever.

With what astonishing apprehensions, then, will the redeemed saints everlastingly behold their Blessed Redeemer! I will not meddle with their vain, audacious question, who must need know whether the glorified body of Christ does yet retain either the wounds or scars. But this is most certain: the memory of it will be as fresh, and the impressions of love as deep, and its working as strong as if His wounds were still in our eyes.

Now His heart is open to us, and ours shut to Him: but when His heart shall be open, and our hearts open. Oh, the blessed congress that there will then be. But I am here at a loss; my apprehensions fail me, and fall so short. Only this, I know; it will be the singular praise of our inheritance, that it was bought with the price of that blood; and the singular joy of the saints, to behold the purchaser and the price, together with the possession!

Neither will the views of the wounds of love renew our wounds of sorrow. How dear forever will the love of Christ be then to us, who stripped Himself, as it were, of His majesty and glory, and put our humble garment of flesh upon Him, that He might put the robes of His own righteousness and glory upon us; and saved us, not from cruel injustice, but from His Father's deserved wrath! Well then, Christians, as you used to do in your books, and on your goods, write down the price they cost you; so do you on your righteousness and on your glory, write down the price: *The precious blood of Christ.*

HEAVEN IS FREE

The second pearl in the saint's diadem is that *it is free.* This seems to devour the former point. But the seeming discord is but a pleasing diversity, composed into that harmony which constitutes the melody. These two attributes, purchased and free, are the two chains of gold, which by their pleasant twisting do make up the wreath for the heads of the pillars in the temple of God. It was dear to Christ, but free to us. Is not every stone that builds this temple a free stone?

Oh, the everlasting admiration that will surprise the saints to think of this freeness. What did the Lord see in me that He should judge me meet for such a state? That I who was but a poor, diseased, despised wretch should be clad in the brightness of His glory? Oh, who can fathom unmeasurable love? There is no talk of our worthiness nor unworthiness; if worthiness were our condition for admittance, we might sit down with St. John and weep, "because none in heaven or earth is found worthy." But the Lion of the tribe of Judah is worthy and has prevailed; and by that title must we hold this inheritance. Here our commission runs: "Freely ye have received, freely give": But Christ has dearly received, yet freely gives. The pope and his servants will be paid for their pardons and indulgences, but Christ will take nothing for His. The commutation of penance must cost men's purses dear, or else they must be cast out of the synagogue, and soul and body delivered up to the devil: but none are shut out of that church for want of money, nor is poverty any eyesore to Christ. An empty heart may bar them out, but an empty purse cannot. His kingdom of grace has always been more consistent with despised poverty than wealth and honor, and riches make entrance to heaven far more difficult than poverty can ever do. That's why it is "the poor of the world, rich in faith, whom God hath chosen to be the heirs of that kingdom, which He hath prepared for them that love Him."

I know the true laborer is "worthy of his hire" and "they that serve at the altar, should live upon the altar." Yet let me desire the right-aiming ministers of Christ to consider what is expedient as well as what is lawful, and that the saving of one soul is better than a thousand pounds a year, and our gain, though due, is a cursed gain, if it causes a stumbling-block to our people's souls. Let us make the free gospel as little burdensome and chargeable as is possible. I would rather never take their tithes while I live, than by those tithes destroy souls for whom Christ died. And though God has ordained that "they which preach the Gospel should live of the Gospel," yet I would rather suffer all things than hinder the gospel. It would be better for me to die than that any man should make this my glorying void. If the necessity of souls and the promoting of the gospel require it, I would rather preach the Gospel in hunger and rags than rigidly contend for what is my due. And if I should do so, still I have no reason to glory. Necessity is laid upon me; yea, *woe* be to me if I preach not the gospel—whether or not I ever receive anything from men.

How unbecoming it is for the messengers of His free grace and kingdom, to risk losing the hearts and souls of their people, rather than to losing a dime of their due. How shameful it is to exasperate people against the message of God, rather than forbear some of their right. What a tragedy to contend with people at law for the wages of the gospel, thus making the glad tidings seem sad tidings to their yet carnal hearts because of this burden! This is not the way of Christ and His apostles, nor adoring to the self-denying, yielding, suffering doctrine which they taught. Away with all those actions that are against the main end of our studies and calling, which is to win souls. And woe be upon that gain which hinders the gaining of men to Christ!

I know flesh will here object necessities, and distrust will have plenty of arguments; but we who have enough to answer to the diffidence of our people, let us take home some of our answers to ourselves, and teach ourselves first before we teach them. How many people have you known whom God allowed to starve in His vineyard?

Since we paid nothing for God's eternal love and nothing for the

Son of His love, and nothing for His Spirit and our grace and faith, and nothing for our pardon—so shall we pay nothing for our eternal rest. The broken heart that has known the dregs of sin will understand and feel what I say. What an astonishing thought it will be to think of the unmeasurable difference between our deservings and our receivings; between the state we should have been in and the state we are in! Oh, how free was all this love, and how free is this enjoyed glory! Infinite wisdom did cast the whole design of man's salvation into the mold of purchase and freeness, that the love and joy of man might be perfected, and the honor of grace most highly advanced; that the thought of merit might neither cloud the one nor obstruct the other, and that on these two hinges the gates of heaven might turn. So then let "Deserved" be written on the floor of hell but on the door of heaven and life, "The Free Gift."

HEAVEN IS THE SAINTS'
OWN POSSESSION

The third comfortable attribute of our heavenly rest is that *it is the saints' proper and peculiar possession.* It belongs to no other of all the sons of men; not that it would have detracted from the greatness or freeness of the gift if God had so pleased that all the world should have enjoyed it. But when God has resolved otherwise, that it must be enjoyed but by few, to find our names among that number should make us the more to value our enjoyment. Distinguishing, separating mercy affects more than any mercy. If it should rain on our grounds alone or the sun shine alone upon our habitations, or the blessing of heaven divide between our flocks and other men's, as between Jacob's and Laban's, then we should more feelingly acknowledge mercy than now, while we possess the same in common. The lower the weighty end of the balance descends, the higher is the other lifted up; and the falling of one of the sails of the windmill is the occasion of the rising of the other.

It would be no extenuation of the mercies of the saints here if all the world were as holy as they; and the communication of their happiness is their greatest desire; yet it might perhaps dull their thankfulness, and distinguishing grace would not be known. But when one should be enlightened and another left in darkness; one reformed and another by his lusts enslaved, it makes them cry out, with the disciple: "Lord, what is it, that thou wilt reveal thyself to us, and not unto the world?" (cf. Jn. 14:22).

By this time the impenitent world will see a reason for the saints' singularity while they were on earth, and will be able to answer their own demands, Why must you be more holy than your neighbors? Even because they would fain be more happy than their neighbors. And why cannot you do as others, and live as the world about you? Sincere singularity in holiness is by this time known to be neither hypocrisy nor folly. If to be singular in that glory be so desirable, surely to be singular in godly living is not contemptible. As every one of them knows his own sore, and his own grief, so shall everyone then feel his own joy; and if they can now call Christ their own, and call God their own God, how much more then upon their full possession of Him! For as He takes His people for His inheritance, so will He Himself be the inheritance of His people forever.

HEAVEN OFFERS
PERFECT FELLOWSHIP

A fourth comfortable adjunct of our heavenly rest is that it is *the fellowship of the blessed saints and angels of God.* The Christian will not be so singular as to be solitary. Though heaven is proper to the saints only, yet is it common to all the saints, for what is it but an association of blessed spirits in God; a corporation of perfected saints, whereof Christ is the head; the communion of saints completed? This does not mean we derive heaven's joys from one another.

Though the strings receive not their sound and sweetness from each other, yet their concurrence causes that harmony which could not be by one alone; for those that have prayed, and fasted, and wept, and watched and waited together, now to joy and enjoy and praise together, should much advance their pleasure. I am certain of this, fellow-Christians, that as we have been together in the labor, duty, danger and distress, so shall we be in the great recompense and deliverance. And as we have been scorned and despised together, so shall we be crowned and honored together; and we who have gone through the day of sadness shall enjoy together that day of gladness; and those who have been with us in persecution and prison shall be with us also in that palace of consolation.

When I look in the faces of the precious people of God, and believingly think of that day, what a refreshing thought it is! Shall we not there remember, think you, the trials which we passed through here; our fellowship in duty and in sufferings; how oft our groans made, as it were, one sound, our tears uniting in one stream, and our desires uniting in one prayer? And now all our praise shall make up one melody, and all our churches one church, and all ourselves but one body; for we shall be one in Christ, even as He and the Father are one.

It is true we must be very careful in this case, that, in our thoughts we look not for that in the saints which is alone in Christ, and that we give them not His own prerogative, nor expect too great a part of our comfort in the fruition of them: we are prone enough to this kind of idolatry. But, yet, He who commands us so to love them now, will give us leave, in the same subordination to Himself, to love them then, when Himself has made them much more lovely. And if we may love them, we shall surely rejoice in them; for love and enjoyment cannot stand without an answerable joy.

I know that Christ is all in all; and that it is the presence of God that makes heaven to be heaven. But yet it much sweetens the thoughts of that place to me to remember that there are such a multitude of my most dear and precious friends in Christ; with whom I took sweet counsel, and with whom I went up to the house of God; who walked with me in the fear of God, and integrity of their hearts. In the face of their lives was written the name of Christ; whose sweet and sensible mention of His excellencies has made my heart to burn within me.

It is a question with some, whether we shall know each other in heaven or not. Surely, there shall no knowledge cease which now we have, but only that which implies our imperfection. And what imperfection can our knowledge of one another imply? Nay, our present knowledge of one other shall be increased beyond belief. It shall indeed be done away, but as the light of candles and stars is done away by the rising of the sun. It is more proper to think of it as a doing away of our ignorance than of our knowledge. Indeed, we shall not know each other after the flesh, not by stature, voice, color, complexion, face, or outward shape. If we had so known Christ, we should know Him no more. We shall know each other not by parts and gifts of learning; nor by titles of honor of worldly dignity; nor by terms of affinity and consanguinity, nor benefits, nor such relations; nor by youth or age—but by the image of Christ, and spiritual relation, and former faithfulness in improving our talents, beyond doubt, we shall know and be known. Nor is it only our old acquaintance, but all the saints of all the ages, whose faces in the flesh we never saw, whom we shall there both know and comfortably enjoy.

Those who now are willingly ministering spirits for our good will willingly then be our companions in joy for the perfecting of our good; and they who had such joy in heaven for our conversion will gladly rejoice with us in our glorification. I think, Christian, this will be a more honorable assembly than ever you beheld, and a more happy society than you were ever of before.

We are come thither already in respect of title, and of earnest and first-fruits; but we shall then come into full possession. Oh,

beloved, if it be a happiness to live with the saints in their imperfection, when they have sin to embitter their society, as well as holiness to sweeten it, what will it be to live with them in their
perfection, where saints are wholly and only saints? If we thought
ourselves in the suburbs of heaven when we heard them set forth
the beauty of our Lord, and speak of the excellencies of His kingdom, what a day will it be when we shall join with them in praises
to our Lord in and for that kingdom! So then I conclude, this is one
singular excellency of the rest of heaven, that we are "fellow-citi-
zens with the saints, and of the household of God."

HEAVEN'S JOYS COME DIRECTLY
FROM THE HAND OF GOD

Another excellent property of our rest will be that *the joys of it are
immediately from God*. We shall see God face to face and stand continually in His presence, and consequently derive our life and
comfort immediately from Him. Whether God will make use of
any creatures for our service then, or, if any, what creatures, and
what use, is more than I yet know. It seems that the creature shall
have a day of deliverance, and that into the glorious liberty of the
sons of God. Our most and great joys will be immediate—directly
from God's own hand. Now we have nothing at all immediately.
From the earth, from man, from sun and moon, from the influence
of the planets, from the ministration of angels, and from the Spirit
and Christ; and, doubtless, the further the stream runs from the
fountain, the more impure it is. It gathers some defilement from
every unclean channel it passes through.

Christ is indeed a precious pearl, but often is held forth in lep-
rous hands. And thus do we disgrace the riches of the Gospel when
it is the work of our calling to make it honorable in the eyes of men.
We dim the glory of that jewel by our dull and low expressions,
whose lustre we do pretend to discover, while the hearers judge of

it by our expressions, and not its proper genuine worth. The truth is the best of men do apprehend but little of what God, in His word, expresses—and what they *do* apprehend they are unable to utter. If an angel from heaven should preach the gospel, yet could he not deliver it according to its glory; much less we, who never saw what they have seen, and keep this treasure in earthen vessels.

The comforts that flow through sermons, through sacraments, through reading, and company, and conference, and creatures are but half comforts. The life that comes by these is but half a life, in comparison of those which the Almighty shall speak with His own mouth and reach forth to us with His own hand. The Christian knows by experience now, that his most immediate joys are his sweetest joys: which have least of man, and are most directly from the Spirit. That is one reason, as I conceive, why Christians who are much in secret prayer, and in meditation and contemplation, rather than they who are more in hearing, reading and conference, are men of greatest life and joy, because they are nearer the source of the fountain, and have all more immediately from God Himself.

We are not yet come to the time and state where we shall have all from God's immediate hand. As God has made all creatures, and instituted all ordinances for us, so will He continue our need of all. We must be content with love-tokens from Him, till we come to receive our all in Him.

There is joy in these remote receivings, but the fullness is in His own presence. Oh, Christians! you will then know the difference between the creature and the Creator, and the content that each of them affords. We shall then have light without a candle, and a perpetual day without the sun. We shall then have rest without sleep, for God will be our rest. We shall then have enlightened understandings without a written law: for the Lord will perfect His law in our hearts, and we shall be all perfectly taught of God. His own will shall be our law, and His own face shall be our light forever. Then shall we have joy, which we drew not from the promises, nor was fetched us home by faith and hope. Beholding and possessing will exclude most of these. We shall then have communion without sacraments, when Christ shall drink with us of the fruit of the vine new; that is, refresh us with the comforting wine of immediate fruition, in the kingdom of His Father.

When we shall live in our Father's house and presence and God shall be all and in all, then we are indeed at home in rest.

HEAVEN WILL BE A SEASONABLE REST

A further excellency is this: it will be unto us *a seasonable rest*. He who expects the fruit of His vineyard in season, and makes His people as trees planted by the waters, fruitful in their season, He will also give them the crown in season. He that will have the words of joy spoken to the weary in season will sure cause that time of joy to appear in His perfect time.

They who knew the season of grace, and did repent and believe in season, shall also, if they faint not, reap in season. If God will not miss the season of common mercies, even to His enemies, but will give both the former and the latter rain in their season, and the appointed weeks of harvest in its season, and by inviolable covenant has established day and night in their seasons, then sure, the harvest of the saints and their day of gladness shall not miss its season.

He who has given the stork, the crane, and the swallow to know their appointed time will surely keep His time appointed. When we have had in this world a long night of sad darkness, will not the day breaking and the rising of the Sun of Righteousness be then seasonable? When we have endured a hard winter in this cold climate will not the reviving spring be then seasonable? When we have sailed (as Paul) slowly many days, and much time spent, and sailing now grown more dangerous; and when neither sun nor stars in many days appear, and no small tempest comes on us and all hope that we shall be saved is almost taken away—do you think that the haven of rest is not seasonable then?

When we have passed a long and tedious journey, and that through no small dangers, is not home then seasonable? When we have had a long and perilous war, and have lived in the midst of furious enemies, and have been forced to stand on a perpetual watch, and received from them many a wound, would not a peace with victory be now seasonable? When we have been captivated in many years' imprisonment, and insulted over by scornful foes, and suffered many pinching wants, and hardly enjoyed bare necessaries, would not a full deliverance to a most plentiful state, even from this prison to a throne, be now seasonable?

Surely, a man would think, who looks upon the face of the world, that rest should seem seasonable to all men. Some of us are languishing under continual weakness and groaning under most grievous pains, crying in the morning. "Would God it were evening!" and in the evening, "Would God it were morning!"—weary of going, weary of sitting, weary of standing, weary of lying, weary of eating, weary of speaking, weary of walking, weary of our very friends, weary of ourselves. Oh! how often has this been mine own case!

And is not rest yet seasonable? Some are complaining under the pressure of the times; weary of their taxes, weary of their dwellings, weary of crime, weary of their fears and dangers, weary of their poverty and wants. And is not rest yet seasonable?

Where can you go, and into what company can you come, where the voice of complaining does not show that men live in a continual weariness—but especially the saints, who are most weary of that which the world cannot feel? What godly society can you fall into, but you shall hear by their moans that something ails them? Some are weary because of a blind mind, doubting the way they walk, unsettled in almost all their thoughts. Some are weary because of a hard heart, some because of pride, some because of passion—and some from all these, and much more. Some are weary because of their daily doubtings and fear concerning their spiritual estate; some because of a shortage of spiritual joys; and some because of the sense of God's wrath. And is not rest now seasonable?

When a poor Christian has desired and prayed and waited for deliverance many a year, is it not then seasonable? When he is ready almost to give up, and saith, "I am afraid I shall not reach the end, and my faith and patience will not hold out"; is not this a fit season for rest?

If the voice of the king were seasonable to Daniel, early in the morning calling him from his den, that he might advance him to more than former dignity, then surely that morning voice of Christ our King, calling us from our terrors among lions, to possess his rest among His saints, should be to us a very seasonable voice.

Now we are often grudging that we have not a greater share of comforts; that our deliverances are not more speedy and eminent; that the world prospers more than we; that our prayers are not presently answered. But our portion is kept to a fitter season. When the winter comes we shall have our harvest. We grudge that we do not find a Canaan in the wilderness, or cities of rest in Noah's Ark, and the songs of Zion in a strange land; that we have not a harbor in the main ocean, or find not our home in the middle way, and are not crowned in the midst of the fight, and have not our rest in the heat of the day, and have not our inheritance before we are at age, and have not heaven before we leave the earth: and would not all this be very unreasonable?

I confess, in regard of the church's service, the removing of the saints may sometimes appear to us unseasonable. I must confess it is one of my saddest thoughts, to reckon up the useful instruments, whom God has lately called out of His vineyard, when the loiterers are many, and the harvest great and very many congregations desolate, and the people as sheep without shepherds, and yet the laborers called from their work, especially when a door of liberty and opportunity is open; we cannot but lament so sore a judgment, and think the removal, in regard of the church, unseasonable.

But whatever it is to those that are left behind; yet the saints' departure, to themselves, is usually seasonable.

HEAVEN WILL BE A SUITABLE REST

A further excellency of this rest is this: as it will be seasonable, so *a suitable rest,* suited to the natures, to the desires, and to the necessity of the saints.

To their *natures.* If suitableness concur not with excellency, the best things may be bad to us; for it is that which makes things good in themselves to be good to us. In our choice of friends we often pass by the more excellent, to choose the more suitable. Every good agrees not with every nature. To live in a free and open air, under the warming rays of the sun, is excellent to man because suitable; but the fish, which is of another nature does rather choose another element; and that which is to us so excellent would quickly be to it destructive.

In heaven, suitableness and excellency will finally be conjoined. The new nature of saints suits their spirits to this rest; and indeed their holiness is nothing else but a spark taken from this element, and by the Spirit of Christ kindled in their hearts, the flame whereof, as mindful of its own divine original, ever mounts the soul aloft, and tends to the place from whence it comes. It works toward its own center, and makes us restless, till there we rest. Gold and earthly glory, temporal crowns and kingdoms, could not make a rest for saints. As they were not redeemed with so low a price, so neither are they endued with so low a nature.

As God will have from them a spiritual worship, suitable to His own spiritual being, so will He provide them a spiritual rest, suitable to His people's spiritual nature. As spirits have not fleshly substances, so neither delight they in fleshly pleasures; these are too gross and vile for them.

A heaven of the knowledge of God and His Christ; a delightful contentment in that mutual love; an everlasting rejoicing in the fruition of our God; a perpetual singing of His high praises; this is heaven for a saint, a spiritual rest suitable to a spiritual nature. Were not our own nature in some sort divine, the enjoyment of the true divine nature could not be to us a suitable rest.

It is suitable also to the *desires* of the saints. As their natures, so will be their desires; and as their desires, so will be their rest. Indeed, we have now a mixed nature; and from contrary principles, do arise contrary desires; as they are flesh, they have desires of flesh; and as so they have sinful desires. These are not the desires that this rest is suited to, for they will accompany them to their rest. But it is the desires of our renewed natures, and those which the Christian will ordinarily own, which this rest is suited to. While our desires remain uncorrupted and misguided, it is a far greater mercy to deny them, yea, to destroy them, than to satisfy them; but those which are spiritual are of His own planting, and He will surely water them and give the increase. Is it so great a work to raise them in us, and shall they after all this vanish and fail?

He quickened our hungering and thirsting for righteousness, so that He might make us happy in a full satisfaction. Christian, this is a rest after your own heart; it contains all that your heart can wish; that which you long for, pray for, labor for, there you shall find it all. You would rather have God in Christ than all the world. There you shall have Him! What would you not give for assurance of His love? There you shall have assurance beyond suspicion. Nay, your desires cannot now extend to the height of what you shall there obtain.

This is a life of desire and prayer; but *that* is a life of satisfaction and enjoyment. Oh! that sinners would also consider that seeing God will not give them a felicity suitable to their sensual desires; it is therefore their wisdom to endeavor for desires suitable to the true felicity, and to direct their ship to the right harbor, seeing they cannot bring the harbor to their ship.

The rest is very suitable to the saints' necessities also as well as to their natures and desires. It contains whatsoever they truly wanted. It was Christ and perfected holiness which they most needed, and with these shall they here be principally supplied. The rain which Elijah's prayer procured was not more seasonable, after the three years' drought, than this rest will be to this thirsty soul.

HEAVEN WILL BE PERFECT
IN EVERY WAY

Another excellency of our rest will be this, that *it will be absolutely perfect and complete;* and this both in the sincerity and universality of it. We shall then have joy without sorrow, and rest without weariness. As there is no mixture of corruption with our graces, so no mixture of sufferings with our solace. There are none of those waves in that harbor, which now so toss us up and down. There will be a universal perfecting of all our parts and powers, and a universal removal of all our evils. And though the positive part be the sweetest, and that which draws the other after it, even as the rising of the sun excludes the darkness; yet is not the negative part to be slighted, even our freedom, from so many and great calamities.

Heaven excludes nothing more directly than sin; whether original and of nature, or actual and of behavior. For there enters nothing that defiles, nor that works abomination, nor that makes a lie. When they are there, the saints are saints indeed. He that will wash them with His heart-blood, rather than suffer them to enter unclean, will now perfectly see to that; He who has undertaken to present them to His Father, "not having spot or wrinkle or any such thing, but perfectly holy, and without blemish," will now most certainly perform His undertaking.

I know if it were offered to your choice, you wouldst rather choose to be freed from sin than to be made heir of all the world. Wait till then, and you shall have that desire: your hard heart, those vile thoughts that lay down and rose up with you, which accompanied you to every duty, which you could no more leave behind you than you could leave yourself behind, shall now be left behind forever. They might accompany you to death, but they cannot proceed a step farther.

Your understanding shall nevermore be troubled with darkness. Ignorance and error are inconsistent with this light. Now you walk like a man in the twilight, always afraid of being out of the way; but then will all this darkness be dispelled, and our blind understandings fully opened, and we shall have no more doubts of our way. We shall know which was the right side, and which the wrong; which was the truth, and which the error. What would we not give to see all dark Scriptures made plain, to see all seeming contradictions reconciled! When glory has taken the veil from our eyes, all this *will* be known in a moment; we shall then see clearly into all the controversies about doctrine or discipline that now perplex us. The poorest Christian is presently there a more perfect divine than any is here.

When our ignorance is perfectly healed, then we shall be settled, resolved men; then shall our reproach be taken from us, and we shall never change our judgments more. Oh! that happy, approaching day, when error shall vanish away forever; when our understanding shall be filled with God Himself, whose light will leave no darkness in us! His face shall be the Scripture, where we shall read the truth; and Himself, instead of teachers and counsels, to perfect our understandings, and acquaint us with Himself, who is the perfect truth. No more error, no more scandal to others, no more disquiet to our own spirits, no more mistaking zeal for falsehood; because our understandings have no more sin. Many a godly man has been a means to deceive and pervert his brethren, and when he sees his own error, cannot again tell how to undeceive them; but there we shall all conspire in one truth, as being one in Him who is that truth.

And as we shall rest from all the sin of our understandings, so of our wills, affection, and conversation. We shall no more retain this rebelling principle, which is still withdrawing us from God. Doubtless, we shall no more be oppressed with the power of our corruptions, nor vexed with their presence; no pride, passion, slothfulness, senselessness, shall enter with us; no strangeness to God, and the things of God; no coldness of affections, nor imperfection in our love; no uneven walking, nor grieving of the Spirit; no scandalous action, or unholy living. We shall rest from all these forever. Then shall our understandings receive light from the face of God, as the full moon from the open sun, where there is no earth to interpose between them; then shall our wills correspond to the divine will, as face answers to face in a glass; and the same, His will, shall be our law and rule, from which we shall never swerve again.

HEAVEN IS A REST FROM SUFFERING

Heaven is *a perfect rest from suffering*. When the cause is gone, the effect ceases. Our sufferings were but the consequences of our sinning, and here they both shall cease together.

We shall rest from all our perplexing doubts and fears; it shall no more be said that doubts are like the thistle, a bad weed, but growing in good ground; they shall now be weeded out, and trouble the gracious soul no more. No more need of so many sermons, books, and signs to resolve the poor doubting soul. The full fruition of love itself will resolve all doubts forever.

We shall rest from all that sense of God's displeasure, which was our greatest torment, whether manifested mediately or immediately. Sorrowful complaints will be turned into admiring thankfulness. All sense of God's displeasure will be swallowed up in that ocean of infinite love, when sense shall convince us that fury dwelleth not in God (cf. Isa. 27:4). Though for a little moment He hides His face, yet with everlasting compassion will He receive and embrace us.

We shall rest from all the temptations of Satan, whereby he continually disturbs our peace. What a grief is it to a Christian, though he yield not to the temptation, yet to be still solicited to deny his Lord. That such a thought should be cast into his heart; that he can set about nothing that is good, but Satan is still dissuading him from it, distracting him in it, or discouraging him after it! What a torment as well as a temptation is it to have such horrid motions made to his soul!

Here we are too prone to entertain cruel thoughts of God, undervaluing thoughts of Christ, unbelieving thoughts of Scripture, injurious thoughts of Providence. We are so easily tempted to turn to present things, to play with the baits of sin, to venture on the delights of the flesh, and to flat atheism itself! We know the treachery of our own hearts that they are as tinder and gunpowder, ready to take fire, as soon as one of these sparks shall fall upon them. How the poor Christian lives in continual disquietness, to feel these motions! But more that his heart should be the soil for this seed, and the too-fruitful mother of such an offspring. And, most of all, he is disquieted by the fear that they will at last prevail, and these cursed motions should procure his consent.

But here is our comfort; as we now stand not by our own strength, and shall not be charged with any of this; so when the day of our deliverance comes, we shall fully rest from these temptations. Satan is then bound up; the time of tempting is done. Now we do walk among his snares, and are in danger of being circumvented with his methods and wiles; but then we are quite above his snares, and out of the hearing of his enticing charms. He has power here to tempt us in the wilderness, but he enters not into the Holy City. There will be no more work for Satan then.

We shall rest also from all our temptations which we now undergo from the world and the flesh, as well as Satan; and that is a number inexpressible, and a weight, were it not that we are beholden to supporting grace, utterly intolerable. Every sense is a snare; every member a snare; every creature a snare; every mercy a snare; and every duty a snare to us. We can scarce open our eyes, but we are in danger. If we behold them above us, we are in danger of envy; if below us, we are in danger of contempt. If we see sumptuous buildings, pleasant habitations, honor and riches we are in danger to be drawn away with covetous desires; if the rags and beggary of others, we are in danger of self-applauding thoughts and unmercifulness. If we see beauty, it is a bait to lust; if deformity, loathing and disdain.

We can scarcely hear a word spoken but contains to us a matter of temptation. How soon do slanderous reports, vain jests, wanton speeches, by that passage creep into the heart! How strong and prevalent a temptation is our appetite, and how constant and strong a watch does it require! Have we comeliness and beauty? What fuel for pride. Are we deformed? What occasion of repining! Have we strength of reason, and gifts of learning? How hard it is not to be puffed up! To seek ourselves; to hunt after applause; to despise our brethren; to mislike the simplicity that is in Christ. Both in the matter and manner of Scripture, in doctrine, in discipline, in worship, and in the saints; to affect a pompous, specious, fleshly service of God, and to exalt reason above faith. Are we unlearned and of shallow heads and slender parts? How apt then to despise what we have not, and to undervalue that which we do not know; and to err with confidence, because of our ignorance. Conceitedness and pride become a zealous enemy to truth, and a leading troubler of the church's peace, under pretenses of truth and holiness. Are we men of eminence and in place of authority? How strong is our temptation to slight our brethren, to abuse our trust, to seek ourselves, to stand upon our honor and privileges; to forget ourselves, our poor brethren, and the public good. How hard it is to devote our power to His glory from whom we have received it! How prone we are to make our wills our law and to cut out all the enjoyments of others, both religious and civil, by the cursed rules and model of our own interest and policy! Are we inferiors and subject? How prone to judge at others' pre-eminence, and to take liberty to bring all their actions to the bar of our incompetent judgment; and to censure and slander them, and murmur at their proceedings! Are we rich and not too much exalted? Are we poor and not discontented, and make our worldly necessities a pretense for robbing God of all His service?

But forever blessed be omnipotent love which saves us out of all these, and makes our straits but the advantages of the glory of His saving grace. In heaven the danger and trouble is over; there is nothing but what will advance our joy.

As we rest from the temptations, so also from all the abuses and persecutions which we suffer at the hands of wicked men. We shall be scorned, derided, imprisoned, banished, butchered by them no more. The prayers of the souls under the altar will then be answered and God will avenge their blood on these that dwell on the earth. This is the time for crowning with thorns, buffeting, spitting on; that will be the time for crowning with glory.

Now we must be hated of all men for Christ's name's sake, and the gospel; then will Christ be admired in His saints that were thus hated. Now because we are not of the world, therefore doth the world hate us; then, because we are not of the world, therefore will the world admire us. Now, as they hated Christ, they will also hate us; then, as they will honor Christ, so will they also honor us. When their flood of persecution is dried up, and the church called out of the wilderness, and the New Jerusalem come down from heaven, and mercy and justice are fully glorified, then shall we feel their fury no more. We leave all this behind us, when once we enter the City of our Rest: the names of Lollard, Huguenots, Roundheads are not there used; the inquisition of Spain is there condemned; the statute of the Six Articles is there repealed.[2] There are no Bishops' or Chancellor's Courts; no visitations nor High Commission judgments; no censures to loss of members, perpetual imprisonment, or banishment.

Christ is not there clothed in a mock robe and blindfolded. Nor is truth clothed in the robes of error, and smitten for that which it most directly contradicts. Nor is a schismatic wounded, and a saint found bleeding; nor our friends smite us, mistaking us for their enemies. There is none of all this blind, mad work there.

Till then possess your souls in patience; bind all reproaches as a crown to our heads; esteem them greater riches than the world's treasures; account it a matter of joy when you fall into tribulation. You have seen in these days that our God can deliver us; but this is nothing to our final conquest. He will recompense tribulation to them that trouble you; and to you who are troubled rest with Christ.

We shall then also rest from our sad divisions, and unchristian quarrels with one another. There is no contention, because none of this pride, ignorance, or other corruption. Paul and Barnabas are now fully reconciled. There they are, not every man conceited of his own understanding and in love with the issue of his own brain, but all admiring the divine perfection, and in love with God and one another. Luther and Zwingli will be agreed. There shall be a full reconciliation between Calvinists and Lutherans; Remonstrants and Contra-remonstrants;[3] Conformists and Nonconformists. Antinomians and Legalists are terms there not known: Presbyterians and Independents are perfectly agreed. There is no discipline erected by state policy, nor any disordered popular rule; no government but that of Christ!

And is it not shame that our course is now so contrary? Is it not enough that all the world is against us, but we must also be against one another? Did I ever think to have heard Christians so to reproach and scorn Christians; and men professing the fear of God, to make so little conscience of censuring, vilifying, slandering and disgracing one another? Alas! Once discernment has been perverted and error has possessed the supreme faculty, where will men go and what will they do? Nay! What will they *not* do? Oh, what a potent instrument for Satan is a misguided conscience! Today they may be orthodox, unanimous, and joined in love, and perhaps within a few weeks will be divided, and at bitter enmity, through their doting about questions that tend not to edify.

Oh happy day of the rest of the saints in glory! when as there is one God, one Christ, one Spirit, so we shall have one judgment, one heart, one church, one employment forever! When there will be no more circumcision and uncircumcision, Jew and Gentile, Anabaptist, Paedobaptist, Brownist, Separatist, Independent, Presbyterian, Episcopal: but Christ is All in All. We shall not there scruple our communion, nor any of the ordinances of divine worship. There will not be one for singing and another against it. But even those who have jarred in discord shall all conjoin in blessed concord, and make one melodious choir.

We shall then rest from all the sorrowful hours and sad thoughts we now undergo, by participating with our brethren in their calamities. Alas! If we had nothing upon ourselves to trouble us, yet what heart could lay aside sorrows, that lives in the sound of the church's sufferings? The church on earth is a mere hospital. Whichever way we go, we hear complaining, and into whatsoever corner we cast our eyes, we behold objects of pity and grief. Who weeps not when all these bleed? As now our friends' distresses are our distresses, so then our friends' deliverance will be part of our own deliverance. How much more comfortable to see them perfected than now to see them wounded, weak, sick and afflicted? Our day of rest will free both them and us from all this.

Oh, the sad and heart-piercing spectacles that my eyes have seen in four years' space![4] In this fight scarce a month, scarce a week, without the sight or noise of blood. Surely there is none of this in heaven. Our black raiment and mourning attire will then be turned into the white robes and garments of gladness. How hardly can my heart now hold when I think of such, and such, and such a dear Christian friend slain or departed! How glad must the same heart needs be when I see them all alive and glorified!

But a far greater grief it is to our spirits, to see the spiritual miseries of our brethren; to see our dearest and most intimate friends to be turned aside from the truth of Christ; to see many near us in the flesh continue their neglect of Christ and their souls. Oh, what continual sorrows do all these sad sights and thoughts fill our hearts with from day to day! And will it not be a blessed day when we shall rest from all these? What heart is not wounded to think on Germany's long desolations? Look on England's four years' blood, a flourishing land almost made ruined! Look to Scotland, look to Ireland; look almost everywhere! Blessed be that approaching day, when our eyes shall behold no more such sights, nor our ears hear any more such tidings!

We shall rest also from all our personal sufferings, whether natural or ordinary, or extraordinary, from the afflicting hand of God. And though this may seem a small thing to those who live in continual ease, and abound in all kind of prosperity, yet, to the daily afflicted soul, it should make all thoughts of heaven delightful.

As all our senses are the inlets of sin, so are they become the inlets of our sorrow. Grief creeps in at our eyes, at our ears, and almost everywhere. Fears do devour us, and darken our delights, as the frosts nip the tender buds, our cares consume us, and feed upon our spirits, as the scorching sun withers the delicate flowers. What tender pieces are these dusty bodies! What brittle glasses do we bear about us; and how many thousand dangers are they hurried through, and how hardly cured if once cracked!

Whatever it is to the sound and healthful, to such as myself this rest should be acceptable, who in ten or twelve years' time have scarce had a whole day free from some sorrow. Oh, the weary nights and days; oh, the unserviceable, languishing weakness; oh, the restless working vapors; oh, the tedious, nauseous medicines, beside the daily expectation of worse! Will it not be desirable to rest from all these?

Oh, the blessed tranquility of that region where there is nothing but sweet continued peace! Our lives will be but one joy, as our time will be changed into one eternity. For it shall come to pass, that in that day the Lord shall give us rest from our sorrow, and our fear, and from the hard bondage wherein we served. The poor man shall no more be tired with his incessant labors: no more use of the plough, or flail, or scythe, or sickle; no stooping of the servant to the master, or the tenant to the landlord; no hunger, or thirst, or cold, or nakedness; no pinching frosts or scorching heats. No more parting of friends asunder, nor voice of lamentation heard in our dwellings; no more breaches nor disproportion will be in our friendship, nor any trouble accompanying our relations.

Then shall the "the ransomed of the Lord . . . return, and come to Zion with songs and everlasting joy upon their heads: they shall obtain joy and gladness, and sorrow and sighing shall flee away" (Isa. 35:10). Hold out then a little longer, oh, my soul; bear with the infirmities of thine earthly tabernacle. It will be thus but a little while; the sound of our Redeemer's feet are even at the door, and your own deliverance nearer than many others. And you who have often cried shall then feel that God and joy fill all your soul. The fruition of heaven, with your freedom from all these sorrows, will more sincerely and feelingly make you know, and to His eternal praise acknowledge, that you live.

We shall rest also from all the trouble and pain of duty. The conscientious magistrate now cries out, "Oh, the burden that lies upon me!" The conscientious parents, who know the preciousness of their children's souls and the constant pains required to their godly education, cry out, "Oh, the burden!" The conscientious minister when he reads his charge and views his pattern; when he has tried awhile what it is to study, and pray and preach; to go from house to house, and from neighbor to neighbor, and to beseech them night and day with tears, and, after all, be hated and persecuted for so doing—no wonder if he cries out, "Oh, the burden!"

And seldom does a minister live to see the ripeness of his people. But one sows and plants, another waters, and a third reaps and receives the increase. To inform the old ignorant sinner, to convince the stubborn and worldly wise, to persuade a willful, resolved wretch, to prick a stony heart to the quick, to make a rock to weep and tremble, to set forth Christ according to our necessity and His excellency, to comfort the soul whom God dejects, to clear up dark and difficult truths, to oppose with convincing arguments all gainsayers, to credit the gospel with exemplary conversations, when multitudes do but watch for our halting.

Oh, who is sufficient for these things? So that every conscientious Christian cries out, "Oh, the burden! Oh, my weakness that makes it so burdensome!" But our eternal rest will ease us of the burden.

Lastly, we shall rest from all those sad affections which necessarily accompany our absence from God. We shall no more look into our cabinet and miss our treasure; look into our hearts and miss our Christ; nor no more seek Him from ordinance to ordinance, and inquire for our God of those we meet; our heart will not lie in our knee, nor our souls be breathed out in our request, but all conclude in a most full and blessed fruition.

HEAVEN IS AN ETERNAL REST

The last jewel in our crown, and blessed attribute of this rest, is that *it is an eternal rest.* This is the crown of our crown; without which all were comparatively little or nothing. The very thought of once leaving it would else embitter all our joys; and the more would it pierce us because of the singular excellencies which we must forsake.

Mortality is the disgrace of all sublunary delights. It makes our present life of little value—were it not for the reference it has to God and eternity—to think that we must shortly lay it down. Surely, were it not for eternity, I should think man a silly piece; and all his life and honor but contemptible; a vain shadow. I can value nothing that shall have an end, except as it leads to that which has no end; or as it comes from that love which has neither beginning nor end.

What do I say when I talk of eternity? Can my shallow thoughts conceive at all what that most high expression contains? To be eternally blessed, and so blessed! Why, surely this, if anything, is the resemblance of God: eternity is a piece of infiniteness. Oh, then, my soul, let go thy dreams of present pleasures, and loose thy hold of earth and flesh. Fear not to enter that estate where thou shalt ever after cease thy fears. Sit down and think about this eternity. Study frequently, study thoroughly, this one word: *eternity*. And when you have learned thoroughly that one word, you will never look on books again! What! live, and never die? Rejoice, and ever rejoice! Oh, what sweet words are those, *never* and *ever*.

Oh, that the gracious soul would believingly study this word *everlasting*. That should revive him in his deepest agony! Must I, Lord, thus live forever? Then will I also love forever. Must my joys be immortal; and shall not my thanks be also immortal? Surely, if I shall never lose my glory, I will also never cease Thy praises. If Thou wilt both perfect and perpetuate me and my glory, as I shall be Thine, and not my own, so shall my glory be Thy glory. And as all did take their spring from Thee, so shall all devolve into Thee again; and as Thy glory was Thine ultimate end in my glory, so shall it also be mine when Thou hast crowned me with that glory which has no end. And unto Thee, "eternal, immortal, invisible, the only wise God, be honour and glory for ever and ever. Amen." (1 Tim. 1:17).

And thus I have endeavored to show you a glimpse of the approaching glory. But oh, how short are my expressions of its excellency! Reader, if you are a humble, sincere believer, and wait with longing and laboring for this rest, you will shortly see and feel the truth of all this. In the meantime, let this much kindle your desires, and quicken your endeavors. Up, and be doing; run and strive and fight and hold on, for you have a certain, glorious prize before you. God will not mock you: do not mock yourself, nor betray your own soul, by delay or dallying.

THE
KINGDOM OF HEAVEN

BY THOMAS BOSTON[1]

"Then shall the King say unto them on his right hand, Come, ye blessed of my Father, inherit the kingdom prepared for you from the foundation of the world."

—Mt. 25:34

Having from this portion of Scripture, which the text is a part of, discoursed of the general judgment; and having now to speak of the everlasting happiness of the saints, and the everlasting misery of the wicked, from the respective sentences to be pronounced upon them in the great day, I shall take them in the order wherein they lie before us; and the rather that, as sentence is first passed upon the righteous, so the execution thereof is first begun, though probably the other may be fully executed before it is completed.

The words of the text contain the joyful sentence itself, together with a historical introduction thereto, which gives us an account of the Judge pronouncing the sentence; "the King," Jesus Christ; the parties on whom it is given, "them on His right hand;" and the time when, "then," as soon as the trial is over. Of these I have spoken already. It is the sentence itself we are now to consider, "Come, ye blessed of my Father," etc. Stand back, oh ye profane goats! away all unregenerate souls not united to Jesus Christ! This is not for you. Come, oh ye saints, brought out of your natural state into the state of grace! Behold here the state of glory awaiting you. Here is glory let down to us in words and syllables; a looking-glass, in which you may see your everlasting happiness; a scheme or draft of Christ's Father's house, wherein there are many mansions.

This glorious sentence bears two things. 1. The complete happiness to which the saints are adjudged, "the kingdom." 2. Their solemn admission to it, "Come, ye blessed of my Father, inherit," etc.

1. Their complete happiness is a kingdom. A kingdom is the height of worldly felicity; there is nothing on earth greater than a kingdom. Therefore the hidden weight of the glory in heaven is held forth to us under that notion. But it is not an ordinary kingdom, it is "the kingdom;" the kingdom of heaven, surpassing all the kingdoms of the earth in glory, honor, profit, and pleasure—infinitely more than they excel the low and inglorious condition of a beggar in rags, and on a dunghill.

2. There is a solemn admission of the saints into this their kingdom, "Come ye, inherit the kingdom." In view of angels, men, and devils, they are invested with royalty, and solemnly inaugurated before the whole world, by Jesus Christ, the Heir of all things, who hath "all power in heaven and in earth." Their right to the kingdom is solemnly recognized and owned. They are admitted to it as undoubted heirs of the kingdom, to possess it by inheritance, or lot, as the word properly signifies, because, in biblical times, inheritances were designed by lot, as Canaan to Israel, God's "first-born," as they are called (Exod. 4:22). And because this kingdom is the Father's kingdom, therefore they are openly acknowledged, in their admission to it, to be the blessed of Christ's Father: which blessing was given them long before this sentence, but it is now solemnly recognized and confirmed to them by the Mediator, in His Father's name. Observe, He says not, Ye blessed of *the* Father, but, Ye blessed of *my* Father; to show us, that all blessings are derived by us from

the Father, the fountain of blessing, as He is "the God and Father of our Lord Jesus Christ," through whom we are blessed (Eph 1:3). And, finally, they are admitted to this kingdom, as that which was "prepared for them from the foundation of the world," in God's eternal purpose, before they, or any of them, were; that all the world may see eternal life to be the free gift of God.

DOCTRINE

The saints shall be made completely happy in the possession of the kingdom of heaven.

Two things I shall here inquire into: 1. The nature of this kingdom. 2. The admission of the saints thereto. And then I shall make some practical improvement of the whole.

The Nature of the Kingdom of Heaven

As to the nature of the kingdom of heaven, our knowledge of it is very imperfect; for "Eye hath not seen, nor ear heard, neither have entered into the heart of man, the things which God hath prepared for them that love him" (1 Cor. 2:9). As, by familiar resemblances, parents instruct their little children concerning things of which otherwise they can have no tolerable notion; so our gracious God, in consideration of our weakness, is pleased to represent to us heaven's happiness under similitudes taken from earthly things, glorious in the eyes of men; since discoveries of the heavenly glory, divested of earthly resemblances, would be too bright for our weak eyes, and we would but lose ourselves in them. Wherefore now we can but speak as children of these things, which the day will fully discover.

The state of glory is represented under the idea of a kingdom, a kingdom, among men, being that in which the greatest number of earthly good things center. Now, every saint shall, as a king, inherit a kingdom. All Christ's subjects shall be kings, each one with his crown upon his head: not that the great King shall divest himself of His royalty, but He will make all His children partakers of His kingdom.

The saints shall have kingly power and authority given them. Our Lord gives not empty titles to His favorites; He makes them kings indeed. The dominion of the saints will be a dominion far exceeding that of the greatest monarch who ever was on earth. They will be absolute masters over sin, which had the dominion over them. They will have a complete rule over their own spirits; an entire management of all their affections and inclinations, which now create them so much molestation: the turbulent root of corrupt affections shall be forever expelled out of that kingdom, and never be able any more to give them the least disturbance. They shall have power over the nations, the ungodly of all nations, and "shall rule them with a rod of iron" (Rev. 2:26-27).

The whole world of the wicked shall be broken before them: Satan shall be bruised under their feet (Rom. 16:20). He shall never be able to fasten a temptation on them any more: but he will be judged by them, and, in their sight, cast with the reprobate crew into the lake of fire and brimstone. So shall they rule over their oppressors. Having fought the good fight, and got the victory, Christ will entertain them as Joshua did his captains, causing them to "[come] near, and put their feet upon the necks of them" (Josh. 10:24).

They shall have the ensigns of royalty. For a throne, Christ will grant them to sit with Him in his throne (Rev. 3:21). They will be advanced to the highest honor and dignity that they are capable of; and in the enjoyment of it, they will have an eternal undisturbed repose, after all the tossings which they met with in the world, in their way to the throne. For a crown, they "shall receive a crown of glory that fadeth not away" (1 Pet 5:4). Not a crown of flowers, as subjects, being conquerors or victors, sometimes have got; such a

crown quickly fades, but their crown never fades. Not a crown of
gold, such as earthly kings wear; even a crown of gold is often tar-
nished, and at best can never make those who wear it happy.

But the heavenly crown will be a crown of *glory*. A crown of
glory is "a crown of life" (Rev. 2:10), that life which knows no end:
a crown which death can never make to fall off one's head. It must
be an abiding crown; for it is "a crown of righteousness" (2 Tim.
4:8). It was purchased for them by *Christ's* righteousness, which is
imputed to them. They are qualified for it by inherent righteousness. And God's own righteousness, or faithfulness, secures it to
them. They shall have a scepter, a rod of iron (Rev. 2:27), terrible
to all the wicked world. And a sword too, "a twoedged sword in
their hand; to execute vengeance upon the heathen, and punish-
ments upon the people" (Ps. 149:6-7). They shall have royal
apparel. The royal robes in this kingdom are white robes (Rev. 3:4):
"They shall walk with me in white," which, in a very particular
manner, points at the inconceivable glory of the state of the saints
in heaven.

The Saints Arrayed in White

The Lord is pleased often to represent to us the glorious state of the
saints, by speaking of them as clothed in "white garments." It is
promised to the conqueror, that he shall be "clothed in white raiment" (Rev. 3:5). The elders about the throne are "clothed in white
raiment" (4:4). The multitude before the throne are "clothed with
white robes" (7:9); "arrayed in white robes" (v. 13); "made . . . white
in the blood of the Lamb" (v. 14).

No more servitude. The Romans, when they set their bond-ser-
vants free, gave them a white garment as a badge of their freedom.
So shall the saints that day receive their white robes; for it is the day
of "the glorious liberty of the children of God" (Rom. 8:21), the
day of "the redemption of our body" (v. 23). They shall no more

see the house of bondage, nor be any more among the pots. If we compare the state of the saints on earth with that of the wicked, it is indeed a state of freedom, whereas the other is a state of slavery: but, in comparison with their state in heaven, it is but a servitude. A saint on earth is indeed a young prince, and heir to the crown; but his motto may be, "I serve;" for he "differeth nothing from a servant, though he be lord of all" (Gal. 4:1).

What are the groans of a saint, the sordid and base work which he is sometimes found employed in, the black and tattered garments which he walks in, but the badges of this comparative servitude? But from the day the saints come to the crown, they receive their complete freedom, and serve no more. They shall be fully freed from sin, which of all evils is the worst, both in itself, and in their apprehension too; how great then must that freedom be, when these Egyptians, whom they see today, they shall see again no more forever! (cf. Exod. 14:13). They shall be free from all temptation to sin: Satan can have no access to tempt them any more, by himself, or by his agents. A full answer will then be given to that petition they have so often repeated, "Lead us not into temptation." No hissing serpent can come into the paradise above: no snare or trap can be laid there, to catch the feet of the saints: they may walk there without fear, for they can be in no hazard: there are no lions' dens, no mountains of leopards, in the promised land.

Nay, they shall be set beyond the possibility of sinning, for they shall be confirmed in goodness. It will be the consummate freedom of their will, to be forever unalterably determined to do good. And they shall be freed from all the effects of sin: "there shall be no more death, neither sorrow, nor crying, neither shall there be any more pain: for the former things are passed away" (Rev. 21:4).

What kingdom is like unto this? Death makes its way now into a palace, as easily as into a cottage: sorrow fills the heart of one who wears a crown on his head: royal robes are no defense against pain, and crying by reason of pain. But in this kingdom no misery can have place. All reproaches shall be wiped off, and never shall a tear drop any more from their eyes, They shall not complain of desertions again; the Lord will never hide His face from them: but the Sun of Righteousness shining upon them in his meridian brightness, will dispel all clouds, and give them an everlasting day, without the least mixture of darkness. A deluge of wrath, after a fearful thunder-clap from the throne, will sweep away the wicked from before the judgment-seat, into the lake of fire: but the righteous are, in the first place, like Noah, brought into the ark and out of harm's way.

Unspotted purity. White raiment was a token of purity. Therefore the Lamb's wife is "arrayed in fine linen, clean and white" (Rev. 19:8). And those who stood before the throne "washed their robes, and made them white in the blood of the Lamb" (7:14). The saints shall then put on the robes of perfect purity, and shine in spotless holiness, like the sun in its strength, without the least cloud to intercept its light. Absolute innocence shall then be restored, and every appearance of sin banished far from this kingdom. The guilt of sin, and the reigning power of it are even now taken away in the saints. Nevertheless, sin dwells in them (Rom. 7:20). But then it shall be no more in them: the corrupt nature will be quite removed; that root of bitterness will be plucked up, and no vestiges of it left in their souls: their nature shall be altogether pure and sinless. There shall be no darkness in their minds; but the understanding of every saint, when he is come to his kingdom, will be as a globe of pure and unmixed light.

There shall not be the least aversion to good, nor the least inclination to evil, in their wills, but they will be brought to a perfect conformity to the will of God; blessed with angelic purity, and fixed therein. Their affections shall not be liable to the least disorder or irregularity; it will cost no trouble to keep them right: they will get such a fixed habit of purity as they can never lose. They will be so refined from all earthly dross as never to savor more of any thing but of heaven. Were it possible for them to be set again amidst the ensnaring objects of an evil world, they would walk among them without the least defilement—as the sun shines on the dunghill, yet is untainted, and as the angels preserved their purity in the midst of Sodom. Their graces shall then be perfected; and all the imperfections now cleaving to them done away. There will be no more ground for complaints of weakness of grace. None in that kingdom shall complain of an ill heart, or a corrupt nature. "It doth not yet appear what we shall be: but we know that, when he shall appear, we shall be like him" (1 Jn. 3:2).

An eternal priesthood. Among the Jews, those who desired to be admitted into the priestly office, being tried, and found to be of the priest's line and without blemish, were clothed in white, and enrolled among the priests. This seems to be alluded to: "He that overcometh, the same shall be clothed in white raiment; and I will not blot out his name out of the book of life" (Rev. 3:5). So the saints shall not be kings only, but priests also; for they are "a royal priesthood" (1 Pet. 2:9).

They will be priests upon their thrones. They are judicially found descended from the Great High Priest of their profession, begotten of Him by His Spirit, of the incorruptible seed of the Word, and without blemish: so the trial being over, they are admitted to be priests in the temple above, that they may dwell in the house of the Lord forever. There is nothing upon earth more glorious than a kingdom; nothing more venerable than the priesthood; and both meet together in the glorified state of the saints. "The general assembly of the first-born" (Heb. 12:23), whose is the priesthood and the double portion, appearing in their white robes of glory, will be a reverend and glorious company. That day will show them to be the persons whom the Lord has chosen out of all the tribes of the earth, to be near unto Him, and to enter into His temple, even into His holy place. Their priesthood, begun on earth, shall be brought to its perfection, when they shall be employed in offering the sacrifice of praise to God and the Lamb forever and ever. They got not their portion in the earth with the rest of the tribes; but the Lord Himself was their portion, and will be their double portion, through the ages of eternity.

A triumphant throng. They were wont to wear white raiment in a time of triumph; to which also there seems to be an allusion: "He that *overcometh,* the same shall be clothed in white raiment" (Rev. 3:5). And what is heaven but an everlasting triumph? None get thither but such as fight, and overcome too. Though Canaan was given to the Israelites as an inheritance, they were required to conquer it, before they could be possessors of it. The saints, in this world, are in the field of battle; often in red garments, garments rolled in blood. But the day approaches in which they shall stand "before the throne, and before the Lamb, clothed with white robes, and palms in their hands" (Rev. 7:9), having obtained a complete victory over all their enemies.

The palm was used as a sign of victory, because that tree, though oppressed with weights, yet yields not, but rather shoots upward. And palm trees were carved on the doors of the most holy place (1 Ki. 6:32), which was a special type of heaven; for heaven is the place which the saints are received into as conquerors.

Behold the joy and peace of the saints in their white robes!

The joys arising from the view of past dangers, and of riches and honors gained at the very door of death, do most sensibly touch one's heart: and this will be an ingredient in the everlasting happiness of the saints, which could have had no place in the heaven of innocent Adam, and his sinless offspring, supposing him to have stood.

Surely the glorified saints will not forget the entertainment which they met with in the world; it will be to the glory of God to remember it, and will also heighten their joy. The Sicilian king, by birth the son of a potter, acted a wise part, in that he would be served at his table with earthen vessels; which could not but put an additional sweetness in his meals, not to be relished by one born heir to the crown. Can ever meat be so sweet to any as to the hungry man? Or can any have such a relish of plenty as he who has been under pinching straits? The more difficulties the saints have passed through in their way to heaven, the place will be the sweeter to them when they come to it.

Every happy stroke, struck in the spiritual warfare, will be a jewel in their crown of glory. Each victory obtained against sin, Satan, and the world will raise their triumphant joy the higher. The remembrance of the cross will sweeten the crown; and the remembrance of their travel through the wilderness will put an additional verdure on the fields of glory, while they walk through them, looking back on the day when they went mourning without the sun.

And now that they appear triumphing in white robes, it is a sign they have obtained an honorable peace; such a peace as their enemies can disturb no more. So everything peculiarly adapted to their militant condition is laid aside. The sword is laid down; and they betake themselves to the pen of a ready writer, to commemorate the praises of Him by whom they overcame.

Public ordinances, preaching, sacraments, shall be honorably laid aside; there is no temple there (Rev. 21:22). On earth these were sweet to them: but the travelers being all got home, the inns, appointed for their entertainment by the way, are shut up; the candles are put out when the sun is risen; and the tabernacle used in the wilderness is folded up, when the temple of glory is come in its room.

Many of the saints' duties will then be laid aside, as one gives his staff out of his hand, when he is come to the end of his journey. Praying shall then be turned to praising: and there being no sin to confess, no wants to seek the supply of, confession and petition shall be swallowed up in everlasting thanksgiving.

There will be no mourning in heaven. They have sown in tears: the reaping time of joy is come, "And God shall wipe away all tears from their eyes" (Rev. 21:4). No need of mortification there; and self-examination is then at an end. They will not need to watch any more; the danger is over. Patience has had its perfect work, and there is no use for it there. Faith is turned into sight, and hope is swallowed up in the ocean of sensible and fun enjoyment. All the rebels are subdued, and the saints quietly sit on their throne. The forces, needful in the time of the spiritual warfare, are disbanded, and they carry on their triumph in the profoundest peace.

A perpetual Sabbath festival. White garments were worn on festival days, in token of joy. And so shall the saints be clothed in white raiment; for they shall keep an everlasting Sabbath to the Lord (Heb. 4:9). "There remaineth therefore a rest," or keeping of a Sabbath, "to the people of God." The Sabbath, in the esteem of saints, is the queen of days; and they shall have an endless Sabbath in the kingdom of heaven, so shall their garments be always white.

They will have an eternal rest, with an uninterrupted joy; for heaven is not a resting place, where men may sleep out an eternity; there they rest not day nor night, but their work is their rest, and continual recreation. Toil and weariness have no place there. They rest there in God, who is the center of their souls. Here they find the completion, or satisfaction, of all their desires, having the full enjoyment of God, and uninterrupted communion with Him.

This is the point to which, till the soul come, it will always be restless: but that point reached, it rests; for God is the last end, and the soul can go no further. It cannot understand, will, nor desire more; but in Him it has what is commensurable to its boundless desires. This is the happy end of all the labors of the saints; their toil and sorrows issue in a joyful rest.

The Chaldeans, measuring the natural day, put the day first, and the night last: but the Jews counted the night first, and the day last. So the wicked begin with a day of rest and pleasure, but end with a night of everlasting toil and sorrow. But God's people have their gloomy night first, and then comes their day of eternal rest.

This, Abraham, in the parable, observed to the rich man in hell (Lk. 16.25): "Son, remember that thou in thy lifetime receivedst thy good things, and likewise Lazarus evil things: but now he is comforted, and thou art tormented."

A Whole Different Realm

If any inquire where the kingdom of the saints lies, it is not in this world; it lies in "a better country, that is, an heavenly" (Heb. 11:16), a country better than the best of this world; namely, the heavenly Canaan, Immanuel's land, where nothing is wanting to complete the happiness of the inhabitants. This is the happy country, blessed with a perpetual spring, and yielding all things for necessity, convenience, and delight.

There men shall eat angels' food; they shall be entertained with "the hidden manna" (Rev. 2:17) without being set to the painful task of gathering it. They will be fed to the full, with the product of the land falling into their mouths, without the least toil to them.

That land enjoys everlasting day, for there is "no night there" (Rev. 21:25). Eternal sunshine beautifies this better country, but there is no scorching heat there. No clouds shall be seen there forever: yet it is not a land of drought; the trees of the Lord's planting are set by the rivers of water, and shall never want moisture, for they will have an eternal supply of the Spirit, by Jesus Christ, from His Father.

This is the country whence our Lord came, and where He is gone again; the country which all the holy patriarchs and prophets had their eye upon while on earth; and which all the saints, who have gone before us, have fought their way to; and to which the martyrs have joyfully swum through a sea of blood. This earth is the place of the saints' pilgrimage; heaven is their country, where they find their everlasting rest.

New Jerusalem. The royal city is that great city, the holy

Jerusalem, described at large in Revelation 21:10-27. The saints shall reign in that city, whose wall is of "jasper" (v. 18); "And the foundations of the wall of the city [are] garnished with all manner of precious stones" (v. 19); and "the street of the city [is] pure gold" (v. 21)—so that their feet shall be set on that which the men of this world set their hearts upon.

This is the city which God has "prepared for them" (Heb. 11:16); "a city which hath foundations" (v. 10); a "continuing city" (13:14), which shall stand and flourish, when all the cities of the world are laid in ashes; and which shall not be moved, when the foundations of the world are overturned.

It is a city that never changes its inhabitants. None of them shall ever be removed out of it; for life and immortality reign there, and no death can enter into it. It is blessed with a perfect and perpetual peace, and can never be in the least disturbed. Nothing from without can annoy it; the gates therefore are not shut at all by day, and there is no night there (Rev. 21:25). There can nothing from within trouble it.

No want of provision there, no scarcity, no discord among the inhabitants. Whatever contentions are among the saints now, no vestige of their former jarrings shall remain there. Love to God and to one another shall be perfected; and those of them who stood at the greatest distance from one another here will joyfully embrace and delight in one another there.

The Father's house. The royal palace is Christ's Father's house, in which "are many mansions" (Jn. 14:2). There shall the saints dwell forever. This is the house prepared for all the heirs of glory, even those of them who dwell in the meanest cottage now, or have not where to lay their heads. As the Lord calls His saints to a kingdom, He will provide them a house suitable to the dignity He puts upon them. Heaven will be a convenient, spacious, and glorious house for those whom the King delights to honor.

Never was a house purchased at so great a rate as this, being the purchase of the Mediator's blood; and for no less could it be afforded to them.

Never was there so much to do to fit the inhabitants for a house. The saints were, by nature, utterly unfit for this house, and human art and industry could not make them meet for it. But the Father gives the designed inhabitants to the Son, to be by Him redeemed. The Son pays the price of their redemption, even His own precious blood. Justice gives them access to the house. And the Holy Spirit sanctifies them by His grace; that they may be meet to come in thither, where no unclean thing can enter.

And no wonder, for it is the King's palace they enter into (Ps. 45:15). Here is where the great King keeps his court, where He has set His throne, and shows forth His glory in a singular manner, beyond what mortals can conceive.

Limitless delights. Paradise is their palace garden. "To day shalt thou be with me in paradise," said our Saviour to the penitent thief on the cross (Lk. 23:43). Heaven is a paradise for pleasure and delight, where there is both wood and water: "A pure river of water of life, clear as crystal, proceeding out of the throne of God and of the Lamb. In the midst of the street of it, and on either side of the river, was there the tree of life, which bare twelve manner of fruits, and yielded her fruit every month" (Rev. 22:1-2).

How happy might innocent Adam have been in the earthly paradise, where there was nothing wanting for use or delight! Eden was the most pleasant spot of the uncorrupted earth, and paradise the most pleasant spot of Eden: but what is earth in comparison of heaven? The glorified saints are advanced to the heavenly paradise. There they shall not only see, but "eat of the tree of life, which is in the midst of the paradise of God" (Rev. 2:7).

They shall behold the Mediator's glory, and be satisfied with His goodness. No flaming sword shall be there, to keep the way of that tree of life. But they shall freely eat of it, and live forever. They shall "drink of the river of [God's own] pleasures" (Ps. 36:8), the sweetest and purest delights which Immanuel's land affords, and shall swim in an ocean of unmixed pleasures for evermore.

Treasures in heaven. They shall have royal treasures, sufficient to support the dignity to which they are advanced. Since the street of the royal city is pure gold, and the twelve gates thereof are twelve pearls, their treasure must be of that which is better than gold or pearl. It is "a far more exceeding and eternal weight of glory" (2 Cor. 4:17). Oh, precious treasure! A treasure not liable to insensible corruption, by moths or rust; a treasure which none can steal from them (Mt. 6:20).

Never did any kingdom afford such a precious treasure, nor a treasure of such variety; for "He that overcometh shall inherit all things" (Rev. 21:7). No treasures on earth are stored with *all things*. If all the treasures of earth were put together in one store, there would be far more valuable things missing there than found in it.

This then is the peculiar treasure of the kings who inherit the kingdom of heaven. They shall want nothing that may contribute to their full satisfaction. Now they are rich in hope; but then they will have their riches in hand. Now all things are theirs in respect of right; then all shall be theirs in possession. They may go forever through Immanuel's land and behold the glory and riches thereof, with the satisfying thought that all they see is their own. Christians should never be uneasy under the want of earthly good things; because they may be sure they shall inherit all things at length.

Heavenly worship. Though there is no material temple therein, no serving of God in the use of ordinances, as here on earth; yet, as for this kingdom, "the Lord God Almighty and the Lamb are the temple of it" (Rev. 21:22). As the temple was the glory of Canaan, so will the celestial temple be the glory of heaven. The saints shall be brought in thither as a royal priesthood, to dwell in the house of the Lord forever; for Jesus Christ will then make every saint "a pillar in the temple of . . . God, and he shall go no more out" (Rev.

3:12), as the priests and Levites did, in their courses, go out of the material temple.

There the saints shall have the cloud of glory, the divine presence, with most intimate, uninterrupted communion with God. There they shall have Jesus Christ, as the true Ark, wherein the fiery law shall be forever hid from their eyes. He is also the mercy-seat, from which nothing shall be breathed but everlasting peace and goodwill toward them. The cherubim, the society of holy angels, shall join with them in eternal admiration of the mystery of Christ. The golden candlestick, with its seven lamps, "the glory of God [will] lighten it, and the Lamb is the light thereof" (Rev. 21:23). The incense altar, in the intercession of Christ, who "ever liveth to make intercession for them" (Heb. 7:25), eternally exhibiting the manner of His death and suffering, and efficaciously willing forever, that those whom the Father has given Him, be with Him. And the shewbread table, in the perpetual feast they shall have together in the enjoyment of God.

Life in This Kingdom

What would royal power and authority, ensigns of royalty, richest treasures, and all other advantages of a kingdom, avail without comfortable society? Some crowned heads have had but a wretched life, through the want of it. Their palaces have been unto them as prisons, and their badges of honor, as chains on a prisoner. Hated of all, they had none they could trust in, or whom they could have comfortable fellowship with.

But the chief part of heaven's happiness lies in the blessed society which the saints shall have there.

Fellowship with one another. The society of the saints among themselves will be no small part of heaven's happiness. The communion of saints on earth is highly prized by all those who are traveling through the world to Zion. Companions in sin can never have such true pleasure and delight in one another as sometimes the Lord's people have in praying together, and in conversing about those things to which the world is a stranger.

Here on earth the saints are but few in a company at best. And some of them are so situated that they seem to themselves to dwell alone, having no access to such as they would freely embosom themselves to in spiritual matters. They sigh and say, "Woe is me! for I am as when they have gathered the summer fruits. . . . There is no cluster to eat . . . . The good man is perished out of the earth" (Mic. 7:1-2).

But in the general assembly of the firstborn in heaven, none of all the saints who ever were or will be on the earth shall be missing. They will be all of them together in one place, all possess one kingdom, and all sit down together to the marriage supper of the Lamb.

On earth even the best of the saints struggle with sinful imperfections, making their society less comfortable. But there they shall be perfect—"not having spot, or wrinkle, or any such thing" (Eph. 5:27). All natural, as well as sinful, imperfections will be done away; they "shall shine as the brightness of the firmament" (Dan. 12:3).

There we shall see Adam and Eve in the heavenly paradise, freely eating of the tree of life; Abraham, Isaac, and Jacob, and all the holy patriarchs, no more wandering from land to land, but come to their everlasting rest; all the prophets feasting their eyes on the glory of Him of whose coming they prophesied; the twelve apostles of the Lamb, sitting on their twelve thrones; all the holy martyrs in their long white robes, with their crowns on their heads; the godly kings advanced to a kingdom which cannot be moved; and those that turn many to righteousness, shining as the stars forever and ever.

There we shall see our godly friends, relations, and acquaintances, pillars in the temple of God, to go no more out from us. And it is more than probable that the saints will know one another in heaven; at least they will know their friends, relatives, and those they were acquainted with on earth, and such as have been most eminent in the Church; yet that knowledge will be purified from all earthly thoughts and affections. This seems to be included in that perfection of happiness to which the saints shall be advanced. If Adam knew who and what Eve was, at first sight, when the Lord God brought her to him (Gen. 2:23-24), why should one question but husbands and wives, parents and children, will know one another in glory?

If the Thessalonians, converted by Paul's ministry, shall be his hope, and joy, and crown of rejoicing "in the presence of our Lord Jesus Christ at his coming" (1 Thess. 2:19), why may we not conclude that ministers shall know their people, and people their ministers, in heaven? And if the disciples, on the Mount of Transfiguration, knew Moses and Elijah, whom they had never seen before (Mt. 17:4), we have reason to think that we shall know them too, and such as them, when we come to heaven.

The communion of saints shall be most intimate there. We "shall sit down with Abraham, and Isaac, and Jacob, in the kingdom of heaven" (Mt. 8:11). Lazarus was carried by the angels into Abraham's bosom (Luke 16:23), which denotes most intimate and familiar society.

And though diversity of tongues shall cease (1 Cor. 13:8), I make no question, but there will be the use of speech in heaven; and that the saints will glorify God in their bodies there, as well as in their spirits, speaking forth His praises with an audible voice. As for the language, we shall understand what it is, when we come thither. When Paul was caught up to the third heaven, the seat of the blessed, he heard there unspeakable words, which it is not lawful for a man to utter (2 Cor. 12:4). Moses and Elijah, on the mount with Christ, talked with Him (Mt. 17:3), and "spake of his decease which he should accomplish at Jerusalem" (Lk. 9:31).

Fellowship with the angels. The saints will have the society of all the holy angels there. An innumerable company of angels shall be companions to them in their glorified state. Happy were the shepherds who heard the song of the heavenly host when Christ was born but thrice happy they, who shall join their voices with them in the choir of saints and angels in heaven, when He shall be glorified in all who shall be about Him there! Then shall we be brought acquainted with those blessed spirits who never sinned. How bright will those morning stars shine in the holy place! They were ministering spirits to the heirs of salvation: loved them for their Lord and Master's sake; encamped round about them, to preserve them from danger. How joyfully will they welcome them to their everlasting habitations, and rejoice to see them come at length to their kingdom, as the tutor does in the prosperity of his pupils!

The saints shall be no more afraid of them, as at times they were wont to be: they shall then have put off mortality, and the infirmities of the flesh, and be themselves as the angels of God, fit to enjoy communion and fellowship with them. And both being brought under one head, the Lord Jesus Christ, they shall join in the praises of God and of the Lamb, saying, with a loud voice, "Worthy is the Lamb that was slain," etc. (Rev. 5:11-12).

Whether the angels shall, as some think, assume ethereal bodies, that they may be seen by the bodily eyes of the saints, and be in a nearer capacity to converse with them, I know not: but, as they want not ways of converse among themselves, we have reason to think that conversation between them and the saints shall not be forever blocked up.

Fellowship with the Lord. They shall have society with the Lord Himself in Heaven, glorious communion with God in Christ, which is the perfection of happiness. I choose to speak of communion with God and the man Christ, together; because, as we derive our grace from the Lamb, so we shall derive our glory from Him too, the man Christ being, if I may be allowed the expression, the center of the divine glory in heaven, from whence it is diffused unto all the saints.

This seems to be taught us by the Scriptures which express heaven's happiness by being with Christ: "To day thou shalt be with me in paradise" (Lk. 23:43). "Father, I will that they also, whom thou hast given me, be with me where I am" (John 17:24). And remarkably to this purpose is what follows: "that they may behold my glory." "So shall we ever be with the Lord" (1 Thess. 4:17)—that is, the Lord Christ, whom we shall meet in the air.

This also seems to be the import of the Scriptures wherein God and the Lamb, the slain Saviour, are jointly spoken of, in point of the happiness of the saints in heaven: "For the Lamb which is in the midst of the throne shall feed them, and shall lead them unto living fountains of waters: and God shall wipe away all tears from their eyes" (Rev. 7:17). "Behold, the tabernacle of God is with men, and he will dwell with them" (21:3)—as in a tabernacle. The same word signifies the flesh of Christ (cf. John 1:14). "The Lord God Almighty and the Lamb are the temple of it" (Rev. 21:22).

The Blessing of the Divine Presence

Here lies the chief happiness of the saints in heaven, without which they never could be happy, though lodged in that glorious place, and blessed with the society of angels there. What I will venture to say of it, shall be comprised in three things:

The perpetual presence of God and Christ in full glory. First, the saints in heaven shall have the glorious presence of God and of the Lamb: God Himself shall be with them (Rev. 21:3), and they shall ever be with the Lord.

God is everywhere present in respect of His essence. The saints militant already enjoy His special gracious presence. But in heaven they have His glorious presence. There they are brought near to the very throne of the great King, and stand before Him, where he shows His inconceivable glory.

There they have the actual heavenly tabernacle of God, on which the cloud of glory rests, the all-glorious human nature of Christ, wherein the fullness of the Godhead dwells; not veiled, as in the days of His humiliation, but shining through that blessed flesh, that all His saints may behold His glory, and making that body more glorious than a thousand suns—so that "the city [has] no need of the sun, neither of the moon, to shine in it: for the glory of God [will] lighten it, and the Lamb is the light thereof"—literally, "the candle thereof" (Rev. 21:23).

That is, the Lamb is the luminary or luminous body, which gives light to the city, as the sun and moon now give light to the world, or as a candle lightens a dark room. And the light proceeding from the glorious luminary of the city is the glory of God. Sometimes on earth that candle burned very dimly; it was hid under a bushel in the time of His humiliation; only now and then it darted out some rays of this light, which dazzled the eyes of the spectators: but now it is set on high, in the city of God, where it shines, and shall shine forever in perfection of glory. It was sometimes laid aside, as a stone disallowed of the builders: but now it is and forever will be, "the light," or luminary of that city; and that "like unto a stone most precious, even like a jasper stone, clear as crystal" (21:11).

Who can conceive the happiness of the saints in the presence chamber of the great King, where He sits in His chair of state, making His glory eminently to appear in the man Christ? His gracious presence makes a mighty change upon the saints in this world. His glorious presence in heaven, then, must needs raise their graces to perfection, and elevate their capacities.

The saints here on earth experience something of the presence of God, now with them in His grace, and know how it can make a little heaven of a sort of hell. How great then must the glory of heaven be, by His presence there in His glory! If a candle, in some sort, beautifies a cottage or prison, how will the shining sun beautify a palace or paradise! The gracious presence of God made a wilderness lightsome to Moses; the valley of the shadow of death, to David; a fiery furnace, to the three children: what a ravishing beauty then shall arise from the Sun of Righteousness, shining in His meridian brightness on the street of the city paved with pure gold!

This glorious presence of God in heaven, will put a glory on the saints themselves. The most pleasing garden is devoid of beauty when the darkness of the night sits down on it; but the shining sun puts a glory on the blackest mountains: so those who are now as bottles in the smoke, when set in the glorious presence of God, will be glorious both in soul and body.

Perfect satisfaction. The saints in heaven shall have the full enjoyment of God and of the Lamb. This is it that perfectly satisfies the rational creature; and here is the saints' everlasting rest.

This will make up all their wants, and fill the desires of their souls, which, after all here obtained, still cry, "Give, give," not without some anxiety, because though they do enjoy God, yet they do not enjoy Him fully. As to the way and manner of this enjoyment, our Lord tells us: "This is life eternal, that they might know thee the only true God, and Jesus Christ, whom thou hast sent" (Jn. 17:3). Now there are two ways in which a desirable object is known most perfectly and satisfyingly; the one is by sight, the other by experience. Sight satisfies the understanding, and experience satisfies the will.

An Intimate Knowledge of God

Accordingly, one may say that the saints enjoy God and the Lamb in heaven, by *an intuitive knowledge;* and *by an experiential knowledge;* both of them perfect (I mean in respect of the capacity of the creature; for otherwise a creature's perfect knowledge of an infinite Being is impossible.)

The saints below enjoy God, in that knowledge they have of Him by report, from His holy Word, which they believe; they see Him likewise darkly in the glass of ordinances, which do, as it were, represent the Bridegroom's picture, or shadow, while He is absent. They have also some experiential knowledge of Him; they taste that God is good, and that the Lord is gracious. But the saints above shall not need a good report of the King, they shall see Him; therefore faith ceaseth. They will behold His own face; therefore ordinances are no more. There is no need of a glass. They shall drink, and drink abundantly, of that whereof they have tasted; and so hope ceaseth, for they are at the utmost bounds of their desires.

We will see Him face to face. But the saints in heaven shall enjoy God and the Lamb by sight, and that in a most perfect manner: "For now we see through a glass, darkly; but then face to face: now I know in part; but then shall I know even as also I am known" (1 Cor. 13:12). Here our sight is but mediate, as by a glass, in which we see not things themselves, but the images of things! But there we shall have an immediate view of God and the Lamb. Here our knowledge is but obscure. There it shall be clear, without the least mixture of darkness. The Lord now converses with His saints through the lattices of ordinances; but then shall they be in the presence chamber with Him. There is a veil now on the glorious face, as to us. But when we come to the upper house, that veil, through which some rays of beauty are now darted, will be found entirely taken off; and then shall glorious excellencies and perfections, not seen in Him by mortals, be clearly discovered, for we shall see His face: "And they shall see his face" (Rev. 22:4). The phrase seems to be borrowed from the honor put on some in the courts of monarchs, to be attendants on the king's person. We read of seven men that were "near the king's person" (Jer. 52:25—lit., "seers of the king's face"). Oh, unspeakable glory! the great King keeps His court in heaven: and the saints shall all be His courtiers ever near the King's person, seeing His face. "The throne of God and of the Lamb shall be in it; and his servants shall serve him: and they shall see his face" (Rev. 22:3-4).

The vision of Christ. They shall see Jesus Christ, God and man, with their bodily eyes, as He will never lay aside the human nature. They will behold that glorious, blessed body, which is personally united to the divine nature, and exalted above principalities and powers and every name that is named. There we shall see, with our eyes, that very body which was born of Mary at Bethlehem and crucified at Jerusalem between two thieves: the blessed head that was crowned with thorns; the face that was spit upon; the hands and feet that were nailed to the cross; all shining with inconceivable glory. The glory of the man Christ will attract the eyes of all the saints, and He will be forever "admired in all them that believe" (2 Thess. 1:10).

Were each star in the heavens shining as the sun in its meridian brightness, and the light of the sun so increased, as the stars, in that case, should bear the same proportion to the sun, in point of light, that they do now; it might possibly be some faint resemblance of the glory of the man Christ in comparison with that of the saints; for though the saints "shine forth as the sun," yet not they but the Lamb shall be "the light of the city."

The wise men fell down, and worshiped Him, when they saw Him a young child, with Mary His mother (Mt. 2:11). But oh, what a ravishing sight will it be to see Him in His Kingdom, on His throne, at the Father's right hand! "The Word was made flesh" (John 1:14), and the glory of God shall shine through that flesh, and the joys of heaven spring out from it, unto the saints, who shall see and enjoy God in Christ. For since the union between Christ and the saints is never dissolved, but they continue His members forever; and the members cannot draw their life but from their head, seeing that which is independent of the head, as to vital influence, is no member; therefore Jesus Christ will remain the everlasting bond of union between God and the saints; from whence their eternal life shall spring. "As thou hast given him power over all flesh, that he should give eternal life to as many as thou hast given him. And this is life eternal, that they might know thee the only true God, and Jesus Christ, whom thou hast sent" (Jn. 17:1-2). "And the glory which thou gavest me I have given them; that they may be one, even as we are one: I in them, and thou in me, that they may be made perfect in one" (vv. 22-23).

Wherefore the immediate enjoyment of God in heaven is to be understood in respect of the laying aside of Word and sacraments, and such external means as we enjoy God by in this world; but not as if the saints should then cast off their dependence on their Head for vital influences: nay, "The Lamb which is in the midst of the throne shall feed them, and shall lead them unto living fountains of waters" (Rev. 7:17).

Now when we shall behold Him, who died for us, that we might live for evermore, whose matchless love made Him swim through the Red Sea of God's wrath, to make a path in the midst of it for us, by which we might pass safely to Canaan's land; then we shall see what a glorious One he was, who suffered all this for us; what entertainment He had in the upper house; what hallelujahs of angels could not hinder Him from hearing the groans of a perishing multitude on earth, and from coming down for their help; and what glory He laid aside for us. Then shall we be more "able to comprehend with all saints what is the breadth, and length, and depth, and height; and to know the love of Christ, which passeth knowledge" (Eph. 3:18-19).

When the saints shall remember that the waters of wrath which He was plunged into are the wells of salvation from whence they draw all their joy; that they have got the cup of salvation in exchange for the cup of wrath His Father gave Him to drink, which His sinless human nature shivered at; how will their hearts leap within them, burn with seraphic love, like coals of juniper, and the arch of heaven ring with their songs of salvation!

The Jews, celebrating the feast of tabernacles, which was the most joyful of all their feasts, and lasted seven days, went once every day about the altar, singing hosanna, with their myrtle, palm, and willow branches in their hands (the two former being signs of victory, the last, of chastity) in the meantime bending their boughs toward the altar. When the saints are presented as a chaste virgin to Christ, and as conquerors have got their palms in their hands, how joyfully will they compass the altar evermore, and sing their hosannas, or rather their hallelujahs about it, bending their palms toward it, acknowledging themselves to owe all unto the Lamb that was slain, and who redeemed them with His blood! To this agrees what John saw: "A great multitude, which no man could number, of all nations, and kindreds, and people, and tongues, stood before the throne, and before the Lamb, clothed with white robes, and palms in their hands; and cried with a loud voice, saying, Salvation to our God which sitteth upon the throne, and unto the Lamb" (Rev. 7:9-10).

The vision of God. They shall see God (Mt. 5:8). They will be happy in seeing the Father, Son, and Holy Ghost, not with their bodily eyes, in respect of which, God is invisible (1 Tim. 1:17), but with the eyes of their understanding; being blessed with the most perfect, full, and clear knowledge of God, and of divine things, which the creature is capable of. This is called *the beatific vision,* and is the perfection of understanding, the utmost term thereof. It is but an obscure delineation of the glory of God, that mortals can have on earth; a sight, as it were, of his "back parts" (Exod. 33:23). But there they will see His face (Rev. 22:4).

They shall see Him in the fullness of His glory, and behold Him fixedly; whereas it is but a passing view they can have of Him here (cf. Exod. 34:6). There is a vast difference between the sight of a king in casual attire, quickly passing by us; and a fixed leisurely view of him, sitting on his throne in his royal robes, his crown on his head, and his scepter in his hand. Such a difference will there be between the greatest manifestation of God that ever a saint had on earth, and the display of His glory in heaven.

There the saints shall eternally, without interruption, feast their eyes upon Him, and be ever viewing His glorious perfections. And as their bodily eyes shall be strengthened, and fitted to behold the glorious majesty of the man Christ, as eagles gaze on the sun without being blinded thereby, so their minds shall have such an elevation as will fit them to see God in His glory: their capacities shall be enlarged, according to the measure in which He shall be pleased to communicate Himself to them, for their complete happiness.

This blissful sight of God being quite above our present capacities, we must needs be much in the dark about it. But it seems to be something else than the sight of that glory, which we shall see with our bodily eyes, in the saints, and in the man Christ, or any other splendor or refulgence from the Godhead whatever; for no created thing can be our chief good and happiness, nor fully satisfy our souls; and it is plain that these things are somewhat different from God Himself.

Therefore I conceive, that the souls of the saints shall see God Himself. So the Scriptures teach us that we shall see face to face, and know even as we are known (1 Cor. 13:12); and that we shall see Him as He is (1 John 3:2).

A field of delights to walk in forever. Yet the saints can never have an adequate conception of God. They cannot comprehend that which is infinite. They may touch the mountain, but cannot grasp it in their arms. They cannot, with one glance of their eye, behold what grows on every side. But the divine perfections will be an unbounded field, in which the glorified shall walk eternally, seeing more and more of God, since they can never come to the end of that which is infinite. They may bring their vessels to this ocean every moment, and fill them with new waters.

What a ravishing sight would it be, to see all the perfections and

lovely qualities that are scattered here and there among the creatures, gathered together into one! But even such a sight would be
infinitely below this blissful sight the saints shall have in heaven.
For they shall see God, in whom all these perfections shall eminently appear infinitely more, whereof there is no vestige to be
found in the creatures. In Him shall they see everything desirable,
and nothing but what is desirable.

Satisfied with His love. Then shall they be perfectly satisfied as
to the love of God toward them, which they are now ready to question on every turn. They will no more find any difficulty to persuade themselves of it, by marks, signs, and testimonies. They will
have an intuitive knowledge of it. They shall, with the profoundest reverence be it spoken, look into the heart of God, and there see
the love He bore to them from all eternity, and the love and goodness He will bear to them for evermore.

Living in the light of His truth. The glorified shall have a most
clear and distinct understanding of divine truths, for in His light we
shall see light (Ps. 36:9). The light of glory will be a complete com-
mentary on the Bible, and untie all the hard and knotty questions
in divinity. There is no joy on earth comparable to that which arises
from the discovery of truth, no discovery of truth comparable to the
discovery of Scripture truth, made by the Spirit of the Lord to the
soul. "I rejoice at thy word," says the psalmist, "as one that findeth
great spoil" (Ps. 119:162). Yet, while here, it is but an imperfect discovery. How ravishing then will it be, to see the opening of all the
treasure hid in that field! They shall also be led into the understanding of the works of God. The beauty of the works of creation
and providence will then be set in due light. Natural knowledge
will be brought to perfection by the light of glory. The web of providence, concerning the church, and all men whatever, will then be
cut out, and laid before the eyes of the saints. And it will appear a
most beautiful mixture; so as they shall all say together, on the view
of it, "He hath done all things well" (cf. Mk. 7:37).

Celebrating forever our redemption. But, in a special manner, the work of redemption shall be the eternal wonder of the saints, and they will admire and praise the glorious contrivance forever. Then shall they get a full view of its suitableness to the divine perfections and to the case of sinners, and clearly read the covenant that passed between the Father and the Son from all eternity concerning their salvation. They shall forever wonder and praise, and praise and wonder, at the mystery of wisdom and love, goodness and holiness, mercy and justice appearing in the glorious scheme. Their souls shall be eternally satisfied with the sight of God Himself, of their election by the Father, their redemption by the Son, and application thereof to them by the Holy Spirit.

Partakers of the divine nature. The saints in heaven shall enjoy God in Christ by experiential knowledge, which is, when the object itself is given and possessed. This is the participation of the divine goodness in full measure; which is the perfection of the will, and utmost term thereof. "The Lamb which is in the midst of the throne shall feed them, and shall lead them unto living fountains of waters" (Rev. 7:17). These are no other but God Himself, "the fountain of living waters," who will fully and freely communicate Himself to them. He will pour out of His goodness eternally into their souls.

Then shall they have a most lively sensation, in the innermost part of their souls, of all that goodness they heard of, and believe to be in Him, and of what they shall see in Him by the light of glory. This will be an everlasting practical exposition of that word which men and angels cannot sufficiently unfold, namely, "He will dwell with them, and they shall be his people, and God himself shall be with them, and be their God" (Rev. 21:3).

God will communicate Himself to them fully. They will no more be set to taste of the streams of divine goodness in ordinances, as they were wont, but shall drink at the fountain head. They will be no more entertained with sips and drops, but filled with all the fullness of God. And this will be the entertainment of every saint.

For though, in created things, what is given to one is withheld from another, yet this infinite good can fully communicate itself to all, and fill all. Those who are heirs of God, the great heritage, shall then enter into a full possession of their inheritance. And the Lord will open His treasures of goodness to them, that their enjoyment may be full. They shall not be stinted in any measure, but the enjoyment shall go as far as their enlarged capacities can reach. As a narrow vessel cannot contain the ocean, so neither can the finite creature comprehend the infinite good.

But no measure shall be set to the enjoyment, but what ariseth from the capacity of the creature. So that, although there be degrees of glory, yet all shall be filled, and have what they can hold; though some will be able to hold more than others. There will be no want to any of them; all shall be fully satisfied, and perfectly blessed in the full enjoyment of divine goodness, according to their enlarged capacities. As when bottles of different sizes are filled, some contain more, others less; yet all of them have what they can contain. The glorified shall have all in God, for the satisfaction of all their desires.

No created thing can afford satisfaction to all our desires; clothes may warm us, but they cannot feed us; the light is comfortable, but cannot nourish us. But in God we shall have all our desires, and we shall desire nothing without Him. They shall be the happy ones, that desire nothing but what is truly desirable; they shall have all they desire. God will be all in all to the saints: He will be their life, health, riches, honor, peace, and all good things. He will communicate Himself freely to them. The door of access to Him shall never be shut again for one moment. They may, when they will, take of the fruits of the tree of life, for they will find it on each side of the river (Rev. 22:2). There will be no veil between God and them, to be drawn aside; but His fullness shall ever stand open to them. No door to knock at in heaven; no asking to go before receiving; the Lord will allow His people an unrestrained familiarity with Himself there.

Now they are in part made "partakers of the divine nature" (2 Pet. 1:4), but then they shall *perfectly* partake of it. That is to say, God will communicate to them His own image, make all His goodness not only pass before them, but pass into them, and stamp the image of all His own perfections upon them, so far as the creature is capable of receiving the same; from whence shall result a perfect likeness to Him in all things in or about them; which completes the happiness of the creature.

This is what the psalmist seems to have had in view: "I shall be satisfied, when I awake, with thy likeness" (Psa. 17:15). The perfection of God's image follows upon the beatific vision. And so says John: "We shall be like him; for we shall see him as he is" (1 Jn. 3.2). Hence there shall be a most close and intimate union between God and the saints. God shall be in them, and they in God, in a glorious and most perfect union: for then shall their dwelling in love be made perfect. "God is love; and he that dwelleth in love dwelleth in God, and God in him" (1 Jn. 4:16).

How will the saints be united to God and He to them, when He shall see nothing in them but His own image; when their love shall arrive at its perfection, no nature but the divine nature being left in them; and all imperfection being swallowed up in their glorious transformation into the likeness of God! Their love to the Lord, being purified from the dross of self-love, shall be most pure; so as they shall love nothing but God, and in God. It shall no more be faint and languishing, but burn like coals of juniper. It will be a light without darkness, a flaming fire without smoke. As the live coal, when all the moisture is gone out of it, is all fire, so will the saints be all love, when they come to the full enjoyment of God in heaven, by intuitive and experiential knowledge of Him, by sight and full participation of the divine goodness.

Fullness of joy. From this glorious presence and enjoyment shall arise an unspeakable joy, which the saints shall be filled with. "In thy presence is fulness of joy" (Ps. 16:11). The saints sometimes enjoy God in the world; but when their eyes are held, so as not to perceive it, they have not the comfort of the enjoyment. But then, all mistakes being removed, they shall not only enjoy God, but rest in the enjoyment with inexpressible delight and satisfaction. The desire of earthly things causes torment, and the enjoyment of them often ends in loathing. But though the glorified saints shall ever desire more and more of God, their desires shall not be mixed with the least anxiety, since the fullness of the Godhead stands always open to them. Therefore they shall hunger no more, they shall not have the least uneasiness in their eternal appetite after the hidden manna. Neither shall continued enjoyment cause loathing. They shall never think they have too much; therefore it is added, "Neither shall the sun light on them, nor any heat" (Rev. 7:16).

The enjoyment of God and the Lamb will be ever fresh and new to them, through the ages of eternity: for they shall drink of living fountains of waters, where new waters are continually springing up in abundance (v. 17). They shall eat of the tree of life, which, for variety, affords twelve manner of fruits, and these always new and fresh, for it yields every month (Rev. 22:2). Their joy shall be pure and unmixed, without any dregs of sorrow; not slight and momentary, but solid and everlasting, without interruption. They will enter into the joy of the Lord (Mt. 25:21).

The expression "enter into joy" is somewhat unusual, and brings to my recollection this word of our suffering Redeemer: "My soul is exceeding sorrowful unto death" (Mk. 14:34). His soul was beset with sorrows, as the word there used will bear; the floods of sorrow went round about Him, encompassing Him on every hand. Wherever He turned His eyes, sorrow was before Him; it flowed in upon Him from heaven, earth, and hell, all at once. Thus was He *entered into* sorrow, and therefore saith, "I am come into deep waters, where the floods overflow me" (Ps. 69:2).

Now, wherefore all this, but that His own might enter into joy? Joy sometimes enters into us now, but has much to do to get access, while we are encompassed with sorrows. But then joy shall not only enter into us, but we shall enter into it, and swim forever in an ocean of joy, where we shall see nothing but joy wherever we turn our eyes. The presence and enjoyment of God and the Lamb will satisfy us with pleasures for evermore. And the glory of our souls and bodies, arising from thence, will afford us everlasting delight. The spirit of heaviness, however closely it cleaves to any of the saints now, shall drop off then. Their weeping shall be turned into songs of joy, and bottles of tears shall issue in rivers of pleasure. Happy they who now sow in tears, which shall spring up in joy in heaven, and will encircle their heads with a weight of glory.

Perfect security. This kingdom will endure forever. Since everything in heaven is eternal, the saints shall have undoubted certainty, and full assurance, of its eternal duration. This is a necessary ingredient in perfect happiness; for the least uncertainty causes fear, anxiety, and torment—and therefore is utterly inconsistent with perfect happiness.

But the glorified shall never have fear, nor cause of fear. They shall be "ever with the Lord" (1 Thess. 4:17). They shall all attain the full persuasion, that nothing shall be able to separate them from the love of God, nor from the full enjoyment of Him forever. The inheritance reserved in heaven is incorruptible; it has no principle of corruption in itself, to make it liable to decay, but endures for evermore. It is undefiled; nothing from without can mar its beauty, nor is there any thing in itself to offend those who enjoy it. Therefore it fades not away; but ever remains in its native lustre, and primitive beauty (1 Pet. 1:4).

Entrance into the Kingdom

We now proceed to speak of the admission of the saints into this their new kingdom. Their admission, the text shows, is by a voice from the throne—the King calling to them, from the throne, before angels and men, to come to their kingdom. *Come* and *go* are but short words: but they will be such as will afford matter of thought to all mankind, through the ages of eternity; since everlasting happiness turns upon one, and everlasting misery on the other.

Come. Now our Lord bids the worst of sinners, who hear the Gospel, Come; but the most part will not come unto Him. Some few, whose hearts are touched by His Spirit, embrace the call, and their souls within them say, "Behold, we come unto Thee." They give themselves to the Lord, forsake the world and their lusts for Him. They bear His yoke, and cast it not off, no, not in the heat of the day when the weight of it, perhaps, makes them sweat the blood out of their bodies. "Behold the fools!" says the carnal world. "Where are they going?" But stay a little, oh foolish world! From the same mouth whence they had the call they are now following, another call shall come, that will make amends for all: "Come, ye blessed of my Father, inherit the kingdom prepared for you from the foundation of the world" (Mt. 25:34).

The saints shall find an inexpressible sweetness in this call, "Come." Hereby Jesus Christ shows His desire for their society in the upper house, that they may be ever with Him there. Thus He will open His heart to them, as sometimes He did to His Father concerning them, saying, "Father, I will that they also, whom thou hast given me, be with me where I am" (Jn. 17:24). Now the travail of His soul stands before the throne, not only the souls, but the bodies He has redeemed; and they *must* come, for He must be completely satisfied.

Hereby they are solemnly invited to the marriage supper of the Lamb. They were invited to the lower table by the voice of the servants, and the sacred workings of the Spirit within them; and they came, and did partake of the feast of divine communications in the lower house. But Jesus Christ in person shall invite them, before all the world, to the higher table.

By this He admits them into the mansions of glory. The keys

of heaven hang at the girdle of our royal Mediator. "All power . . . in heaven" is given to Him (Mt. 28:18). And none get in thither but whom He admits. When they were living on earth with the rest of the world, He opened the doors of their hearts, entered into them, and shut them again, so that sin could never re-enter, to reign there as formerly. Now He opens heaven's doors to them, draws His doves into the ark, and shuts them in; so that the law, death, and hell can never get them out again.

The saints in this life were still laboring to enter into that rest; but Satan was always pulling them back, their corruptions always drawing them down, insomuch that they have sometimes been left to hang by a hair of promise (if I may be allowed the expression) not without fear of falling into the lake of fire. But now Christ gives the word for their admission, they are brought in, and put beyond all hazard.

He speaks to them as the person introducing them into the kingdom, into the presence-chamber of the great King, and to the throne. Jesus Christ is the great Secretary of heaven, whose office it is to bring the saints into the gracious presence of God now, and to whom alone it belongs to bring them into the glorious presence of God in heaven. Truly heaven would be a strange place to them if Jesus were not there; but the Son will introduce His brethren into His Father's kingdom; they shall go in with Him to the Marriage (Mt. 25:10).

Ye blessed of my Father. Consider in what quality they are introduced by Him: "Come, ye blessed of my Father, inherit the kingdom prepared for you from the foundation of the world" (Mt. 25:34). It is Christ's Father's house they are to come into. Therefore He puts them in mind that they are blessed of the Father, dear to the Father, as well as Himself. This it is that makes heaven home to them, namely, that it is Christ's Father's house, where they may be assured of welcome, being married to the Son, and being His Father's choice for that very end.

He brings them in for His Father's sake, as well as for His own. They are the blessed of His Father; who, as He is the fountain of the Deity, is also the fountain of all blessings conferred on the children of men. They are those whom God loved from eternity. They were blessed in the eternal purpose of God, being elected to everlasting life. At the opening of the book of life, their names were found written therein: so that by bringing them to the kingdom, He does but bring them to what the Father, from all eternity, designed for them.

Being saved by the Son, they are saved according to His (that is, the Father's) purpose (2 Tim. 1:9). They are those to whom the Father has spoken well. He spoke well to them in His Word, which must now receive its full accomplishment. They had His promise of the kingdom, lived and died in the faith of it; and now they come to receive the thing promised. Unto them He has done well. A gift is often in Scripture called a blessing; and God's blessing is ever real, like Isaac's blessing, by which Jacob became his heir.

They were all by grace justified, sanctified, and enabled to persevere to the end; now they are raised up in glory, and being tried, stand in the judgment. What remains, then, but that God should crown His work of grace in them, in giving them their kingdom, in the full enjoyment of Himself forever?

Finally, they are those whom God has *consecrated;* which also is a Scripture term of blessing (1 Cor. 10:16). God set them apart for Himself, to be kings and priests unto Him; and the Mediator introduces them, as such, to their kingdom and priesthood.

Joint heirs with Christ. Christ introduces them, as heirs of the kingdom, to the actual possession of it. "Inherit the kingdom prepared for you from the foundation of the world." They are the children of God by regeneration and adoption. "And if children, then heirs; heirs of God, and joint-heirs with Christ" (Rom. 8.17).

Now is the general assembly of the firstborn before the throne. Their minority is overpast; and the time appointed of the Father for their receiving their inheritance is come. The Mediator purchased the inheritance for them with His own blood; their rights and evidences were drawn long ago, and registered in the Bible; nay, they have investment of their inheritance in the person of Christ, as their proxy, when He ascended into heaven, "Whither the forerunner is for us entered" (Heb. 6:20).

Nothing remains, but that they enter into personal possession thereof, which, begun at death, is perfected at the last day, when the saints in their bodies, as well as their souls, go into their kingdom.

The kingdom prepared for you. They are introduced to it as those it was prepared for, from the foundation of the world. The kingdom was prepared for them in the eternal purpose of God, before they, or any of them, had a being; which shows it to be a gift of free grace to them. It was from eternity the divine purpose that there should be such a kingdom for the elect; and that all impediments which might oppose their access to it should be removed out of the way. By the same eternal decree, everyone's place in it was determined and set apart, to be reserved for him, that each of the children coming home at length into their Father's house, might find his own place awaiting him, and ready for him, as at Saul's table David's place was empty when he was not there to occupy it himself (1 Sam. 20:25). And now the appointed time is come, they are brought in, to take their several places in glory.

USE

I shall conclude my discourse on this subject with a word of application.

To All Who Claim a Right to This Kingdom

Since it is evident there is no promiscuous admission into the kingdom of heaven, and none obtain it but those whose claim to it is solemnly tried by the great judge, and, after trial, supported as good and valid; it is necessary that all of us impartially try and examine whether, according to the laws of the kingdom contained in the Holy Scriptures, we can verify and make good our claim to this kingdom. The hopes of heaven which most men have, are built on such sandy foundations as can never abide the trial. Having no ground whatever but in their own deluded fancy, such hopes will leave those who entertain them miserably disappointed at last. Wherefore, it is not only our duty, but our interest, to put the matter to a fair trial in time.

If we find we have no right to heaven, we are yet in the way, and what we have not, we may obtain; but if we find we have a right to it, we shall then have the comfort of a happy prospect into eternity, which is the greatest comfort one is capable of in the world. If you inquire how you may know whether you have a right to heaven or not, I answer, you may know that by the state you are now in.

If you are yet in your natural state, you are children of wrath, and not children of this kingdom; for that state, to those who live and die in it, issues in eternal misery.

If you are brought into the state of grace, you have a just claim to the state of glory; for grace will certainly issue in glory at length. This kingdom is an inheritance which none but the children of God can justly claim. We become the children of God by regeneration, and union with Christ His Son; "And if children, then heirs; heirs of God, and joint-heirs with Christ" (Rom. 8:17). These, then, are the great points upon which our evidences for the state of glory depend. Therefore, I refer you to what is said on the state of grace, for satisfying you as to your right to glory.

If you be heirs of glory, "the kingdom of God is within you" (Lk. 17:21) by virtue of your regeneration and union with Christ. The kingdom of heaven has the throne in your heart, if you have a right to that kingdom. Christ is in you, and God is in you; and having chosen Him for your portion, your soul has taken up its everlasting rest in Him, and gets no true rest but in Him; as the dove, until she came into the ark. To Him the soul habitually inclines, by virtue of the new nature, the divine nature, which the heirs of glory are partakers of. "Whom have I in heaven but thee? and there is none upon earth that I desire beside thee" (Ps. 73:25).

The laws of heaven are in your heart, if you are an heir of heaven: "I will put my laws into their mind, and write them in their hearts: and I will be to them a God, and they shall be to me a people" (Heb. 8:10). Your mind is enlightened in the knowledge of the laws of the kingdom by the Spirit of the Lord, the instructor of all the heirs of glory; for whoever may lack instruction, surely a true heir to a crown shall not lack it. "It is written in the prophets, And they shall be all taught of God" (Jn. 6:45). Therefore, though father and mother leave them early, or be in no concern about their Christian education, and they be soon put to work for their daily bread, yet they shall not lack teaching.

Your heart is changed, and you bear God's image, which consists in "righteousness and true holiness" (Eph. 4:24). Your soul is reconciled to the whole law of God, and at war with all known sin. In vain do they pretend to the holy kingdom, who are not holy in heart and life; for "without [holiness] no man shall see the Lord" (Heb. 12:14).

If heaven is a rest, it is for spiritual laborers, not for loiterers. If it is an eternal triumph, they are not in the way to it who avoid the spiritual warfare, and are in no care to subdue corruption, resist temptation, and to cut their way to it through the opposition made by the devil, the world, and the flesh.

The treasure in heaven is the chief in your esteem and desire; for it is your treasure, and "For where your treasure is, there will your heart be also" (Mt. 6:21). If it is not the things that are seen, but the things that are not seen, which your heart is in the greatest care and concern to obtain; if you are driving a trade with heaven, and your chief business lies there; it is a sign that your treasure is there, for your heart is there. But if you are of those who wonder why so much ado is made about heaven and eternal life, as if less might serve the turn, you are like to have nothing to do with it at all. Carnal men value themselves most on their treasures upon earth; with them, the things that are not seen are weighed down by the things that are seen, and no losses so much affect them as earthly losses. But the heirs of the crown of glory value themselves most on their treasures in heaven, and will not put their private estate in the balance with their kingdom; nor will the loss of the former go so near their hearts as the thoughts of the loss of the latter.

Where these first-fruits of heaven are to be found, the eternal weight of glory will surely follow after; while the want of them must be admitted according to the Word, to be an incontestible evidence of an heir of wrath.

To Those Who Have Indeed a Right To It

Let the heirs of the kingdom behave themselves suitably to their character and dignity. Live as having the faith and hope of this glorious kingdom: let your conversation be in heaven (Phil. 3:20).

Let your souls delight in communion with God while you are on earth, since you look for your happiness in communion with Him in heaven. Let your speech and actions savor of heaven; and in your manner of life, look like the country to which you are going—so that it may be said of you, as of Gideon's brethren "each one resembled the children of a king" (Judg. 8:18).

Maintain a holy contempt of the world, and of the things of the world. Although others, whose earthly things are their best things, set their hearts upon them, yet it becomes you to set your *feet* on them, since your best things are above. This world is but the country through which lies your road to Immanuel's land. Therefore pass through it as pilgrims and strangers; and dip not into the encumbrances of it, so as to retard you in your journey. It is unworthy of one born to a palace, to set his heart on a cottage to dwell there—and of one running for a prize of gold, to go off his way to gather the stones of the brook. But much more it is unworthy of an heir of the kingdom of heaven to be hid among the stuff of this world, when he should be going on to receive his crown.

The prize set before you challenges your utmost zeal, activity, and diligence. Holy courage, resolution, and magnanimity become those who are to inherit the crown. You cannot come at it without fighting your way to it, through difficulties from without and from within: but the kingdom before you is sufficient to balance them all, though you should be called to resist even unto blood. Prefer Christ's cross before the world's crown, and wants in the way of duty, before ease and wealth in the way of sin. Choose rather to suffer affliction with the people of God, than to enjoy the pleasures of sin for a season (Heb. 11:25).

In a common inn, strangers perhaps fare better than the children; but here lies the difference: the children are to pay nothing for what they have got; but the strangers get their bill, and must pay completely for all they have had. Did we consider the after-reckoning of the wicked for all the smiles of common providence they meet with in the world, we should not grudge them their good things here, nor take it amiss that God keeps our best things last. Heaven will make up all the saints' losses, and there all tears will be wiped away from their eyes.

It is worth observing, that there is such a variety of Scripture notions of heaven's happiness, as may suit every afflicted case of the saints. Are they oppressed? The day cometh in which they shall have the dominion. Is their honor laid in the dust? A throne to sit upon, a crown on their head, and a scepter in their hand, will raise it up again. Are they reduced to poverty? Heaven is a treasure. If they be forced to quit their own habitations, yet Christ's Father's house is ready for them. Are they driven to the wilderness? There is a city prepared for them. Are they banished from their native country? They shall inherit a better country. If they are deprived of public ordinances, the Lord God Almighty and the Lamb are the temple there, whither they are going; a temple, the doors of which none can shut. If their life be full of bitterness, heaven is a paradise for pleasure. If they groan under the remains of spiritual bondage, there is glorious liberty abiding them. Do their defiled garments make them ashamed? The day is coming in which their robes shall be white, pure, and spotless. The battle against flesh and blood, principalities and powers, is indeed sore: but a glorious triumph awaits them. If the toil and labors of the Christian life be great, there is an everlasting rest for them in heaven. Are they judged unworthy of the society of angels in heaven? Do they complain of frequent interruptions of their communion with God? There they shall go no more out, but shall see His face for evermore. If they are in darkness here, eternal light is there. If they grapple with death, there they shall have everlasting life.

And, to sum up all in one word, "He that overcometh shall inherit all things" (Rev. 21:7). He shall have peace and plenty, profit and pleasure, everything desirable; full satisfaction of his most enlarged desires. Let the expectants of heaven, then, lift up their heads with joy; let them gird up their loins, and so run that they may obtain, trampling on everything that may hinder them in their way to the kingdom. Let them never account any duty too hard, nor any cross too heavy, nor any pains too great, so that they may attain the crown of glory.

To Those Who Have No Right Thereto

Let those who have no right to the kingdom of heaven be stirred up to seek it with all diligence. Now is the time wherein the children of wrath may become heirs of glory.

When the way to everlasting happiness is opened, it is no time to sit still and loiter. Raise up your hearts toward the glory that is to be revealed; and be not always in search of rest in this perishing earth. What can all your worldly enjoyments avail you, while you have no solid ground to expect heaven after this life is gone? The riches and honors, profits and pleasures, that must be buried with us, and cannot accompany us into another world, are but a wretched portion, and will leave men comfortless at length. Ah! why are men so eager in their lifetime to receive their good things? Why are they not rather careful to secure an interest in the kingdom of heaven, which would never be taken from them but afford them a portion to make them happy through the ages of eternity?

If you desire honor, there you may have the highest honor, which will last when the world's honors are laid in the dust; if riches, heaven will yield you a treasure; and there are pleasures for evermore. Oh, be not despisers of the pleasant land, neither judge yourselves unworthy of eternal life; close with Christ, as He is offered to you in the Gospel, and you shall inherit all things. Walk in the way of holiness, and it will lead you to the kingdom. Fight against sin and Satan, and you shall receive the crown. Forsake the world, and the doors of heaven will be opened to receive you.

THE SYMPATHY OF THE TWO WORLDS

A SERMON
BY CHARLES H. SPURGEON

There is joy in the presence of the angels of God over one sinner that repenteth.

—*Luke 15:10*

Man's heart is never big enough to hold either its joys or its sorrows. You never heard of a man whose heart was exactly full of sorrow, for no sooner is it full than it overflows. The first prompting of the soul is to tell its sorrow to another. The reason is that our hearts are not large enough to hold our grief; we need to have another heart to receive a portion thereof. It is even so with our joy. When the heart is full of joy, it always allows its joy to escape. It is like the fountain in the marketplace; whenever it is full, it runs away in streams, and so soon as it ceases to overflow, you may be quite sure that it has ceased to be full. The only full heart is the overflowing heart.

You know this, beloved, you have proved it to be true, for when your soul has been full of joy, you have first called together your own kindred and friends, and you have communicated to them the cause of your gladness. And when those vessels have been full even to the brim, you have been like the woman who borrowed empty vessels of her neighbors, for you have asked each of them to become partakers in your joy, and when the hearts of all your neighbors have been full, you have felt as if they were not large enough, and the whole world has been called upon to join in your praise. You bade the fathomless ocean drink in your joy; you spoke to the trees and bade them clap their hands while the mountains and hills were invoked by you to break forth into singing; the very stars of heaven seemed to look down upon you, and you bade them sing for you, and all the world was full of music through the music that was in your heart.

And, after all, what is man but the great musician of the world? The universe is a great organ with mighty pipes. Space, time, eternity are like the throats of this great organ, and man, a little creature, puts his fingers on the keys and wakes the universe to thunders of harmony, stirring up the whole creation to mightiest acclamations of praise. Know you not that man is God's high priest in the universe? All things else are the sacrifice, but he is the priest—carrying in his heart the fire and in his hand the wood and in his mouth the two-edged sword of dedication with which he offers up all things to God.

But I have no doubt, beloved, the thought has sometimes struck us that our praise does not go far enough. We seem as if we dwelt in an isle cut off from the mainland. This world, like a fair planet, swims in a sea of ether unnavigated by mortal ship. We have sometimes thought that surely our praise was confined to the shores of this poor, narrow world, that it was impossible for us to pull the ropes that might ring the bells of heaven, that we could by no means whatever reach our hands so high as to sweep the celestial chords of angelic harps.

We have said to ourselves there is no connection between earth and heaven. A huge black wall divides us. A strait of unnavigable waters shuts us out. Our prayers cannot reach to heaven, neither can our praises affect the celestials.

Let us learn from our text how mistaken we are. We are, after all, however much we seem to be shut out from heaven and from the great universe, but a province of God's vast, united empire, and what is done on earth is known in heaven, what is sung on earth is sung in heaven, and there is a sense in which it is true that the tears of earth are wept again in paradise, and the sorrows of mankind are felt again, even on the throne of the Most High.

My text tells us, "There is joy in the presence of the angels of God over one sinner that repenteth." It seems as if it showed me a bridge by which I might cross over into eternity. It does, as it were, exhibit to me certain magnetic wires that convey the intelligence of what is done here to spirits in another world. It teaches me that there is a real and wonderful connection between this lower world and that which is beyond the skies where God dwells in the land of the happy.

We shall talk about that subject a little this morning. My first head will be *the sympathy of the world above with the world below;* the second, *the judgment of the angels*—they rejoice over repenting sinners; we shall see what is their ground for so doing. The third will be *a lesson for the saints; if* the angels in heaven rejoice over repenting sinners, so should we.

THE SYMPATHY OF THE TWO WORLDS

Imagine not, oh son of man, that you are cut off from heaven, for there is a ladder, the top whereof does rest at the foot of the throne of the Almighty, the base whereof is fixed in the lowest place of man's misery!

Conceive not that there is a great gulf fixed between you and the Father across which His mercy cannot come and over which your prayers and faith can never leap. Oh, think not, son of man, that you dwell in a storm-girt island cut off from the continent of eternity. I beseech you, believe that there is a bridge across that chasm, a road along which feet may travel.

This world is not separated, for all creation is but one body. And know then, oh son of man, though you in this world do but dwell as it were on the foot, yet from the feet even to the head there are nerves and veins that do unite the whole. The same great heart that beats in heaven beats on earth. The love of the Eternal Father that cheers the celestial makes glad the terrestrial too. Rest assured that though the glory of the celestial is one and the glory of the terrestrial is another, yet are they but another in appearance, for after all, they are the same.

Oh! listen, son of man, and you will soon learn that you are no stranger in a strange land—a houseless Joseph in the land of Egypt, shut out from his father and his brothers, who still remain in the happy paradise of Canaan. No, your Father loves you still. There is a connection between you and Him. Strange that though leagues of distance lie between the finite creature and the infinite Creator, yet there are links that unite us!

When a tear is wept by you, think not your Father does not behold, for, "Like as a father pitieth his children, so the Lord pitieth them that fear him." Your sigh is able to move the heart of Jehovah, your whisper can incline His ear to you, your prayer can stay His hands, your faith can move His arm. Oh! think not that God sits on high in an eternal slumber, taking no account of you.

"Can a woman forget her sucking child, that she should not have compassion on the soil of her womb? yea, they may forget, yet will I not forget thee." Engraven upon the Father's hand your name remains, and on His heart recorded there your person stands. He thought of you before the worlds were made; before the channels of the sea were scooped or the gigantic mountains lifted their heads in the white clouds, He thought of you. He thinks on you still. "I the Lord do keep it; I will water it every moment: lest any hurt it, I will keep it night and day." For the eyes of the Lord run to and fro in every place, to show Himself strong on the behalf of all them that fear Him. You are not cut off from Him. You do move in Him: in Him you do live and have your being. He is a very present help in time of trouble.

Remember, oh heir of immortality, that you are not only linked to the Godhead, but there is another One in heaven with whom you have a strange yet near connection. In the center of the throne sits One who is your Brother, allied to you by blood. *The Son of God,* eternal, equal with His Father, became in the fullness of time the son of Mary, an infant of a span long. He was, yes is, bone of your bone and flesh of your flesh. Think not that you are cut off from the celestial world while He is there, for is He not your head, and has He not Himself declared that you are a member of His body, of His flesh, and of His bones? Oh, man, you are not separated from heaven while Jesus tells you—

> *I feel at my heart all thy sighs and thy groans,*
> *For thou art most near me, my flesh and my bones,*
> *In all thy distresses, thy Head feels the pain,*
> *They all are most needful, not one is in vain.*

> *Oh, poor, disconsolate mourner,*
> *Christ remembers you every hour*
> *Your sighs are His sighs, your groans are His groans,*
> *your prayers are His prayers.*
> *He in his measure feels afresh,*
> *What every member bears.*

Crucified He is when you are crucified; He dies when you die, you live in Him, and He lives in you, and because He lives shall you live also; you shall rise in Him, and you shall sit together in the heavenly places with Him. Oh, never was husband nearer to his wife and never head nearer to the members and never soul nearer to the body of this flesh than Christ is to you, and while it is so, think not that heaven and earth are divided.

They are but kindred worlds, two ships moored close to one another; one short plank of death will enable you to step from one into the other; this ship, all black and coaly, having done the coast-

ing trade, the dusty business of today, and being full of the black-
ness of sorrow; that ship all golden, with its painted pennon flying
and its sail all spread, white as the down of the seabird, fair as the
angel's wing. I tell you, man, the ship of heaven is moored side-
by-side with the ship of earth, and rock though this ship may and
careen though she will on stormy winds and tempests, yet the
invisible and golden ship of heaven sails by her side never sun-
dered, never divided, always ready in order that when the hour
shall come, you may leap from the black, dark ship and step upon
the golden deck of that thrice happy one in which you shall sail
forever.

But, oh man of God, there are other golden links besides this
that bind the present to the future and time to eternity. And what
are time and eternity, after all, to the believer, but like Siamese
twins, never to be separated? This earth is heaven below, the next
world is but a heaven above; it is the same house—this is the lower
room and that the upper, but the same roof covers both, and the
same dew falls upon each. Remember, beloved, that *the spirits of the
just made perfect* are never far from you and me if we are lovers of
Jesus. All those who have passed the flood wait expectantly for full
communion with us. Do we not sing—

> *The saints on earth, and all the dead,*
> *But one communion make;*
> *All join in Christ, the living Head,*
> *And of his grace partake.*

We have but one Head for the church triumphant and for the
church militant:

> *One army of the living God,*
> *To his command we bow;*
> *Part of the host have cross'd the flood,*
> *And part are crossing now.*

The saints of the living God, I doubt not, still remember us, still look for us, for this is ever upon their hearts—the truth that they without us cannot be made perfect. They cannot be a perfect church until we are gathered in, and therefore do they long for our appearing.

But to come to our text a little more minutely, it assures us that the angels have communion with us. Bright spirits, firstborn sons of God, do you think of me? Oh, cherubim great and mighty, seraphim burning, winged with lightning, do you think of us? Gigantic is your stature. Our poet tells us that the wand of an angel might make a mast for some tall admiral, and doubtless he was right when he said so. Those angels of God are creatures mighty and strong, doing His commandments, hearkening to His word—and do they take notice of us?

Let the Scripture answer: "Are they not all ministering spirits, sent forth to minister for them who shall be heirs of salvation?" "The angel of the Lord encampeth round about them that fear him." "For he shall give his angels charge over thee, to keep thee in all thy ways. They shall bear thee up in their hands, lest thou dash thy foot against a stone." Yes, the brightest angels are but the serving men of the saints; they are our lackeys and our footmen. They wait upon us, they are the troops of our bodyguard, and we might, if our eyes were opened, see what Elisha saw, horses of fire and chariots of fire round about us, so that we should joyously say, "They that be with us are more than they that be with them."

Our text tells us that the angels of God rejoice over repenting sinners. How is that? They are always as happy as they can be; how can they be any happier? The text does not say that they are any happier, but perhaps that they show their happiness more.

"A merry heart hath a continual feast"; but then even the merry heart has some special days on which it feasts well. To the glorified every day is a Sabbath, but of some it can be said, "That sabbath day was a high day." There are days when the angels sing more loudly than usual; they are always harping well God's praise, but some-times the gathering hosts who have been flitting far through the universe come home to their center, and around the throne of God, standing in serried ranks, marshaled not for battle but for music, on certain set and appointed days they chant the praise of the Son of God, who loved us and gave himself for us.

And do you ask me when those days occur? I tell you, the birth-day of every Christian is a sonnet day in heaven. There are Christmas days in paradise, where Christ's high mass is kept, and Christ is glorified not because He was born in a manger but because He is born in a broken heart. There are days—good days in heaven, days of sonnet, red letter days of overflowing adoration. And these are days when the shepherd brings home the lost sheep upon His shoulder, when the church has swept her house and found the lost piece of money, for then are these friends and neighbors called together, and they rejoice with joy unspeakable and full of glory over one sinner that repents.

I have thus, I hope, shown you that there is a greater connec-tion between earth and heaven than any of us dreamed. And now let none of us think, when we look upward to the blue sky, that we are far from heaven; it is a very little distance from us. When the day comes, we shall go posthaste there, even without horses and chariots of fire. Balaam called it a land that is very far off; we know better—it is a land that is very near. Even now,

> By faith we join our hands
> With those that went before,
> And greet the blood-besprinkled bands
> Upon the eternal shore.

All hail, bright spirits! I see you now. All hail, angels! All hail, you brethren redeemed! A few more hours or days or months and we shall join your happy throng; until then your joyous fellowship, your sweet compassion shall ever be our comfort and our consolation—and having weathered all storms of life, we shall at last anchor with you within the port of everlasting peace.

THE JUDGMENT OF THE ANGELS

Why do angels rejoice over penitent sinners? In the first place, I think it is because they remember the days of creation. You know, when God made this world and fixed the beams of the heavens in sockets of light, the morning stars sang together, and the sons of God shouted for joy; as they saw star after star flying abroad like sparks from the great anvil of Omnipotence, they began to sing; every time they saw a new creature made upon this little earth, they praised afresh. When first they saw light, they clapped their hands and said, "Great is Jehovah; for He said 'Light be!' and light was." And when they saw sun and moon and stars, again they clapped their hands, and they said, He has "made great lights: for his mercy endureth forever: The sun to rule by day: for his mercy endureth forever: The moon to rule by night: for his mercy endureth forever." And over everything He made, they chanted evermore that sweet song, "Creator, You are to be magnified, for Your mercy endureth forever."

Now, when they see a sinner returning, they see the creation over again, for repentance is a new creation. No man ever repents until God makes in him a new heart and a right spirit. I do not know that ever since the day when God made the world, with the exception of new hearts, the angels have seen God make anything else. He may, if He has so pleased, have made fresh worlds since that time. But perhaps the only instance of new creation they have ever seen since the first day is the creation of a new heart and a right spirit within the breast of a poor penitent sinner. Therefore do they rejoice because creation comes over again.

I doubt not, too, that they celebrate because they behold God's works afresh shining in excellence. When God first made the world, He said of it, "It is very good"—He could not say so now. There are many of you that God could not say that of. He would have to say the very reverse. He would have to say, "No, that is very bad, for the trail of the serpent has swept away your beauty, that moral excellence which once dwelt in manhood has passed away"; but when the sweet influences of the Spirit bring men to repentance and faith again, God looks upon man, and He says, "It is very good." For what His Spirit makes is like Himself—good and holy and precious, and God smiles again over His twice-made creation and says once more, "It is very good." Then the angels begin again and praise His name whose works are always good and full of beauty.

But, beloved, the angels exult over sinners that repent because they know what that poor sinner has escaped. You and I can never imagine all the depths of hell. Shut out from us by a black veil of darkness, we cannot tell the horrors of that dismal dungeon of lost souls. Happily, the wailings of the damned have never startled us, for a thousand tempests were but a maiden's whisper compared with one wail of a damned spirit. It is not possible for us to see the tortures of those souls who dwell eternally within an anguish that knows no alleviation. These eyes would become sightless balls of darkness if they were permitted for an instant to look into that ghastly shrine of torment. Hell is horrible, for we may say of it, eye has not seen, nor ear heard, neither has it entered into the heart of man to conceive the horrors that God has prepared for them that hate Him.

But the angels know better than you or I could guess. They know it; not that they have felt it, but they remember that day when Satan and his angels rebelled against God. They remember the day when the third part of the stars of heaven revolted against their liege Lord, and they have not forgotten how the red right hand of Jehovah Jesus was wrapped in thunder. They do not forget that breach in the battlements of heaven when, down from the greatest heights to the lowest depths, Lucifer and his hosts were hurled. They have never forgotten how with sound of trumpet they pursued the flying foe down to the gulfs of black despair; and, as they neared that place where the great serpent is to be bound in chains, they remember how they saw Tophet, which was prepared of old. And they recollect how, when they winged back their flight, every tongue was silent, although they might well have shouted the praise of Him who conquered Lucifer, but on them all there did sit a solemn awe of one who could smite a cherub and cast him into hopeless bonds of everlasting despair.

They knew what hell was, for they had looked within its jaws and had seen their own brothers fast enclosed within them; therefore, when they see a sinner saved they rejoice because there is one less to be food for the never-dying worm—one more soul escaped out of the mouth of the lion.

There is yet a better reason. The angels know what the joys of heaven are, and therefore, they rejoice over one sinner that repents. We talk about pearly gates and golden streets and white robes and harps of gold and crowns of amaranth and all that; but if an angel could speak to us of heaven, he would smile and say, "All those fine things are but child's talk, and you are little children, and you cannot understand the greatness of eternal bliss, and therefore God has given you a child's hornbook and an alphabet in which you may learn the first rough letters of what heaven is, but what it is you do not know.

"Oh mortal, your eye has never yet beheld its splendors, your ear has never yet been ravished with its melodies, your heart has never been transported with its peerless joys." You may talk and think and guess and dream, but you must never measure the infinite heaven that God has provided for His children. And therefore it is when they see a soul saved and a sinner repenting that they clap their hands, for they know that all those blessed mansions are theirs, since all those sweet places of everlasting happiness are the entail of every sinner that repents.

But I want you just to read the text again, while I dwell upon another thought. There is joy in the presence of the angels of God over one sinner *that repenteth*. Now, why do they not save their joy until that sinner dies and goes to heaven? Why do they rejoice over him when he repents?

My Arminian friend, I think, ought to go to heaven to set them right upon this matter. According to his theory, it must be very wrong of them because they rejoice prematurely. According to the Arminian doctrine, a man may repent, and yet he may be lost; he may have grace to repent and believe, and yet he may fall from grace and be a castaway. Now, angels, don't be too fast. Perhaps you may have to repent of this one day if the Arminian doctrine is true; I would advise you to save your song for greater joys. Why, angels, perhaps the men that you are singing over today you will have to mourn over tomorrow.

I am quite sure that Arminius never taught his doctrine in heaven. I do not know whether he is there—I hope he is, but he is no longer an Arminian. But if he ever taught his doctrine there, he would be put out. The reason why angels rejoice is because they know that when a sinner repents, he is absolutely saved—or else they would rejoice prematurely and would have good cause for retracting their merriment on some future occasion. But the angels know what Christ meant when He said, "I give unto them eternal life, and they shall never perish, neither shall any man pluck them out of my hand"; therefore they rejoice over repenting sinners because they know they are saved.

There is yet one more fact I will mention before I leave this point. It is said that the angels rejoice over *one* sinner that repenteth. Now this evening it shall be my happy privilege to give the right hand of fellowship to no less than forty-eight sinners that have repented, and there will be great joy and rejoicing in our churches tonight because these forty-eight have been immersed on a profession of their faith. But how loving are the angels to men, for they rejoice over *one* sinner that repents.

There she is in that garret where the stars look between the tiles. There is a miserable bed in that room with but one bit of covering, and she lies there to die! Poor creature! many a night she has walked the streets in the time of her merriment, but now her joys are over; a foul disease, like a demon, is devouring her heart! She is dying fast, and no one cares for her soul! But there in that chamber she turns her face to the wall, and she cries, "O Thou that saved Magdalene, save me; Lord, I repent, have mercy upon me, I beseech You."

Did the bells ring in the street? Was the trumpet blown? Ah! no. Did men rejoice? Was there a sound of thanksgiving in the midst of the great congregation? No, no one heard it, for she died unseen. But stay! There was one standing at her bedside who noted well that tear—an angel who had come down from heaven to watch over this stray sheep and mark its return, and no sooner was her prayer uttered than he clapped his wings, and there was seen flying up to the pearly gates a spirit like a star.

The heavenly guards came crowding to the gate, crying, "What news, oh son of fire?"

He said, "'Tis done."

"And what is done?" they said.

"Why, she has repented."

"What! she who was once a chief of sinners? Has she turned to Christ?"

"'Tis even so," said he.

And then they told it through the streets, and the bells of heaven rang marriage peals, for Magdalene was saved, and she who had been the chief of sinners was turned to the living God.

It was in another place. A poor neglected little boy in ragged clothing had run about the streets for many days. Tutored in crime, he was paving his path to the gallows. But one morning he passed by a humble room where some men and women were sitting together teaching poor ragged children. He stopped in there, a wild Bedouin of the streets; they talked to him; they told him about a soul and about an eternity—things he had never heard before; they spoke of Jesus and of good tidings of great joy to this poor friend-less lad. He went another Sabbath and another, his wild habits hanging about him, for he could not got rid of them.

At last it happened that his teacher said to him one day, "Jesus Christ receives sinners." That little boy ran, but not home, for it was but a mockery to call it so—where a drunken father and a las-civious mother kept a hellish riot together. He ran, and under some dry arch or in some wild unfrequented corner he bent his little knees, and there he cried, that poor creature in his rags, "Lord, save me, or I perish"; and the little urchin was on his knees—the little thief was saved! He said, "Jesus, lover of my soul, let me to your bosom fly."

And up from that old arch, from that forsaken hovel, there flew a spirit glad to bear the news to heaven that another heir of glory was born to God.

I might picture many such scenes, but will each of you try to picture your own? You remember the occasion when the Lord met with you. Ah! little did you think what a commotion there was in heaven! If the queen had ordered out all her soldiers, the angels of heaven would not have stopped to notice them, if all the princes of earth had marched in pageant through the streets, with all their robes and jewelry and crowns and all their regalia and their chari-ots and their horsemen—if the pomps of ancient monarchies had risen from the tomb—if all the might of Babylon and Tyre and Greece had been concentrated into one great parade—yet not an angel would have stopped in his course to smile at those poor tawdry things.

But over you, the vilest of the vile, the poorest of the poor, the most obscure and unknown—over you angelic wings were hovering, and concerning you it was said on earth and shouted aloud in heaven, "Hallelujah, for a child is born to God today."

A LESSON TO THE SAINTS

I think, beloved, the lesson will not be hard for you to learn. The angels of heaven rejoice over sinners who repent. Saints of God, will not you and I do the same? I do not think the church rejoices enough. We all grumble enough and groan enough, but very few of us rejoice enough. When we take a large number into the church, it is spoken of as a great mercy, but is the greatness of that mercy appreciated?

I will tell you who they are that can most appreciate the conversion of sinners. They are those that are just converted themselves or those that have been great sinners themselves. Those who have been saved themselves from bondage, when they see others coming who have so lately worn the chains, are so glad that they can well take the tabret and the harp and the pipe and the psaltery and praise God that there are other prisoners who have been emancipated by grace.

But there are others who can do this better still, and they are the parents and relations of those who are saved. You have thanked God many times when you have seen a sinner saved, but mother, did not you thank Him most when you saw your son converted? Oh! those holy tears, they are not tears—they are God's diamonds—the tears of a mother's joy when her son confesses his faith in Jesus. Oh! that glad countenance of the wife when she sees her husband, long bestial and drunken, at last made into a man and a Christian! Oh! that look of joy that a young Christian gives when he sees his father converted, who had long oppressed and persecuted him.

I was preaching this week for a young minister, and being anxious to know his character, I spoke of him with apparent coolness to an estimable lady of his congregation.

In a very few moments she began to warm in his favor. She said, "You must not say anything against him. Sir; if you do, it is because you do not know him."

"Oh," I said, "I knew him long before you did: he is not much, is he?"

"Well," she said, "I must speak well of him, for he has been a blessing to my servants and family."

I went out into the street and saw some men and women standing about, so I said to them, "I must take your minister away."

"If you do," they said, "we will follow you all over the world, if you take away a man who has done so much good to our souls."

After collecting the testimony of fifteen or sixteen witnesses, I said, "If the man gets such witnesses as these, let him go on; the Lord has opened his mouth, and the devil will never be able to shut it."

These are the witnesses we want—men who can rejoice with the angels because their own households are converted to God. I hope it may be so with all of you. If any of you are yourselves brought to Christ today—for He is willing to receive you—you will go out of this place singing, and the angels will sing with you. There shall be joy in earth and joy in heaven—on earth peace, and glory to God in the highest. The Lord bless you one and all, for Jesus' sake.

HOME AT LAST!

A SERMON BY J.C. RYLE

There shall in no wise enter into it any thing that defileth, neither whatsoever worketh abomination, or maketh a lie: but they which are written in the Lamb's book of life.

—Rev. 21:27

Brethren, there can be no question about the place described in our text: it is heaven itself, that holy city, the new Jerusalem, which is yet to be revealed.

I begin this my last Sunday among you by speaking of heaven. Before I depart and leave you in the wilderness of this world, I would dwell a little on that Canaan God has promised to them that love Him; *there* it is the last and best wish of my heart you may all go; *there* it is my consolation to believe I shall at all events meet some of you again.

Brethren, you all hope to go to heaven yourselves. There is not one of you but wishes to be in happiness after death. But on what are your hopes founded? Heaven is a prepared place; they that shall dwell there are all of one character. The entrance into it is only by one door. Brethren, remember that.

And then, too, I read of two sorts of hope: a good hope and a bad hope; a true hope and a false hope; a lively hope and a dead hope; the hope of the righteous and the hope of the wicked, of the believer and of the hypocrite. I read of some who have hope through grace, a hope that maketh not ashamed, and of others who have no hope and are without God in the world. Brethren, remember that.

Surely it were wise and prudent and safe to find out what the Bible tells you on the subject, to discover whether your confidence is indeed well founded; and to this end I call your attention to the doctrine of my text.

The Lord grant you may consider well your own fitness for heaven. There must be a certain meetness for that blessed place in our minds and characters. It is senseless, vain, and absurd to suppose that all shall go there, whatever their lives have been. May God the Holy Ghost incline you to examine yourselves faithfully while you have time, before that great day cometh when the unconverted shall be past all hope and the saints past all fear.

THE PLACE ITSELF

There is such a place as heaven. No truth is more certain in the whole of Scripture than this: "There remaineth . . . a rest to the people of God" (Heb. 4:9). This earth is not our rest; it cannot be; there breathes not man or woman who ever found it so.

Go, build your happiness on earth, if you are so disposed; choose everything you can fancy would make life enjoyable. Take money, house, and lands; take learning, health, and beauty; take honor, rank, obedience, troops of friends; take everything your mind can picture to itself or your eye desire. Take all, and yet I dare to tell you even then you would not find rest. I know well that a few short years, and your heart's confession would be, it is all hollow, empty, and unsatisfying; it is all weariness and disappointment; it is all vanity and vexation of spirit. I know well you would feel within a hungering and famine, a leanness and barrenness of soul; and ready indeed would you be to bear your testimony to the mighty truth: This earth is not our rest.

Oh, brethren, how faithful is that saying, "If in this life only we have hope in Christ, we are of all men most miserable" (1 Cor. 15:19). This life, so full of trouble and sorrow and care, of anxiety and labor and toil; this life of losses and bereavements, of partings and separations, of mourning and woe, of sickness and pain; this life of which even Elijah got so tired that he requested he might die; truly I should be crushed to the very earth with misery, if I felt this life were all. If I thought there was nothing for me beyond the dark, cold, silent, lonely grave, I should indeed say it would be better never to have been born.

Thanks be to God this life is not all. I know and am persuaded there is a glorious rest beyond the tomb; this earth is only the training-school for eternity, these graves are but the stepping-stone and half-way house to heaven. I feel assured this my poor body shall rise again; this corruptible shall yet put on incorruption, and this mortal immortality, and be with Christ forever. Yes, heaven is truth and no lie. I will not doubt it. I am not more certain of my own existence than I am of this: There does remain a rest for the people of God.

And, brethren, what sort of a place shall heaven be? Before we pass on and consider its inhabitants, let us just pause an instant and think on this. What sort of a place shall heaven be? Heaven shall be a place of perfect rest and peace. They who dwell there have no more conflict with the world, the flesh, and the devil; their warfare is accomplished, and their fight is fought; at length they may lay aside the armor of God, at last they may say to the sword of the Spirit, Rest and be still.

They watch no longer, for they have no spiritual enemies to fear; they fast and mortify the flesh no longer, for they have no vile earthy body to keep under; they pray no more, for they have no evil to pray against. There the wicked must cease from troubling; there sin and temptation are forever shut out; the gates are better barred than those of Eden, and the devil shall enter in no more. Oh,

Christian brethren, rouse ye and take comfort; surely this shall be indeed a blessed rest.

There faith shall be swallowed up in sight, and hope in certainty, and prayer in praise, and sorrow in joy. Now is the school-time, the season of the lesson and the rod, then will be the eternal holiday. Now we must endure hardness and press on faint yet pursuing.

Then we shall sit down at ease, for the Canaanite shall be expelled forever from the land. Now we are tossed upon a stormy sea, then we shall be safe in harbor. Now we have to plough and sow, then we shall reap the harvest; now we have the labor, but then the wages; now we have the battle, but then the victory and reward. Now we must needs bear the cross, but then we shall receive the crown. Now we are journeying through the wilderness, but then we shall be at home.

Oh, Christian brethren, well may the Bible tell you, "Blessed are the dead which die in the Lord" (Rev. 14:13). Surely you must feel that witness is true.

But again. Heaven shall be a place of perfect and unbroken happiness. Mark what your Bible tells you in the very chapter which contains my text, "And God shall wipe away all tears from their eyes; and there shall be no more death, neither sorrow, nor crying, neither shall there be any more pain: for the former things are passed away" (Rev. 21:4). Hear what the prophet Isaiah says:

> *He will swallow up death in victory; and the Lord God will wipe away tears from off all faces; and the rebuke of his people shall he take away from off all the earth: for the Lord hath spoken it. And it shall be said in that day, Lo, this is our God; we have waited for him, and he will save us: this is the Lord; we have waited for him, we will be glad and rejoice in his salvation.*
>
> —Isa. 25:8-9

Brethren, think of an eternal habitation in which there is no sorrow. Who is there here below that is not acquainted with sorrow? It came in with thorns and thistles at Adam's fall; it is the bitter cup that all must drink; it is before us and behind us; it is on the right hand and the left; it is mingled with the very air we breathe. Our bodies are racked with pain, and we have sorrow; our worldly goods are taken from us, and we have sorrow; we are encompassed with difficulties and troubles, and we have sorrow; our friends forsake us and look coldly on us, and we have sorrow; we are separated from those we love, and we have sorrow; those on whom our hearts' affections are set go down to the grave and leave us alone, and we have sorrow.

And then, too, we find our own hearts frail and full of corruption, and that brings sorrow; we are persecuted and opposed for the Gospel's sake, and that brings sorrow; we see those who are near and dear to us refusing to walk with God, and that brings sorrow. Oh, what a sorrowing, grieving world we live in!

Blessed be God! there shall be no sorrow in heaven. There shall not be one single tear shed within the courts above. There shall be no more disease and weakness and decay; the coffin, and the funeral, and the grave, and the dark-black mourning shall be things unknown. Our faces shall no more be pale and sad; no more shall we go out from the company of those we love and be parted asunder—that word, *farewell,* shall never be heard again. There shall be no anxious thought about tomorrow to mar and spoil our enjoyment, no sharp and cutting words to wound our souls; our wants will have come to a perpetual end, and all around us shall be harmony and love.

Oh, Christian brethren, what is our light affliction when compared to such an eternity as this? Shame on us if we murmur and complain and turn back, with such a heaven before our eyes! What can this vain and passing world give us better than this? This is the city of our God Himself, when He will dwell among us Himself. The glory of God shall lighten it, and the Lamb is the light thereof. Truly we may say, as Mephibosheth did to David, "Yea, let [the world] take all, forasmuch as my lord the king is come again in peace unto his own house" (2 Sam. 19:30).

Such is the Bible heaven, there is none other; these sayings are faithful and true, not any of them shall fail. Surely, brethren, it is worth a little pain, a little laboring, a little toil, if only we may have the lowest place in the kingdom of God.

WHO SHALL NOT ENTER HEAVEN?

Let us now pass on and see that great thing which is revealed in the second part of our text. You have heard of heaven; but all shall not enter it: and who are the persons who shall not enter in?

Brethren, this is a sad and painful inquiry, and yet it is one that must be made. I can do no more than declare to you Scripture truth: it is not my fault if it is cutting and gives offense. I must deliver my Master's message and diminish nothing; the line I have to draw is not mine, but God's: the blame, if you will lay it, falls on the Bible, not on me. "There shall in no wise enter into it any thing that defileth, neither whatsoever worketh abomination, or maketh a lie" (Rev. 21:27). Verily these are solemn words; they ought to make us think.

"Nothing that defileth." This touches the case of all who are defiled with sins of heart, and yet feel it not, and refuse to be made clean. These may be decent persons outwardly, but they are vile and polluted within. These are the worldly-minded. They live to this world only, and they have no thought of anything beyond it. The care of this world, the money, the politics of this world, the business of this world, the pleasures of this world, these things swallow up their whole attention—and as for St. James' advice to keep ourselves unspotted from the world, they know not what it means.

These are the men who set their affections on earthly things; they have each their idol in the chamber of their imagination, and they worship and serve it more than God. These are the proud and self-righteous, the self-honoring and the self-conceited; they love the praise of men, they like the good opinion of this world, and as for the glorious Lord who made them, His honor, His glory, His house, His Word, His service—these are all things which in their judgment must go down, and take the second place.

Such people know not what sorrow for sin means. They are strangers to spiritual anxiety; they are self-satisfied and content with their condition. And if you attempt to stir them up to zeal and repentance it is more than probable they are offended.

Brethren, you know well there are such people. They are not uncommon; they may be honorable in the eyes of men, they may be wise and knowing in this generation, admirable men of business, they may be first and foremost in their respective callings, but still there is but one account of them; they bring no glory to their Maker, they are lovers of themselves more than of God, and therefore they are counted as defiled in His sight and nothing that is defiled shall enter heaven.

But again: *"Nothing that worketh abomination."* This touches the case of all who practice those sins of life which God has pronounced abominable, and take pleasure in them, and countenance those who practice them. These are the men who work the works of the flesh, each as his heart inclines him. These are the adulterers, fornicators, and unclean livers; these are the drunkards, revelers, and gluttons; these are the blasphemers, swearers, and liars. These are the men who count it no shame to live in hatred, variance, wrath, strife, envyings, quarrelings and the like. They throw the reins on the neck of their lusts; they follow their passions wherever they may lead them; their only object is to please themselves.

Brethren, you know well there are such people. The world may give smooth names to their conduct; the world may talk of them as light and affable, and loose and wild, but it will not do. They are all abominable in the sight of God, and except they be converted and born again, they shall in no wise enter heaven.

Once more: *"Nothing that maketh a lie."* This touches the case of hypocrites. These are the false professors; the lip-servants; they say that they know God, but in works they deny Him; they are like barren fig-trees, all leaves and no fruit; they are like tinkling cymbals, all sound, but hollow, empty and without substance; these have a name to live while they are dead, and a form of godliness without the power. They profess what they do not practice; they speak what they do not think; they say much and do little; their words are most amazing; their actions are most poor. These men can talk most bravely of themselves; no better Christians than they are, if you will take them at their own valuation. They can talk to you of grace, and yet they show none of it in their lives; they can talk to you of saving faith, and yet they possess not that charity which is faith's companion. They can declaim against forms most strongly, and yet their own Christianity is a form and no more; they can cry out loudly against Pharisees, and yet no greater Pharisees than they are themselves.

Oh, no; this religion is of a sort that is public, and not private; plenty abroad, but none at home; plenty without, but none within; plenty in the tongue, but none in the heart. They are altogether unprofitable, good for nothing, they bear no fruit.

Brethren, you must know well there are such miserable persons. Alas! The world is full of them in these latter days. They may deceive ministers; they may deceive their neighbors; they may even deceive their friends and family; they may try hard to deceive themselves; but they are no better than liars in God's sight, and except they repent, they shall in no wise enter heaven.

Brethren, consider well these things: The sin-defiled, the abominable, the hypocrite, shall in no wise enter into heaven. Look well to your own souls; judge yourselves that ye be not judged of the Lord. I call heaven and earth to witness this day, they that will live these bad lives, whether they be Churchmen or dissenters, old or young, rich or poor, they shall in no wise enter in. Go, cleave to the ways of the world if you are so determined; stick to your sins if you must needs keep them; but I warn you solemnly this hour, they that will have these things shall in no wise enter into heaven.

Oh, blame me now for speaking sharply to you—think I am too particular if you like it. But, oh! remember if you ever stand outside the gates, crying, "Lord, open to us," in vain. Remember there was a time when I told you, the worldly-minded and the evil livers shall in no wise enter in. Brethren, I have told you before, and I tell you now again for the last time: If you cling to the things God hates, you shall in no wise enter into heaven.

WHO SHALL ENTER HEAVEN?

Brethren, we must pass on. The text has told you who shall not enter heaven. Oh! what a mighty crowd those words shut out! But it tells you something more: Who are they that shall.

Short is the account and simple: "They only that are written in the Lamb's book of life." And who are written in this precious book? I do not know their names, but I do know their characters, and what those characters are I will endeavor to tell you shortly, for the last time.

They are all true penitents. They have been convinced of their own unworthiness in God's sight; they have felt themselves to be sinners in deed and in truth; they have mourned over their sins, hated their sins, forsaken their sins—the remembrance of them is grievous, the burden of them intolerable. They have ceased to think well of their own condition and count themselves fit to be saved. They have confessed with their whole heart: "Lord, we are indeed unclean."

Again: *they are all believers in Christ Jesus.* They have found out the excellency of the work He did to save them, and cast on Him the burden of their souls. They have taken Christ for their all in all: their wisdom, their righteousness, their justification, their forgiveness, their redemption. Other payment of their spiritual debts they have seen none; other deliverances from the devil they have not been able to find. But they have believed on Christ, and come to Christ for salvation; they are confident that what they cannot do Christ can do for them, and having Jesus Christ to lean on, they feel perfect peace.

Once more: *they are all born of the Spirit and sanctified.* They have all put off the old man with his deeds, and put on the new man, which is after God. They have all been renewed in the spirit of their minds; a new heart and a new nature has been given to them. They have brought forth those fruits which only are the proof of the Spirit being in them. They may have slipped and come short in many things. They may have mourned over their own deficiencies full often. But still, the general bent and bias of their lives has always been toward holiness—*more holiness, more holiness,* has always been their hearts' desire. They love God, and they must live to Him.

Such is the character of them that are written in heaven. These, then, are the men whose names are to be found in the Lamb's book of life.

Once they may have been as bad as the very worst—defiled, abominable, liars. What matter? They have repented and believed, and now they are written in the book of life.

They may have been despised and rejected of this world, poor and mean and lowly in the judgment of their neighbors. What matter? They had repentance and faith and new hearts, and now they are written in the glorious book of life.

They may have been of different ranks and nations; they may have lived at different ages, and never seen each other's faces. What matter? They have one thing at least in common: they have repented and believed, and been born again, and therefore they stand all together in the Lamb's book of life.

Yes, brethren, these are the men and women that enter heaven. Nothing can keep them out.

And now, men and brethren, in conclusion, let me press upon you my old question. How is it with yourselves? What? No answer? Are you ready to depart? Again, no answer? Is your name written in the book of life? Once more, have you no answer?

Oh, think, think, unhappy man or woman, whoever thou art, think what a miserable thing it is to be uncertain about eternity. And then consider, if you cannot give your heart to God now, how is it possible you could enjoy God's heaven hereafter? Heaven is unceasing godliness; it is to be in the presence of God and His Christ for evermore. God is the light, the food, the air of heaven. It is an eternal sabbath. To serve God is heaven's employment, to talk with God is heaven's occupation.

Oh, sinners, sinners, could you be happy there? To which of all the saints would you join yourselves? By whose side would you go and sit down, with whom of all the prophets and apostles would you love to converse? Surely it would be a wearisome thing to you; surely you would soon want to go forth and join your friends outside. Oh, turn ye, turn ye while it is called today! God will not alter heaven merely to please you; better a thousand times to conform to His ways while you can. You must love the things of heaven before your death, or else you cannot enter heaven when ye die.

Christian, look up and take comfort. Jesus has prepared a place for you, and they that follow Him shall never perish, neither shall any man pluck them out of His hands. Look forward to that glorious abode He has provided. Look forward in faith, for it is thine.

Oh, Christian brethren, think what a glorious meeting that shall be! There we shall see the saints of old, of whom we have so often read. There we shall see those holy ministers whose faith and patience we have admired. There we shall see one another round the throne of our common Saviour, and be parted and separated no more. There we shall labor and toil no more, for the days of mourning shall be ended. Oh, but my heart will leap within me, if I see there faces I have known among you; if I hear the names of any of yourselves! The Lord grant it, the Lord bring it to pass. The Lord grant we may some of us, at least, come together in that day, when there shall be one fold and one Shepherd, and with one heart and voice join that glorious song,

> *Worthy is the Lamb that was slain to receive power, and riches and wisdom, and strength, and honour, and glory, and blessing . . . . Blessing, and honor, and glory, and power, be unto him that sitteth upon the throne, and unto the Lamb for ever and ever*
> —*Rev. 5:12-13*

NOTES

Chapter 1
The Modern Romance with Heaven

1. Elisabeth Kubler-Ross, *On Death and Dying* (New York: Simon & Schuster, 1970).

2. Moody, Raymond A. *Life after Life* (New York: Mockingbird, 1975, and Bantam, 1976); *Reflections on Life After Life* (New York: Mockingbird, 1977); *The Light Beyond* (New York: Bantam, 1989); *Coming Back: A Psychiatrist Explores Past-Life Journeys* (New York: Bantam, 1990); *Reunions: Visionary Encounters with Departed Loved Ones* (New York: Villard, 1993).

3. "The conversion of Kubler-Ross: From thanatology to seances and sex," *Time*, (12 Nov. 1979), 81.

4. "Bulletins from Beyond," vol. 1, no. 1, Sept., 1994. http://www.linknet.it/Spirit/bulletins-beyond-sep-94.html.

5. Betty J. Eadie, *Embraced by the Light* (New York: Bantam, 1992), 29.

6. Ibid., 31.

7. Ibid., 31-32.

8. Ibid., 40.

9. Ibid., 42.

10. Ibid., 44.

11. Ibid., 45.

12. Ibid., 45-46.

13. Ibid.

14. Ibid., 85.

15. The Ogden, Utah *Standard-Examiner* (6 March 1993), cited in "News Watch," *The Christian Research Journal* (31 Aug 1994).

16. Doug Groothuis, *Deceived by the Light* (Eugene, Ore.:.Harvest House, 1995), 22.

17. *The Christian Research Journal*.

18. Eadie, 47.

19. Ibid., 43.

20. Ibid., 47.

21. Ibid. (emphasis added).

22. Ibid., 61.

23. 2 Nephi 2:25.

24. Eadie, 109.

25. Not long ago some zealous Mormons created a furor in the Jewish community by taking published lists of Holocaust victims and "baptizing" them by proxy. *The Los Angeles Times* (6 May 1995), 1.

26. Eadie, 85.

27. Ibid., 85.

28. Ibid., 57-58.

29. Ibid., 63.

30. Ibid., 64.

31. Ibid., 58.

32. Ibid., 67.

33. Broadcast on ABC-TV, 13 May 1994.

34. Groothuis, 26-27.

35. Eadie, 50.

36. Ibid., 48-49.

37. Ibid., 81.

38. Ibid., 41.

39. Ibid., 51.

40. Groothuis, 28.

41. Eadie, 50.

42. Ibid., 49-50.

43. Ibid., 70.

44. Ibid., 112.

45. Ibid

46. Ibid., 113.

47. Ibid., 34-35.

48. Ibid., 35.

49. Ibid., 48-49.

50. Ibid., 94.

51. Ibid., 115-116.

52. Ibid., 59.

53. Ibid.

54. Ibid., 114.

55. Ibid.

56. Ibid., 115.

57. Ibid., 90, 103.

58. Ibid., 115, 121.

59. Ibid., 101.

60. Ibid., 95.

61. Ibid., 84.

62. "A Conversation with Dannion Brinkley," *The Monthly Aspectarian* (September 1995) On-line edition.http://www.lightworks.com/MonthlyAspectarian/1995/September/08-LW995.HTM

63. Ibid.

64. Ibid.

65. Eadie, 119 (emphasis added).

66. Ibid., 41.

Chapter 2
No Earthly Idea About Heaven

1. Richard Eby, *Caught Up into Paradise* (Old Tappan, N.J.: Fleming H. Revell, n.d.).

2. Ibid., 228-29.

3. Ibid., 230.

4. Roberts Liardon, *I Saw Heaven* (Tulsa, Okla.: Harrison House, 1983), 6.

5. Ibid., 19.

6. Ibid., 16-22.

7. Ibid., p. 26.

8. Joni Eareckson Tada, *Heaven* (Grand Rapids, Mich.: Zondervan, 1995), 53-55.

9. Richard Baxter, *The Saints' Everlasting Rest,* abridged by John T. Wilkinson (London: Epworth, 1962), 110.

10. Ibid., 118.

11. Ibid., 121.

Chapter 3
What Heaven Will Be Like

1. Wilbur Smith, *Biblical Doctrine of Heaven* (Chicago:Moody, 1968), 155.

Chapter 4
New Jerusalem

1. Joseph Dillow, *The Reign of the Servant Kings* (Miami Springs, Fla.: Schoettle, 1992), 347.

2. Ibid., 481.

3. See John F. MacArthur, *Faith Works* (Dallas, Tex.: Word, 1992), 175-92.

4. Dillow, 348.

5. Ibid., 48-49.

6. Matthew 8:12 says, "*The children of the kingdom* shall be cast out into outer darkness: there shall be weeping and gnashing of teeth" (emphasis added). "Children of the kingdom" refers not to Christians, but to unbelieving Israelites. Their relationship to "the kingdom" is only a line of physical descent—an earthly tie, and not enough to make them spiritually fit for the heavenly kingdom. So Jesus tenderly warns that if they do not repent they will be judged along with the rest of the unbelieving world.

7. J.A. Seiss, *The Apocalypse: Lectures on the Book of Revelation* (Grand Rapids, Mich.: Zondervan, 1970 reprint), 499.

Chapter 5
What We Will Be Like in Heaven

1. C. S. Lewis, *Letters to Malcom* (San Diego: Harcourt Brace, 1973), n.p.

2. A. A. Hodge, *Evangelical Theology* (Carlisle, Penn.: Banner of Truth, 1976), 400.

Chapter 6: The Heavenly Host

1. Alma Daniel, Timothy Wyllie, and Andrew Ramer, *Ask Your Angels* (New York: Ballantine, 1992).

2. Bill Deckard, "Angels We Have Heard?" *Moody* (April 1995), 46.

Appendix 1: The Jewels in Our Heavenly Crown

1. Excerpted from *The Saints' Everlasting Rest*, a classic work first published in 1650.

2. Lollard, Huguenots, and Roundheads were names of derision used by enemies of the Reformation against the followers of Wycliffe, the French Protestants, and the working-class Puritans, respectively. The Spanish Inquisition is well known. The statute of the Six Articles, often called "the whip with six strings" was imposed in 1539, during the reign of Henry VIII, designed to stop the spread of the Reformation to England. It prescribed (among other things) death by burning for anyone who denied the doctrine of transubstantiation.

3. "Remonstrants" refers to the followers of Jacobus Arminius. Their "remonstrance" against the doctrines of divine sovereignty led to the Synod of Dordt, which produced canons outlining the five points commonly referred to as "the five points of Calvinism."

4. This was penned during the time of the English Civil War.

Appendix 2: The Kingdom of Heaven

1. Excerpted from *Human Nature in Its Fourfold State*, a classic work first published in 1720.

SCRIPTURE
INDEX

GENERAL
INDEX

The Glory of Heaven was typeset by the Photocomposition Department of Crossway Books of Wheaton, Illinois.

Manuscript editor: Leonard G. Goss

Production editor: Ted Griffin

Cover designer: Cindy Kiple

The text was set in 11.25/15 point Aldine 401